C000242355

Digital Platforms
and Algorithmic
Subjectivities

Edited by
Emiliana Armano, Marco Briziarelli,
Elisabetta Risi

Critical, Digital and Social Media Studies

Series Editor: Christian Fuchs

The peer-reviewed book series edited by Christian Fuchs publishes books that critically study the role of the internet and digital and social media in society. Titles analyse how power structures, digital capitalism, ideology and social struggles shape and are shaped by digital and social media. They use and develop critical theory discussing the political relevance and implications of studied topics. The series is a theoretical forum for internet and social media research for books using methods and theories that challenge digital positivism; it also seeks to explore digital media ethics grounded in critical social theories and philosophy.

Editorial Board

Thomas Allmer, Mark Andrejevic, Miriyam Aouragh, Charles Brown, Melanie Dulong De Rosnay, Eran Fisher, Peter Goodwin, Jonathan Hardy, Kylie Jarrett, Anastasia Kavada, Arwid Lund, Maria Michalis, Stefania Milan, Vincent Mosco, Safiya Noble, Jack Qiu, Jernej Amon Prodnik, Sarah Roberts, Marisol Sandoval, Sebastian Sevignani, Pieter Verdegem, Bingqing Xia, Mariano Zukerfeld

Published Titles

Critical Theory of Communication: New Readings of Lukács, Adorno, Marcuse, Honneth and Habermas in the Age of the Internet
Christian Fuchs
https://doi.org/10.16997/book1

Knowledge in the Age of Digital Capitalism: An Introduction to Cognitive Materialism
Mariano Zukerfeld
https://doi.org/10.16997/book3

Politicizing Digital Space: Theory, the Internet, and Renewing Democracy
Trevor Garrison Smith
https://doi.org/10.16997/book5

Capital, State, Empire: The New American Way of Digital Warfare
Scott Timcke
https://doi.org/10.16997/book6

The Spectacle 2.0: Reading Debord in the Context of Digital Capitalism
Edited by Marco Briziarelli and Emiliana Armano
https://doi.org/10.16997/book11

The Big Data Agenda: Data Ethics and Critical Data Studies
Annika Richterich
https://doi.org/10.16997/book14

Social Capital Online: Alienation and Accumulation
Kane X. Faucher
https://doi.org/10.16997/book16

AI for Everyone? Critical Perspectives
Edited by Pieter Verdegem
https://doi.org/10.16997/book55
The Society of the Selfie: Social Media and the Crisis of Liberal Democracy
Jeremiah Morelock and Felipe Ziotti Narita
https://doi.org/10.16997/book59
Paradoxes of Digital Disengagement: In Search of the Opt-Out Button
Adi Kuntsman and Esperanza Miyake
https://doi.org/10.16997/book61

Digital Platforms and Algorithmic Subjectivities

Edited by
Emiliana Armano, Marco Briziarelli, Elisabetta Risi

University of Westminster Press
www.uwestminsterpress.co.uk

Published by
University of Westminster Press
115 New Cavendish Street
London W1W 6UW
www.uwestminsterpress.co.uk

Introduction and editorial arrangement © Emiliana Armano,
Marco Briziarelli, Elisabetta Risi 2022
Text of chapters © Their respective authors 2022

First published 2022

Cover design: www.ketchup-productions.co.uk
Series cover concept: Mina Bach (minabach.co.uk)
Print and digital versions typeset by Siliconchips Services Ltd.

ISBN (Hardback): 978-1-914386-11-4
ISBN (Paperback): 978-1-914386-12-1
ISBN (PDF): 978-1-914386-08-4
ISBN (EPUB): 978-1-914386-09-1
ISBN (Mobi): 978-914386-10-7

DOI: https://doi.org/10.16997/book54

This work is licensed under the Creative Commons
Attribution-NonCommercial-NoDerivatives 4.0 International License.
To view a copy of this license, visit http://creativecommons.org/licenses/by-nc
-nd/4.0/ or send a letter to Creative Commons, 444 Castro Street, Suite 900,
Mountain View, California, 94041, USA. This license allows for copying
and distributing the work, providing author attribution is clearly stated,
that you are not using the material for commercial purposes, and that
modified versions are not distributed.

The full text of this book has been peer-reviewed to ensure
high academic standards. For full review policies,
see: https://www.uwestminsterpress.co.uk/site/publish.

Suggested citation: Armano, E., Briziarelli, M., and Risi, E. (eds.), 2022.
Digital Platforms and Algorithmic Subjectivities. London: University
of Westminster Press. DOI: https://doi.org/10.16997/book54
License: CC-BY-NC-ND 4.0

To read the free, open access version of this book
online, visit https://doi.org/10.16997/book54
or scan this QR code with your mobile device

Contents

List of Illustrations

Figures

Table

Platforms, Algorithms and Subjectivities: Active Combination and the Extracting Value Process – An Introductory Essay

Emiliana Armano, Marco Briziarelli, Joseph Flores and Elisabetta Risi

In the last decade, and in a considerable portion of the world, digital platforms have colonised important areas of social life (Srnicek 2016; van Dijck, Poell and de Waal 2018), from production to services and logistics, from training to communication, and to social reproduction, all of which have remediated (Bolter and Grusin 2003) and remodelled social relations and organisational processes. While predominant theories of mediation of the 1980s and 1990s still presupposed a dichotomy between physical and virtual reality, in the hybrid networks of contemporary digital societies, matter and information are no longer so easily separable (Lupton 2016; Manovich 2013).

Rather than building 'digital doubles' – informational identities that transcend us and ultimately come to dominate us (Haggerty and Ericson 2000) – our subjectivities are both represented and constituted by algorithmic identities (Cheney-Lippold 2011), and then recursively reproduced (Beer 2016; Airoldi and Rokka 2019), which show how machines, in their various

How to cite this book chapter:
Armano, E., Briziarelli, M., Flores, J., and Risi, E. 2022. Platforms, Algorithms and Subjectivities: Active Combination and the Extracting Value Process – An Introductory Essay. In: Armano, E., Briziarelli, M., and Risi, E. (eds.), *Digital Platforms and Algorithmic Subjectivities*. Pp. 1–18. London: University of Westminster Press. DOI: https://doi.org/10.16997/book54.a. License: CC-BY-NC-ND 4.0

components, never really confront us, but appear to be an integral part of our life processes: we rely on intelligent objects, make friends on social networks, take selfies, record voice messages to share online, or perform lifelogging based on our bodies' performance. Algorithms are not to be understood as an abstract entity with purely quantitative relevance; they do not infer only computational processes for the statistical-mathematical knowledge of society, or merely promise to be useful in order to select and constitute some social actors at the expense of others (Morozov 2013; Airoldi and Gambetta 2018). Rather they work in networks of associations that qualitatively modulate the weaving of society (Thrift 2007). As a result, in a variety of self-quantifying practices (Lupton 2016; Moore 2018), data on subjects' practices, produced by tracking and self-tracking, in turn affect those subjects' attitudes, dispositions, relationships, preferences and behaviours by constitutive representations. The pervasive power of these devices attracts, persuades and often forces millions of people, companies and public institutions into having a 'digital presence' as well as into digital self-promoting performances – the screen window display (Codeluppi 2007) as *the* place and way to showcase the performance and network of selves. This inextricable intertwining of such platforms with our lives is now evident in the context of the social, cultural and economic structures of a platform society.

Underlying Tendencies

Different types of 'platforms', according to Srnicek, mark so-called platform capitalism via different processes of value creation, which in some cases rely on production/appropriation processes (Fuchs 2010), in others on income and extraction (Rigi and Prey 2015). Also integrated into such economies are platforms that do not involve a monetised exchange of goods and services, such as platforms that promote peer-to-peer relationships (De Rosnay and Musiani 2020) and are oriented instead toward the pooling of goods, resources and knowledge, towards the production of commons (Teli, Lyle and Sciannamblo 2018). Related to these issues, data metric power has a syntactic and semantic function that can govern us 'at a distance'. The metric power of numbers guides us without emotion or violence (Beer 2016). It is not the numbers that punish us if we do not reach certain standards, it is us blaming ourselves after having measured our defeat (Risi, Briziarelli and Armano 2019). Moreover we emphasise that these socio-technical devices function as black boxes (Pasquale 2015), based on non-transparent algorithms that continuously extract data from subjects.

In such a context, this book, instead of concentrating on the infrastructural and technological dimensions of platform capitalism, emphasises relational and organisational questions, in particular the ambivalent logic of connection/disconnection, the production of the neoliberal subject (Armano, Teli and Mazali 2020; Bartoletti 2020) and its complex intersectional nature in relation to the internet (Benski and Fisher 2013; Risi 2016), issues of what has been termed 'onlife' (Floridi 2015), and the transformative potential of these phenomena. In this regard, a key point worth noting is the active combination (Alquati 1994, 2021) between the capitalist means of production and human activities. Such active combination consists in the concatenation of – *agencement* – (Gherardi 2015) between human and digital machine, or to return to Alquati, it connects the ability of the living human with the procedures encoded in the algorithm, which pervade and structure different productive and reproductive activities, from increasingly digitised work, to social media in urban spaces and in everyday life, (Farooq and Grudin 2016). Active combination is a fundamental part of the process of extracting value (Mezzadra and Neilson 2018) and simultaneously modelling subjectivity.

We are in this sense motivated by a concern with the integral power of platforms and their algorithms in shaping our societies. The power we describe is not explicitly coercive or violent, it does not use disciplinary sanctions in the traditional sense but, by constantly monitoring and surveilling us (Greenfield 2017; Zuboff 2019) it imprisons us through evaluation, reporting and ranking (Merry 2016). Exemplifying this, Ned Rossiter and Soenke Zehle explore this in Chapter 2, critically reflecting on the pervasiveness of algorithmic governance processes, and, in doing so also represent this book's ambition to respond to the call for 'algorithms awareness' (Bucher 2012) and the extent to which people are aware of a life shaped by algorithmic selection (Eslami et al. 2015). In fact, the coding of our data, the rules of algorithms, the identity we are assigned and, in part, the identity we assign ourselves as a 'data subject' (Ruppert 2011) or 'measureable types' (Cheney-Lippold 2017, 47), appear to remain hidden from most of us. The key question is not that platforms, through their own algorithmic logics, determine the polarisation of social and working behaviour, but rather that specific 'modes of feeling', through platforms, become forms of subjectivity, implicit ways of selecting choices and ultimately of looking at the world. After all, subjectivities are not tangible entities but reflective combinations of practicing and experiencing social relations, thus reifying those instrumental social links mostly only adequate for value extraction does not simply mean to give up on our species-being, or subordinate it to fetishism, but to also lose the battle for critical consciousness and radical collective mobilisation against current capitalism. In this way, an algorithmic production of subjectivity constitutes the concrete result of particular relational scenarios, in which each participant adds his/her own contribution to a collective moment. The work of platforms is onto-formative: they circumscribe the boundaries of thought and action as well as define the subjects and objects that belong to them.

Accordingly, in order to start tracking and understanding how this totalising reality operates, we could start by asking what kind of conceptualisation of the digital media environment is needed to tackle this opacity. Most of the chapters included in this edited collection examine digital media as a complex field formed at the intersection of objective structures and subjective practices. In line with such perspectives, Peters claims that media are much more than tools, as they constitute the primary conditions of possibility for people to exist: 'Media are our infrastructures of being, the habitats and materials through which we act and are' (2015, 15). What does this mean in the context of platform capitalism? On the one hand, 'in a time when it is impossible to say whether the nitrogen cycle or the Internet is more crucial to the planet's maintenance' (Peters 2015, 2), digital platforms and the algorithms that power them, could be regarded as organisational and infrastructural environments, co-developing and co-depending on capitalism. Notions such as 'datafication' (van Dijck 2014), 'algorithmic culture' (Striphas 2015) and 'algorithmic life' (Amoore and Piotukh 2016) describe a social imaginary that operates as a social power (Manovich 2001), capable of producing a field where computational logic meets an individual's consciousness (Bucher, 2018) and practical knowledge (Bilić 2016). And most importantly, all these notions point to how coded information as data acquire informational value (Zuboff 2019).

According to van Dijck et al., 'platforms do not reflect the social: they produce the social structures we live in' (van Dijck, Poell and de Waal 2018, 2): platforms intervene (Gillespie 2015) and mix social norms and sociotechnical norms specific to online environments creating a symbolic field and practices that delimit specific ways of relating – often distinct from offline ones – and that preside over new processes of signification of being together. The construction and management of sociality that operates through platforms is therefore not defined by a simple transfer of pre-existing dynamics into technological spaces, but is shaped by the architectures and *affordances* (Papacharissi 2011) of the platforms themselves, which circumscribe the possibilities and forms of relationships between individuals.

Platforms

Affordances can be defined as the 'socio-technical architectures' of platforms (Papacharissi 2011), which imply their 'capacity to shape the agency of human actors' (Caliandro and Gandini 2017, 11). During the Covid-19 crisis, citizens had to stay at home and avoid going out: in that context the affordances of platforms were the boundaries of their territories of self, i.e. the limits within which sociality could take place and be reconstructed. Platforms operate therefore as monitoring systems that quantify and direct people, as the Covid-19 crisis exemplified. Here, Marco Briziarelli and Emiliana Armano's chapter focuses on this new dynamic of platform extension during the pandemic, while Niccolò Cuppini, Mattia Frapporti and Maurillo Pirone's contribution delves into the impact of the pandemic on logistics. Platforms, by remotizing social relations, allow degrees of autonomy even when proximity is not possible. They provide subjectivities with an apparent individual freedom: a well-defined space, with specific technological possibilities and limits (i.e. affordances) that predetermine the margin of people's actions. For example, how the sense of privacy has changed by the interweaving of possibilities of subjectification opened up by specific technological affordances and related practices developed by users, which concern the relationship between online public and private spheres (Boccia Artieri 2014; 2020).

Overall, this edited volume stresses an economic definition of platforms as enterprises (Langlois and Elmer 2013) that, combining digitalisation and commodification (van Dijck, Poell and de Waal 2018), have become the flagship of a new stage in capitalist development (Srnicek 2016). Also, part of the macro-scale infrastructural nature of platform capitalism, and the power to aggregate billions of bits into intelligible and valuable information, is the capability of actors moving in the digital sphere to find each other as 'needles in the hay-stack' (MacCormick 2012, 25). In this regard, an assumption of this book is that platform algorithms give us a location in social space and time; an economic, social, cultural and psychological positionality. As Zittrain (2008) claims, platform economy is generative and dependent on specific kinds of subjects as it relies on the active participation of leisure time users and wage workers (Langlois and Elmer 2013). As a result, everyday life is increasingly experienced as a platform existence (van Dijck, Poell and de Waal 2018) mediated by algorithmic infrastructures. Platforms do not only mediate sociality, but also work as performative intermediaries that co-produce and shape social life, which increasingly takes place in and through algorithmic media (Bucher 2012). In fact, platforms are based on algorithms that gather, aggregate and classify (big) data, spontaneously or unconsciously produced by users, which allow platforms to suggest content to their audience.

In this context, we think two aspects stand out. Firstly, as van Dijck (2014) claims, platforms are more constitutive of the *lived environment* rather than simply reflective of our social context in that they are concurrently defining and setting the limits, as well as providing new opportunities, for most of our mediated social relations. Secondly, most of the contributors to this book share the assumption that one of the most important social situations where we can simultaneously examine how we perform technologically mediated interactions and how such interactions subjectify us is when operating as labouring subjects in social cooperation with others.

Algorithmic Powering

The fact that neoliberal subjects acquire a mentality in which everyone becomes his own entrepreneur, exposing and selling his own social skills and attitudes as if this were a natural fact (Gorz 1994), describes a realm where subjects are considered as responsible for their life opportunities and successes as an entrepreneurial project needing investments.

In that respect, we support Chicchi and Simone's thesis, which effectively describes neoliberal society as a performance society (2017). The new social imperative, based on individual performance, takes on a concrete corporate determination through the generalisation of the enterprise form as a subjective form adapted to the productive needs of post-industrial capitalism. Subjectivities have become fundamental performative agents of new kinds of individuals who, through self-management, can fully realise their own aspirations, express their own personalities, access knowledge and better control their inner emotions (Boltanski and Chiapello 1999). As a result, neoliberalism becomes coextensive with all society by generating one of the great paradoxes of platform-driven subjectivities, i.e. the tension between abstraction and a rich individualisation, exploitation and enjoyment, auto-direction and hetero-direction (Armano, Teli and Mazali 2020). As Lazzarato (2014) understands it, we could define it as the tension between social subjection and machinic enslavement.

As we have already suggested, we assume algorithms do not simply exercise controlling and predicting power, but they also have an *onto-formative* capacity: they organise the relationships between users and the surrounding environment, by selecting and reinforcing a social order that not accidently resembles social platforms (Mackenzie 2015). Such productive capacity is far from being impartial (Gillespie 2015; Airoldi and Gambetta 2018): in fact, algorithmic systems can embed cultural biases and reproduce various kind of social discriminations (e.g. Noble 2018). Furthermore, the protection of users' privacy and the opacity of how users' data are employed is increasingly recognised as of serious, worldwide public concern. While individuals act on platforms within their affordances (Caliandro and Gandini 2017) and relate to algorithms as in a 'love-affair' (Finn 2017), new and complex algorithmic identities are shaped and performed through opaque categorisation processes based on users' gathered data (Cheney-Lippold 2011; Gillespie 2014).

Algorithms powering platforms can systematise and translate users' attitudes, dispositions, relationships and behaviours in functional data in order to favour classifications and micro-targeting. Both discourses and practices around Big Data shape the way individuals are tracked and conceptualised. As we note, companies use algorithms to establish typologies of identities based on gender, race, geographical position and average expenditures (Chiney-Lippold 2011; Ruppert 2012). Search preferences and selected content are shared and combined with reaction feedback, which constitutes the basis for further interaction between users and content as well as between user and user. The subjectivity of the sharing user plays a fundamental role in this process: in fact, based on their identity, users circulate content and join networks with the hope of both shaping their own social networks and joining collective conversations (Payne 2012). People are frequently not aware that while users produce data, that data are appropriated by algorithm developers, in 'cultural environments of growing datafication and automated decision-making' (Markham 2020). Hence the issue of 'algorithms awareness' (Hargittai et al. 2020; Gran, Booth and Bucher 2020; Risi, Bonini and Pronzato 2020) and the extent to which people are conscious of a life shaped by algorithmic selection mechanisms (Eslami et al. 2015).

The feedback cycle is in indeed *recursive* (Airoldi and Rokka 2019) because the algorithm powering these kinds of platforms produces recommendations based on 'my recommendations', when I am asserting my dietary preferences and giving cues regarding my leisure activities. In this encoding and decoding loop, named *recursive* (Beer 2013; 2016), algorithm and subject are fused in a machinic reciprocal learning. Acknowledging the dynamicity of this human-machine relationship, Cheney-Lippold (2011) describes how algorithms construct fairly complex identities: such complexity certainly gets more refined and qualified. In platform capitalism, individuals become multiplicities, endlessly subdividable 'dividuals' (Deleuze 1992). Such 'dividual' status means that we all carry multiple layers of algorithmic identities (Elmer 2004) and we temporally inhabit different categories that are in turn differently constructed by competing interpretive machines (Cheney-Lippold 2017). Therefore, complex processes of the abstraction of subjects are, in our view, a symptom of the subsumption of people (not simply as workers) under platform capitalist forms. As Galloway (2004) claims, we are indeed confronting an abstract subjectivity, perfectly functional because digital platforms do not need our first and last name but merely a cluster of descriptive information. Furthermore, when this external subjectification meets the ways in which platforms *internally* shape individuals by generating motivations and practices, we are still confronting an abstract subjectivity that finds inner drivers to self-govern and self-activate, in agreement with neoliberal governmentality.

Examined in more detail, the neoliberal subject of platform capitalism is the result of the combination of different converging tendencies: the performative propensity to put him/herself on display (Codeluppi 2007), the desiring of conspicuous social visibility (Bucher 2012), and self-branding skills (Marwick 2013); the tendency of establishing and maintaining, through social platforms, a surplus of relational recognition as well as shared content (Bolter and Grusin 2000); and finally, being mobilised by a neoliberal ideology that links the boundless expansion of social platforms with limitless capital accumulation combined with a managerial approach to the management of resources such as social capital (Dardot and Laval 2009).

In our view, these internalised motivations are combined with external compelling pressures. We, for instance, refer to what Dean (2010) defines as the injunction to actively join the constant flow of communication and information (Armano, Teli and Mazali 2020). Furthermore, as a sign of the general neoliberalisation of social life, we receive instigations from multiple sources to remain flexible and to keep improving ourselves in order to better respond to market fluidity and the imperatives of a flexible kind of accumulation (Harvey 1989).

Against Machinic Agency?

This integral mode of subjection combines freedom and subjection, as well as abstraction and elements of a relatively genuine individuation, but also Deleuze and Guattari's (1987) combination of people and technology: the machinic. In this sense, most of the contributions to this edited volume, while not necessarily explicitly drawing on the notion of machinic subjectivity, point to the question of active combination and of agency in the human-machine relationship (Ziewitz 2016), the varying relations of power, and some of the opportunities for both subordination and resistance. Platforms become the stage and their algorithms the choreographers for digital social actors, and, as with any stage, they constrain and simultaneously make possible socially shared practical meanings. On such a stage, we become *identified subjects* and *identifying objects*, we are monitored and we monitor ourselves through tools evaluation, reporting, and ranking (Merry 2016): individuality is understood in a processual sense, since it is partly acquired and partly constructed by the process of algorithmic 'individuation' (Prey 2018).

Agency in the human-machine relationship also means recovering the Marxian take on individuation as a positive process of human assertion: becoming free, critically reflective subjects who can be the 'technologically conscious user' (Beer 2009) and who strive to take ownership of their own data (Nafus and Sherman 2014). In this sense, the question of human-machine agency remains dialectical on both sides of the equation because datafication does not simply provide venues for a quantification of the self critically exemplified by Moore (2018) and Zuboff (2019), it also provides users with enormous informational and knowledge capital.

This ambiguous power relation between platforms and users also speaks to questions of hegemony. As Read (2003) observes, the idea that subjects become productive suggests a capitalist subsumption process that exceeds the formal and real and tends towards what we could call socialised subsumption, a mode of subjection that implies what Gramsci (1975) defines as catharsis – the hegemonic dynamic that transforms coercion and necessity into freedom and deliberation.

The Book and Its Chapters

The book is divided into two main parts: 'Theoretical Foundations' and 'Case Studies.' In the first part of the volume, we provide an overview of some of the main theoretical nodes that define the intersection between platform capitalism and the subjectivities inhabiting it, operating through it and confronting it. The overall narrative that emerges from the first part shows how the logic of platforms, based on algorithmic computing and measurement mechanisms, extends the ethos of the enterprise form to all aspects of subjective existence, bringing to fruition the combination of hi-tech libertarianism and economic liberalism, which has characterised digital culture since its origins. Assuming the active combination between such subjectivities and information and communication technologies to be a fundamental part of the process of extracting value, the second part of the book examines concrete processes in which neoliberal subjectivity is defined within the digital environments of the platforms' affordances. We thus focus on the spaces of uncertainty of the algorithmic determination of subjectivities and the possible forms and modalities of resistance, experimentation, neo-mutualism and cooperation. Chapters in the first part of the collection share a broader approach to the subject by trying to theorise the social and historic conditions that allow algorithmic subjectivities to emerge, operate, thrive and develop in new directions. In doing so, these contributions deal with digital and platform capitalism as a general stage where dynamics of social reproduction (and partially social transformation) take place.

One important factor of social reproduction in platform capitalism is analysed by Hasmet M. Uluorta and Lawrence Quill in their reexamination of the so-called 'Californian Ideology'. Their chapter offers important insights into how people understand their relationship with their work, technology and history, and how subjects make sense of the tensions between capitalism's crude realities and its utopian thrust. They argue that while the original *telos* of progress of the techno-libertarians has been called into question in recent times, many aspects of the Californian Ideology have been naturalised: for instance, digital connectivity is both problematised and taken for granted; social media may be regarded as dangerous but also necessary; the neoliberal positive prejudice for private market self-regulation is still accompanied by deep scepticism in state institutions.

Californian Ideology naturally combines with what Rossiter and Zehle define as algorithmic governance, because, as they assume, a mode of subjection necessarily implies a mode of governance. As they note, modes of governance within institutional settings are increasingly shaped by algorithmic architectures of organisation, which, while posing limits to political possibility, are nonetheless radically dissimilar from the traditional experience of politics.

While Rossiter and Zehle explore neoliberal governance experienced by neoliberal subjects in their understanding of political power, public services and access to public resources, Briziarelli and Armano investigate the relation of digital labour and urban space production in the context of a crisis of capitalism. They argue that the Covid-19 pandemic-induced circulatory crisis has prompted a compensatory response that can be described as digital spatial fix, which combines measures against the crisis as well as subsumptive phenomena mainly under capitalist forms such as *digital abstract space* and machinic fix capital. They illustrate this by examining how the private residences of many workers are being subsumed as digital abstract space wherein their subjectivities are *domesticated*. Like Briziarelli and Armano, Cuppini, Frapporti and

Pirone examine the Covid-19 pandemic context as a privileged site to study platform capitalism and its operators. They provide an important assessment of the potential consequences of the pandemic on platform workers, specifically in the field of logistics. They suggest that the crisis has resulted in increased platformization (and their algorithmic systems) of society. The forced reorganisation of social spaces (e.g. public and private, work and leisure spaces) has had a considerable impact on how subjects understand their positions in relation to work and work control, social surveillance, but also in the spread of the entrepreneurial culture associated with the Californian Ideology.

Another theoretical aspect examined in the first part of the book is provided by Heiner Heiland's contribution, which returns to the subject of algorithmic governance by employing a black box metaphor. The nature of so-called black boxed algorithmic-driven governance, which is characterised by automatisation, made impersonal, and powered by machines, becomes an abstract political and administrative power. As a result, Heiland describes a permanent asymmetry of knowledge between subjects and governance. Crucially, Heiland also points to the current theoretical gap between logic and control, contending that social processes cannot be controlled in the same way as technical processes.

An issue implicitly examined in all these chapters is the general question of freedom in relation to current information and communication technologies. In this respect, explicitly exploring questions of human-machine agency, Emiliana Armano, Daniela Leonardi and Annalisa Murgia claim that, in delivery platforms, the power of algorithms is implemented through an active combination with living human capacity, which allows the digital machine to reproduce itself. As they argue, in a system of mediated relationships, this process makes subjects particularly exposed to the logic of rating and ranking, which ultimately shapes the formation of (counter)subjectivity. In their relational analysis of digital capitalism, they contend that a virtual space shaped by algorithms can represent a potential space for struggle.

The remaining chapters in this section deal with another fundamental theme examined by this book: the relationship between subjectivity, value and labour. Andrea Miconi reasserts Marx's labour theory of value in order to push back against a general tendency to both underestimate the role played by living labour and the tendency to reify the very notion of the platform. The author detects three main problems: the tendency to ignore labour altogether, the pre-eminence of data extraction over other forms of value production, and the incongruence between the notion of the multi-sided market and commodification. In part responding to Miconi's concerns, Patrick Cingolani's chapter contends that platform capitalism is defined by its ability to thrive on the extraction of free labour. Questioning how capitalism exploits and profits from free activities by making consumers contribute to the improvement of products, techniques and tools, this chapter underscores how capital develops a full range of new methods of exploitation.

In contrast to Part I, the Case Studies section of the book is dedicated to the examination of empirical cases; everyday practices of neoliberal subjects and the constant process of subjection in which they are involved. All of the chapters here provide insights into how, in different social circumstances, the tensions within human-machine agency relations materialises especially in the context of a digital labour process. Alberto Cossu, for example, points to the ambiguous opacity of platform capitalism, echoing Heiland's discussion about the black box, examining individual amateur investors in crypto-financial markets. Based on digital data gathering and content analysis, Cossu claims that such digital traces empower these new investors with unprecedented possibilities for creating value and, at the same time, they become subject to data gathering by companies that analyse and sell their aggregated behaviours. Overall, Cossu sheds light on new forms of 'ideological' currency that places subjectivities within the capitalist relations of production.

While Cossu considers an integration of subjectivities through ideological incorporation, Milena Franke and Valeria Pulignano consider the subordination aspect of such processes of subsumption of subjects. They analyse a deficit of agency within a food delivery platform in Belgium in order to understand how asymmetric power relations unfold within platform work. In interlinking the 'triangular' relationship between platforms, individual clients and workers they claim subordinating social relationships not only reconfirm coercion as a key component of the capitalistic relations of production but illustrate how labour platforms simultaneously empower and disempower actors.

Elisabetta Risi and Riccardo Pronzato examine the role of algorithms in creating prosumers and explore the creation of interlocking roles between user practices, algorithmic hybridisation, programmability and self-quantification. As they argue, as everyday life is currently being datafied and fed into an algorithm that processes and transforms it into behavioural and recursive models, individuals become 'data subjects' and algorithmic prosumers. The authors describe a process of co-development between algorithms and data subjects: while algorithms are in constant need of information in order to understand and predict how platform users utilise these typifications in order to make sense of their daily actions, users are provided with constitutive material for identity formation.

Also examining the topic of identity formation, Jacopo Anderlini and Carlo Milani explore how practices of reappropriation of technology that conceal 'appropriate' social and technical organisation can prefigure new sociotechnical imaginaries, and how they shape digital spaces, infrastructures, social interactions and relations. They examine how practices of reappropriation demonstrate how to envision alternative social organisations, such as mutualism, as well as alternative technology usages more suited for solidarist digital communities.

In a different social arena, but with similar concerns regarding power relations and how they are mediated by platforms, Robert Ovetz deals with the automation of higher education. With the introduction of online technologies such as Learning Management Systems, Zoom and Canvas, Ovetz argues that the automation of higher education efficiently produces self-disciplined workers who work remotely, allowing higher education institutions to remain highly profitable. Ovetz considers how platforms are intended to deskill academic labour, impose new processes of algorithmic management, and control and surveil it, with extractive processes of knowledge enclosure that are separated from the social body. Thus, like Franke and Pulignano, and Cingolani, Ovetz is concerned with the mediating role of online technologies in extracting value.

Interestingly enough, Davide Arcidiacono, Ivana Pais and Flaviano Zandonai examine another way in which platforms are mediating power relations, in this case between the state and its citizens. They turn the focus towards the platformization of welfare services, thus going beyond business-oriented merchant perspectives that dominate the field of Platform Studies. The authors analyse the peculiarities of organisational design when welfare services adopt new platform architecture, examining how algorithms and artificial intelligence upend previously institutionalised forms of social welfare and the ways platforms alter how individuals interact with the state. The platformization of welfare services leads to solutions that overcome the traditional bureaucracy of local welfare systems and, at the same time, redefines the role of social workers not as simple public administrators of welfare, but according to a logic of process and collaboration never experienced before.

Following Risi and Pulignano, Tatiana Mazali and Nicoletta Gay explore further performative aspects of platform subjectivities, exemplified by the functioning of ranking systems on main social networks. They claim that the logic of digital 'positioning' of the self has exacerbated many emerging practices related to the self, such as branding, self-marketing, self-positioning, processes of individualisation, identity fragility, as well as, in the realm of work, precarization and impoverishment of incomes. They point to the need to generate new ranking systems in order to act as countermeasures against the inequalities and the lack of diversity in our society, mitigating them, and providing fairer and less discriminatory outcomes.

Focusing on the aspects of platform work where workers' behaviour is antagonistic to platform logics Maurizio Franzini and Silvia Lucciarini examine gig workers and how their precarious condition becomes politically productive of alternative forms of mobilisation and unionisation of workers, signalling the role of new worker organisations in advocating for them. These workers, despite being particularly exposed to the most troubling aspects of platform capitalism and algorithmic management, are also at the vanguard of envisioning possible forms of resistance.

Cracking Open the Black Box

The various perspectives that this book contains represents a significant addition to the corpus of studies on platform capitalism by offering a critical sociology that, by studying the interactions and productive tensions between digital platforms and their users' practices, achieves a delicate balance between opposing tendencies, such as between the objective or the subjective, the structural and the contingent moment, the particular and the general. It contributes to cracking open the black box by providing a perspective that does not treat technology as a fetish with a life of its own but as a set of social relations, which are mediated by technological hardware, capitalist interests, social and cultural biases and, last but certainly not least, conscious and productive human activity. Thus, while, for instance, many contributions to this collection assume the centrality of digital platforms, which provide a training ground for mass actions that shape users' behaviour in the delineation of a new public space of production and life (Risi, Bonini and Pronzato 2020), and function as surplus value extracting machines (Mezzadra and Neilson 2018), platforms can only achieve this through the active participation of users. After all, the various processes of subjectification the chapters describe imply, more or less explicitly, a double movement: an objectification of the subject – being subjected to platform power – and a subjectification of the object – the platform being empowered by human signification and human praxis. In other words, on the one hand, in interrogating the technology/human agency relationship, this book suggests that human agents interacting through platforms are increasingly conditioned by the ongoing process of capitalist subsumption of their subjectivity, yet on the other hand, such processes make platforms interdependent and interconnected by people's actions. Thus, the more platform capitalism establishes relations of subordination with its operating subjects, the more dependent subjects become on the platform for their agency.

In conclusion, it seems appropriate to emphasise the urgency of continuing to explore and critique digital capitalism, because, like a hegemonic substratum of 'truths', the more its digital totality becomes preponderant, the less visible and less open to critique it becomes. Our tentative remedy against that opacity is to approach technology and the subjects operating through it as social processes, which, we argue, pushes back against the risk of fetishising technology with the mystique of an *arcana imperii* kind of power. The perspectives showcased in this book, ranging from enthusiasm to disappointment, and from involvement to disenchantment with digital technology invite scholars to continue their research into these complex interconnections.

References

Airoldi, M. and Gambetta, D. 2018. Sul Mito della Neutralità Algoritmica. *The Lab's Quarterly*, 20(4), 25–46.

Airoldi, M. and Rokka, J. 2019. Algorithmic Consumer Cultures. Paper presented at the Interpretive Consumer Research Workshop 2019, Lyon, France.

Alquati, R. 1994. *Camminando per Realizzare un Sogno Comune*. Velleità Alternative.

Alquati, R. 2021. *Sulla Riproduzione della Capacità Umana Vivente: L'industrializzazione della Soggettività*. Derive Approdi.

Amoore, L. 2013. *The Politics of Possibility*. Duke University Press.

Amoore, L. and Piotukh, V. (Eds.), 2016. *Algorithmic Life: Calculative Devices in the Age of Big Data*. Routledge.

Armano, E., Teli, M., and Mazali, T. 2020. The Production of Neoliberal Subjectivity in Platform Capitalism: Comparative Interpretative Hypotheses. *Sociologia della Comunicazione*, 59(1), 106–126.

Bartoletti, R. 2020. Le culture del neoliberismo: Discorsi, pratiche e soggettività. *Sociologia della Comunicazione*, 59(1), 5–19.

Beer, D. 2009. Power through the Algorithm? Participatory Web Cultures and the Technological Unconsciousness. *New Media & Society*, 11(3), 985–1002.

Beer, D. 2013. *Popular Culture and New Media: The Politics of Circulation*. Palgrave Macmillan.

Beer, D. 2016. *Metric Power*. Palgrave Macmillan.

Benski, T. and Fisher, E. 2013. *Internet and Emotions*. Routledge.

Berry, D. 2014. *Critical Theory and the Digital*. Bloomsbury.

Bilić, P. 2016. Search Algorithms, Hidden Labour and Information Control. *Big Data and Society*, January–June, 1–9.

Boccia Artieri, G. 2014. La Rete Ropo l'Overload Informative: La Realtà dell'Algoritmo da Macchia Cieca a Bene Comune, *Paradoxa*, VIII(2), 100–113.

Boccia Artieri, G. 2020. Fare sociologia attraverso l'algoritmo: potere, cultura e agency. *Sociologia Italiana*, 15, 137–148.

boyd, d. and Crawford, K. 2012. Critical Questions for Big Data: Provocations for a Cultural, Technological and Scholarly Phenomenon. *Information, Communication and Society*, 15(5), 662–679.

Boltanski, L. and Chiapello, E. 1999. *Le Nouvel Esprit du Capitalism*. Gallimard.

Bolter, D. and Grusin, R. 2003. *Remediation. Competizione e Integrazione tra Media Vecchi e Nuovi*. Guerini e Associati.

Bucher, T. 2012. Want to Be on the Top? Algorithmic Power and the Threat of Invisibility on Facebook. *New Media & Society*, 14(7), 1164–1180. https://doi.org/10.1177/1461444812440159.

Bucher, T. 2018. *If … Then: Algorithmic Power and Politics*. Oxford University Press.

Caliandro, A. and Gandini, A. 2017. *Qualitative Research in Digital Environments: A Research Toolkit*. Routledge.

Cheney–Lippold, J. 2011. A New Algorithmic Identity: Soft Biopolitics and the Modulation of Control. *Theory, Culture & Society*, 28(6), 164–181. https://doi.org/10.1177/0263276411424420.

Cheney-Lippold, J. 2017 *We Are Data: Algorithms and the Making of Our Digital Selves*, New York University Press.

Chicchi, F. and Simone, A. 2017. *La Società della Prestazione*. Ediesse.

Codeluppi, V. 2007. *La Vetrinizzazione Sociale*. Bollati Boringhieri.

Couldry, N. and Powell, A. 2014. Big Data from the Bottom Up. *Big Data and Society*, 1(2), 1–5. https://doi.org/10.1177/2053951714539277.

Dean, J. 2010. Affective Networks. *MediaTropes*, II(2), 19–44.

Dardot, P. and Laval, C. 2009. *La Nouvelle Raison du Monde: Essai sur la Société Néolibérale*. Editions La Découverte.

Deleuze, G. 1992. Postscript on the Societies of Control. *October*, 59, 3–7.

Deleuze, G. and Guattari, F. 1987. *A Thousand Plateaus: Capitalism and Schizophrenia*. University of Minnesota Press.

De Rosnay, M. and Musiani, F. 2020. Alternatives for the Internet: A Journey into Decentralised Network Architectures and Information Commons, *tripleC*, 18(2), 622–629. https://doi.org/10.31269/triplec.v18i2.1201.

Elmer, G. 2004. *Profiling Machines: Mapping the Personal Information Economy*. MIT Press.

Eslami, M. et al. 2015. 'I Always Assumed that I Wasn't Really That Close to [Her]'. Reasoning about Invisible Algorithms in News Feeds. *Proceedings of the 33rd Annual ACM Conference on Human Factors in Computing Systems* (pp. 153–162). Association for Computer Machinery.

Farooq, U. and Grudin, J. 2016. Human-Computer Integration. *Interactions*, 23(6), 26–32.

Finn, E. 2017. *What Algorithms Want: Imagination in the Age of Computing*. MIT Press.

Floridi, L. 2015. *The Onlife Manifesto: Being Human in a Hyperconnected Era*. Springer International Publishing.

Fuchs, C. 2010. Labor in Informational Capitalism and on the Internet, *The Information Society: An International Journal*, 26(3), 179–196.

Galloway, A. 2004. *Protocols. How Control Exists after De-centralization*. MIT Press.

Gherardi, S. 2015. To Start Practice Theorizing Anew: The Contribution of the Concepts of *Agencement* and Formativeness. *Organization*, 23(5), 680–698.

Gillespie, T. 2014. The Relevance of Algorithms. In T. Gillespie, P. Boczkowski, and K. Foot (Eds.), *Media Technologies: Essays on Communication, Materiality, and Society*. MIT Press.

Gillespie, T. 2015. Platforms Intervene. *Social Media + Society*, 1(1), 1–2.

Gillespie, T. 2018. *Custodians of the Internet: Platforms, Content Moderation, and the Hidden Decisions That Shape Social Media*. Yale University Press.

Gorz, A. 1994. *Il Lavoro Debole: Oltre la Società Salariale*. Edizioni Lavoro.

Graham, S. and Marvin, S. 2001. *Splintering Urbanism: Networked Infrastructures, Technological Mobilities and the Urban Condition*. Routledge.

Gramsci, A. 1975. *Quaderni del Carcere*. Einaudi.

Gran, A., Booth, P., and Bucher, T. 2020. To Be or Not to Be Algorithm Aware: A Question of a New Digital Divide? *Information, Communication & Society*, 24(12), 1779–1796. https://doi.org/10.1080/1369118X.2020.1736124.

Greenfield, A. 2017. *Radical Technologies: The Design of Everyday Life*, Verso Books.

Grusin, R. 2010. *Premediation: Affect and Mediality After 9/11*. Palgrave Macmillan.

Kosík, K. 1976. *Dialectics of the Concrete*. D. Reidel.

Haggerty, K., Ericson, D., and Richard, V. 2000. The Surveillant Assemblage. *British Journal of Sociology*, 5(4), 605–622.

Hargittai, E., Gruber, J., Djukaric, T., Fuchs, J., and Brombach, L. 2020. Black Box Measures? How to Study People's Algorithm Skills. *Information, Communication & Society*, 23(5), 764–775. https://doi.org/10.1080/1369118X .2020.1713846.

Helmond, A. 2015. The Platformization of the Web: Making Web Data Platform Ready. *Social Media + Society*, 1(2), 1–11.

Harvey, D. 1989. From Managerialism to Entrepreneurialism: The Transformation in Urban Governance in Late Capitalism. *Geografiska Annaler*, 71(1), 3–17.

Langlois, G. and Elmer, G. 2013. The Research Politics of Social Media Platforms. *Culture Machine*, 14.

Lazzarato, M. 2014. *Signs and Machines: Capitalism and the Production of Subjectivity*. Semiotext(e).

Lupton, D. 2016. The Diverse Domains of Quantified Selves: Self-tracking Modes and Dataveillance. *Economy and Society*, 45(1), 101–122.

Lyle, P., Sciannamblo, M., and Teli, M. 2018. Fostering Commonfare. Infrastructuring Autonomous Social Collaboration. In R. Mandryk et al. *Proceedings of the 2018 CHI Conference on Human Factors in Computing Systems, April 21-26 2018, Montreal, QC*. Association for Computing Machinery. Available at: https://dl.acm.org/doi/pdf/10.1145/3173574.3174026.

Manovich, L. 2001. *Language of New Media*. MIT Press.

Manovich, L. 2013. Media after Software. *Journal of Visual Culture*, 12(1), 30–37.

MacCormick, J. 2012. *Nine Algorithms That Changed the Future*. Princeton University Press.

Mackenzie, A. 2015. The Production of Prediction: What Does Machine Learning Want? *European Journal of Cultural Studies*, 18(4–5), 429–445.

Markham, A. N. 2020. Taking Data Literacy to the Streets: Critical Pedagogy in the Public Sphere. *Qualitative Inquiry*, 26(2), 227–237.

Marwick, A. 2013. Memes. *Contexts*, 12(4), 12–13.

Merry, S. E. 2016. *The Seductions of Quantification: Measuring Human Rights, Gender Violence, and Sex Trafficking*. University of Chicago Press.

Mezzadra, S. and Neilson, B. 2018. Between Extraction and Exploitation: On Mutations in the Organization of Social Cooperation. *Actuel Marx*, 63(1), 97–113.

Montfort, N. and Bogost, I. 2009. *Racing the Beam: The Atari Video Computer System*. MIT Press.

Moore, P. 2018. *The Quantified Self in Precarity: Work, Technology and What Counts*. Routledge.

Morozov, E. 2013. *To Save Everything, Click Here: The Folly of Technological Solutionism*. Public Affairs.

Nafus, D. and Sherman, J. 2014. This One Does Not Go Up To 11: The Quantified Self Movement as an Alternative Big Data Practice. *International Journal of Communication*, 8, 1784–1794.

Noble, S. U. 2018. *Algorithms of Oppression: How Search Engines Reinforce Racism*. New York University Press.

Payne, A. 2012. *Handbook of CRM: Achieving Excellence Through Customer Management*. Routledge.

Pagano, R., Cremonesi, P., Larson, M. et al. 2016. The Contextual Turn: From Context-Aware to Context-Driven Recommender Systems. In S. Shen et al. *Proceedings of the 10th ACM Conference on Recommender Systems*, September 2016. Association for Computing Machinery.

Papacharissi, Z. 2011. *A Networked Self*. Routledge.

Pashukanis, E. 1978. *Law and Marxism: A General Theory*. Routledge.

Pasquale, F. 2015. *The Black Box Society: The Secret Algorithms that Control Money and Information*. Harvard University Press.

Peters, J. D. 2015. *The Marvelous Clouds: Toward a Philosophy of Elemental Media*. University of Chicago Press.

Plantin, J. C. 2018. Google Maps as Cartographic Infrastructure: From Participatory Mapmaking to Database Maintenance. *International Journal of Communication*, 12, 489–506.

Prey, R. 2018. Nothing Personal: Algorithmic Individuation on Music Streaming Platforms. *Media, Culture & Society*, 40(7), 1086–1100.

Read, J. 2003. *The Micro-Politics of Capital: Marx and the Prehistory of the Present*. SUNY Press.

Risi, E. 2016. Intersezioni e Confini del Lavoro, tra Spazi e Tempi Urbani e Digitali: Il Caso dei Knowledge Workers a Milano. In E. Armano and A. Murgia (Eds.), *Le Reti del Lavoro Gratuito: Spazi Urbani e Nuove Soggettività*. Ombre Corte.

Risi, E., Bonini, T., and Pronzato, R. 2020. Algorithmic Media in Everyday Life: An Experience with Auto-Ethnographic Student Diaries. *Etnografia e Ricerca Qualitativa*, 3, 407–422.

Risi, E., Briziarelli, M., and Armano, E. 2019. Crowdsourcing Platforms as Devices to Activate Subjectivities. *Partecipazione & Conflittos*, 12(3), 767–793. https://doi.org/10.1285/i20356609v12i3p767.

Rigi, J. and Prey, R. 2015. Value, Rent, and the Political Economy of Social Media. *The Information Society*, 31(5), 392–406.

Rose, N. 1990. *Governing the Soul: The Shaping of the Private Self*. Routledge.

Ruppert, E. 2011. Population Objects: Interpassive Subjects. *Sociology*, 45(2), 218–233.

Srnicek, N. 2016. *Platform Capitalism*. Polity Press.

Striphas, T. 2015. Algorithmic Culture. *European Journal of Cultural Studies*, 18(4–5), 395–412.

Thrift, N. 2007. *Non-Representational Theory: Space, Politics, Affect*. Routledge.

Turow, J. and Draper, N. 2014. Industry Conceptions of Audience in the Digital Space: A Research Agenda. *Cultural Studies*, 28(4), 643–656.

van Dijck, J. 2014. Datafication, Dataism and Dataveillance: Big Data Between Scientific Paradigm and Ideology. *Surveillance and Society*, 12(2), 197–208.

van Dijck, J., Poell, T., and de Waal, M. 2018. *The Platform Society: Public Values in a Connective World*. Oxford University Press.

Ziewitz, M. 2016. Governing Algorithms: Myth, Mess, and Methods. *Science, Technology, & Human Values*, 41(1), 3–16.

Zittrain, J. 2008. *The Future of the Internet: And How to Stop It*. Allen Lane.

Zuboff, S. 2019. *The Age of Surveillance Capitalism: The Fight for a Human Future at the New Frontier of Power*. Public Affairs.

PART I

Theoretical Foundations

CHAPTER 1

The Californian Ideology Revisited

Hasmet M. Uluorta and Lawrence Quill

Introduction

It is twenty-five years since Richard Barbrook and Andy Cameron's article appeared in *Science and Culture*. In 1996, at a moment of profound socioeconomic change, they identified the geographical epicentre of that change as the West Coast of the United States. Over the previous two decades, a belief system developed that managed to combine contradictory, yet highly appealing elements rooted in a commitment to technological determinism: the idea that technology would make the world a better place for everyone. Identifying an emerging ideology with roots in technological utopianism was not a new idea and it was not exclusive to the Bay Area in California. In the United States during the first few decades of the twentieth century, for example, philosophers, commentators and mainstream politicians made the case for technological solutions to social and political problems that captured the public imagination and did so from New York and Chicago, rather than San Francisco (see Jordan 1994). Nonetheless, Barbrook and Cameron (hereafter B&C) identified historical elements of the new ideology that were West Coast specific, emerging from the cultural politics of the 1960s and 1970s, an emergent yuppie entrepreneurialism in the 1980s along with the research nexus of universities and corporations in and around the Bay Area.

How to cite this book chapter:
Uluorta, H. M. and Quill, L. 2022. The Californian Ideology Revisited. In: Armano, E., Briziarelli, M., and Risi, E. (eds.), *Digital Platforms and Algorithmic Subjectivities.* Pp. 21–31. London: University of Westminster Press. DOI: https://doi.org/10.16997 /book54.b. License: CC-BY-NC-ND 4.0

In the generation since B&C wrote their seminal piece, there has been an evolution in thinking concerning technology and its relation to politics, power and society. This is in no small part due to technological advances and its associated properties of speed and ubiquity. The authors wrote their piece when personal desktop computing had just gained a foothold in the consumer market. The speed of connection to the internet was limited to the bandwidth provided by dial up modems and commercialisation of the web was in its infancy. Today, the iPhone and similar 'affordable' devices have made personal and wireless computing portable. Users are trackable through machine based legible content and Siri's Artificial Intelligence permits the rapid enhancement of applications for intimate queries. This represents a new stage in the Californian Ideology (hereafter CI) that has seemingly emerged naturally and spontaneously. But, as the authors revealed in their original piece, there was very little that was either natural or spontaneous about the CI.

Returning to the authors' original analysis and assessing it in the light of these and other changes seems timely. This chapter revisits two major claims of the original hypotheses. We consider how the electronic agora that emerged to describe a near-future society where personal communication between individuals was possible without the mediating institutions of government, transformed into largely unregulated social media platforms. Relatedly, we examine how the electronic marketplace subsumed the gift economy and morphed into a surveillance economy that nudges individuals into ongoing personal consumption.

The Californian Ideology

B&C's approach to the development of personal computing and networked communications was both descriptive and normative. It described a particular moment in the life-cycle of technologies, the 'convergence of the media, computing, and telecommunication hypermedia...' (44), alongside a set of ideas that embraced this convergence. These ideas had, they claimed, formed a 'heterogeneous orthodoxy' (44) one that managed to combine contradictory elements into a pleasing whole: 'the freewheeling spirit of the hippies and the entrepreneurial zeal of the yuppies' (45).

Optimistic, libertarian, but also bohemian, the CI blended elements of both the New Left and the New Right with a uniform call to withdraw from the public sphere. While much attention has been paid to the emergence of the New Left in places such as Haight-Ashbury and Berkeley, less well known is the New Right's emergence in Southern California. The New Right's free market doctrine sought to counter the gains made by the New Left especially those associated with the Civil Rights Movement (Freund 2007; HoSang 2011). The CI rested, then, on a peculiar alliance between the anti-establishment cultural politics of the 1960s and a reactionary anti-government free market doctrine.

Despite these tensions, both components had enough in common to forge an ambiguous alliance: both were anti-establishment, suspicious of government and advocated self-empowerment. And both groups shared a belief in the liberating power of technology thereby providing a 'mystical resolution of the contradictory attitudes' inherent to the CI (56).

It mattered less that both visions looked nostalgically to the past, to the founding of the American republic, for a vision of the future. For the New Left, it was the ideal of Jeffersonian democracy that provided the model for the electronic agora. For the New Right, it was the freedom of individuals to keep what was theirs against the machinations of a foreign monarch. B&C point out that this was an unsettling view because it ignored the enormous suffering that made the American republic a possibility in the first place. Overlooked was the massive racialised inequality that was, at the time of the first dotcom boom (1995–2001) only deepening in California. And despite libertarian claims to the contrary, the origins of the computing industry relied less on the heroic efforts of computing pioneers and much more on state sponsorship in the form of Defense Department grants and clandestine work for the NSA and CIA (Kaplan 2000). From road networks to irrigation channels, to the university system, and other infrastructure projects, life as it existed in California would not have been possible without massive state funding as part of the mixed economy.

Ignoring this collective history, however, enabled adherents to the CI to oppose regulation and compliance with tax authorities on the one hand, and offer high-tech solutions to intractable problems like racialised poverty on the other. The absence of any sense of a social reality, permitted a 'mish-mash of hippie anarchism and economic liberalism beefed up with lots of technological determinism' (B&C, 56) forming a persuasive and alluring set of self-justificatory ideas. B&C's conclusion was poignant. The CI was not the only path to the future. It was decidedly parochial:

> developed by a group of people living within one specific country with a particular mix of socio-economic and technological choices. Its eclectic and contradictory blend of conservative economics and hippie radicalism reflects the history of the West Coast – and not the inevitable future of the rest of the world. (63)

From the Electronic Agora to Social Media

Early participants in the text-only Bulletin Board Server *Whole Earth 'Lectronic Link* (WELL), like Howard Rheingold, were motivated by a strong sense to 'rediscover the power of cooperation, turning cooperation into a game, a way of life – a merger of knowledge capital, social capital, and communion' (1993, 110). The virtual community, consisting of discussion forums called 'conferences', was contrasted against the corporate power of the mainstream media. Rheingold's (1993) *The Virtual Community*, advocated for participatory democracy and was peppered with references to thinkers such as Jürgen Habermas (1989) and his theory of communicative action. It was precisely those elements of Habermas' theory that emphasised open access, voluntary participation, rational argument, and the freedom to express opinions that was required, Rheingold argued, for 'authentic engagement' (1993, 243–6).

Similar ideas were in circulation at the time that the WELL was established in 1985. Benjamin Barber (1984) noted in *Strong Democracy* that the heart of the political process was 'democratic talk'. Along with the creation of public spaces like parks, urban farms and neighbourhood associations, he recommended the construction of assemblies for between five and twenty-five thousand citizens to engage and deliberate. The electronic agora obviated the need for such costly construction projects. However, by the time B&C wrote their piece, the Habermasian public sphere was under assault. Numerous critics pointed to the exclusionary nature of the public sphere (Fraser 1992). Habermas and his followers were charged with failing to recognise more complex notions of identity given expression within numerous counterpublics (Mouffe 1993).

While some attempt was made to salvage the Habermasian project (see Benhabib 1992), the clash of opinions within the WELL and the (at times) uncivil communicative style of the interlocutors had not gone unnoticed. This tension had, in fact, been identified much earlier. Richard Sennett's (1977) *The Fall of Public Man* considered the problem to be both historical and technological. Historical self-understanding had shifted from a person possessed of 'natural character' concerned with the public good, to the far more private 'personality' concerned only with like minds. Personalised politics, suggested Sennett, was destined to result in *destructive Gemeinschaft* drawing upon the animosities that existed between friends and enemies. This feature of modern life was exacerbated by electronic media: '[t]he media [television and radio] have vastly increased the store of knowledge groups have about each other but have rendered actual contact unnecessary' (282). By 1995, an impasse appeared to have been reached.

And yet, as Fred Turner (2005) notes, the search for the public sphere was only one component of the WELL experiment. Equally important was the commune movement of the 1960s and early 1970s. The 'New Communalists' were inspired less by Jefferson and more by the writings of Alvin Toffler and Buckminster Fuller. Their goal was to retreat from mainstream society and politics and to establish new, isolated communities. Stewart Brand's *Whole Earth Catalog* was intended to provide the raw materials and ideas to make this vision possible and served as the model for the WELL and, later, social networks. Turner (2005, 489) notes, 'the Catalog both depicted the products of an emerging counterculture and linked the scattered members of that culture to one another. In that sense, it became a 'network forum.' From the outset, the idea of 'virtual community' was heralded by those who craved a revitalised public sphere uncorrupted by commercial interests *and* by those who embraced a technology-infused communalism that was libertarian politically and economically.

It is hard to overestimate the impact of Rheingold's notion of virtual community on the political imaginary within the US. Despite numerous theoretical and empirical challenges to Rheingold's (1993) claims, the virtual community took its place – alongside the 'digital agora', 'electronic town-hall meeting' and 'digital public sphere' – as part of the ongoing American political story (see also Kirk and Schill 2011; Kruse, Norris and Flincham 2018).

By the mid 1990s, the popularity of the WELL had peaked. With increasingly sophisticated Graphical User Interfaces (GUI), file sharing programs and platforms that enabled billions of people to 'connect' rather than a few thousand on a variety of devices, bulletin boards and the 'electronic agora' were being displaced. It was Rheingold's influence again this time in a 2002 book, *Smart Mobs*, that analysed the rise of mobile computing and the use of reputation systems to generate trust that helped fuel the rise of social media platforms. Nevertheless, this also coincided with a period of prolonged and steady decline in trust in government that began in the 1960s (Griffin 2015). Americans did not merely 'bowl alone' (Putnam 2000) but 'sorted' themselves into groups in increasingly homogenous communities. As Bill Bishop (2008, 40) noted, by the early 21st century, the United States was a country,

> where everyone can choose the neighbours (and church and news shows) most compatible with his or her lifestyle and beliefs. And we are living with the consequences of this segregation by way of life: pockets of like-minded citizens that have become so ideologically inbred that we don't know, can't understand, and can barely conceive of 'those people' who live just a few miles away.

Despite this, the second wave of digital democracy characterised by networked technologies was heralded by advocates as a step towards the development of critical counterpublics. Social networks contained within them the potential to challenge traditional forms of media via citizen journalism and activism (WikiLeaks), inspiring social movements that precipitated political revolution (the Arab Spring of 2010–11), and highlighted issues like economic and racial inequality (Indignados, #BlackLivesMatter). Scholars noted both the speed and frequency with which protest movements coalesced around transient issues, responding to perceived crises in real time (Castells 2012).

Unfortunately, as with the electronic agora, it is difficult to gauge how far social media measures up to the aspirations of democratic theorists. Digital enclaves have tended to emulate their physical counterparts. In the absence of shared norms that regulate speech online, there has been a marked rise in populist rhetoric and extremism. The inability to determine factual from fake sources of information has further undermined the possibility of shared goals.

Finally, the apparent contradiction between digital public spaces free from monetary interests and social media platforms that are an integral component of 'surveillance capitalism' is an ongoing concern (Zuboff 2019).

From Electronic to Capitalocentrist Marketplace[1]

B&C noted the malleability of the CI as it embraced two seemingly opposing visions of the electronic marketplace. The New Left saw the emergence of a hi-tech 'gift economy' that would, 'replace corporate capitalism and big government' (52). The other adhered to a neoliberal political economy ascendant in the late 1970s culminating with the election of former Republican California Governor Ronald Reagan as President in 1980. Led intellectually by Republican Speaker of the House Newt Gingrich along with Alvin and Heidi Toffler, the New Right envisioned a limitless electronic capitalist marketplace. The entrepreneur hero would be released from the shackles of government regulation and the domination of oligopolistic firms.

Barbrook (2005) would be one of the first scholars to understand that both visions would exist side-by-side, as information would be interchangeably shared and sold. An undertheorised aspect of B&C's analysis, however, was the role played by financial capital, namely venture capitalists, and the implications of financialisation as the dominant logic of capitalist accumulation. Sand Hill Road, near Stanford University, is synonymous with Silicon Valley's start-up culture. Prior to 1993, however, would-be entrepreneurs and venture capitalists were unaware of the financial opportunities that the internet represented (Ferguson 1999). This changed with Netscape's initial stock offering in 1995 where its valuation more than doubled in the first day reaching nearly $1 billion (Kenney 2003).

Four impacts are worth noting. First, this would signal to others that internet start-ups could be extremely lucrative (Zook 2003). Larger companies such as Cisco Systems, for example, began to buy out start-ups paying enormous multiples making early venture fund investors, firm founders and employees immensely wealthy (Mayer and Kenney 2004). This would lead to a new cycle with further investments, employees establishing their own start-ups or moving onto other start-up ventures. Second, Netscape's success cannot be attributed to its profitability as it was not profitable (Amazon, Tesla, Twitter and Uber are other examples of this trend). Instead, it was the perception that the web was a rebellious force irrevocably reshaping the media landscape (Streeter 2010). The term *disruption* would become part of the naturalised ethos of the CI, as technology driven change was seen as inevitable. Third, as Microsoft sought to undermine Netscape's domination of the browser market, it began bundling its Internet Explorer software free of charge within its new operating systems. Preloaded and releasing rapid downloadable updates that expanded its operation and functionality, Microsoft understood that the key to profitability was in keeping users within an ecosystem. In a widely circulated article, Tim O'Reilly (2005) described how the post-bubble internet, dubbed Web 2.0, was emerging where firms sought user participation as a means to profitability. Facebook, for example, is essentially an empty site requiring user-generated content to ensure (on-going) use. Participation, O'Reilly noted, was not linked to democratic aims, but rather to ensure user-generated content even when users were self-interested.

Fourth, unable to compete, in 1998 Netscape began distributing the source code of its browser with the hope that the community of users would help to maintain and improve the browser more quickly and with greater success than its engineers. This seemed to epitomise the electronic agora model espoused by the New Left. It was a do-it-yourself solution that transcended the capitalist marketplace, as it remained free.

What Netscape had effectively done, however, was to reaffirm the CI by shifting away from freeware and shareware to a new hybrid form of sharing and capitalist accumulation in the form of Open Source. This term, and its ensuing practices, were more palatable to corporate interests. Retained would be the idea that the role of technology is to encourage freedom and thereby renew democracy. A critical difference, though, was that with Open Source the labour utilised to change the software could now be claimed as part of the original code and receive copyright protection (Söderberg 2008). Soon other corporations, such as IBM with Apache HTTP Server, would enter the Open Source space as they too saw the profit potential of this new format.

Unable to challenge Microsoft's monopoly, corporations would offset the costs of software development by relying on the gift economy as a means to generate profits (Barbrook 2005). A more recent example is Google's Android. As a Linux based Open Source project, Google has been able to secure third party application development while retaining control over the direction of Android development. Android also collects usage data from its users in order to launch and refine applications as well as to develop location and user specific services and advertising.

Taken together these four points reveal that it was a short step to monetising user content beginning in the early 2000s. New firms sought to keep users engaged on their respective platforms. For example, Facebook's introduction of the 'like' button in 2009, along with Twitter's 'retweet' function, provided a public metric to assess the popularity of online content as well as a means to predict which content a user might prefer in future postings. Kosinski, Stillwell and Graepal (2013) note that clicking the like button can reveal personal information such as sexual orientation, religion and political party affiliation to Facebook without the user's explicit knowledge. Likes then produce commodifiable information that can be packaged and sold to third parties.

Likes also push rationality aside in favour of emotion. As one leading commentator put it, the social media environment provides the ideal context to employ psychological techniques to encourage addictive behaviours thereby '…

suppress[ing] the areas of the brain associated with judgment and reason while activating the parts associated with wanting and desire' (Eyal and Hoover 2014, 10). Likes feed into this as the search for active intensity and distraction, where users pause rather than swipe or scroll away, is now an integral part of social media success (or failure) (Dean 2010; Paasonen 2016).

Social media has evolved since the early 2000s when platforms such as Friendster, MySpace and Facebook first made their appearance. In design, these platforms shared similarities with Rheingold's virtual community offering tools to connect with (albeit) existing friends. But, as a result of a series of enhancements to their services, social media moved closer to elements contained within the New Communalist model. As Tarleton Gillespie (2010) argues, these platforms then model the democratic ideal by giving all participants a voice while simultaneously appealing to advertisers as a safe and productive site to host them. Under a veneer of neutrality, they have also been highly effective in evading governmental regulation (Taplin 2017).

Conclusion

B&C understood how both the New Left and Right envisioned the computer revolution as a moment when the tools of the establishment could be placed in the hands of the people. Once the people knew how to work the machine, they could fix the system. They would possess, in addition, all the information that resided in hitherto closed bureaucracies. The virtual community formed part of the fantasy of liberation within the CI, where techno-populism and counter-cultural techno-fetishism met in the electronic agora and marketplace (Dean 2002, 89).

By the mid-2000s, the original promise of the electronic agora was struggling against competing notions that saw it as a virtual marketplace of ideas and consumables. Rather than promoting an informed and engaged citizenry, social media has also facilitated consumption, gossip and the increased sorting of the population into exclusive ideological groups. In this sense connectivity cannot be disassociated from ambivalence. The promise of a burgeoning gift economy has instead become subsumed within oligopolistic firms. From concerns with surveillance (Zuboff 2019), algorithmic discrimination (Noble 2017), tech-addiction and anxiety (Dean 2010), the creation of enormous wealth disparities in places such as the Bay Area (O'Neil 2017) and the possibility of technological mass underemployment and unemployment (Gray and Suri 2019) the CI has been challenged. These ruptures trigger new political claims that require a re-imagining of subjectivities.

The 'Big Five' of Alphabet-Google, Amazon, Facebook, Apple and Microsoft (GAFAM) nevertheless continue to extend their capabilities and reach (van Dijck, Nieborg and Poell 2019). Implicit in this latest iteration of the CI is the imperative force of risk mitigation and management, corporate-technocratic control and a new understanding that the lifeworld is irrevocably integrated into digital systems. Implied here is the modification of behaviours both for individuals and groups at scale. What is being produced is a neoliberal subjectivity whereby 'the good' is increasingly shifted away from the individual. Social media platforms function simultaneously as a 'virtual community' and a laboratory for psychological and economic modelling. The widespread monitoring of online sentiment, and the collection of emotional and biometric data through cameras as well as through wearable technologies, is a development unforeseen in B&C's original analysis. The holy grail of platform capitalism today is ubiquitous data collection delivering real-time information about customers' desires and emotions. As McStay (2016, 5) notes, 'data and understanding of emotions are of the highest importance to help give people what they really want, rather than what they say they want.' In this way algorithms remove agency (a key component of the original CI) and empower others who profess to know a person's individual preferences better than they do themselves. Connecting with individuals in ways that extend beyond ones' perception of self, these technologies render the possibility of greater insight as well as error.

Twenty-five years on from the publication of 'The Californian Ideology', techno-utopians have altered their message to account for the move out of the agora to the surveilled space of social media. Public reason, they complain, has been replaced by an advertiser-driven media space that devalues the most important aspects of 'humanity' (Lanier 2011). Conversation has been replaced by electronic forms of communication that are fragmented and exhibit a forced intimacy, collapsing the distinction between private and public (Turkle 2017). It is no little irony that some of the founders of social media networks have abandoned them, barring their children from using the technologies that they helped develop.

Note

[1] The term capitalocentric/ist used in the subheading for this section was taken from Gibson-Graham (1996).

References

Barber, B. 1984. *Strong Democracy: Participatory Politics for a New Age*. University of California Press.

Barbrook, R. and Cameron, A. 1996. The Californian Ideology. *Science and Culture*, 6(1), 44–72.

Barbrook, R. 2005. The Hi-Tech Gift Economy. *First Monday Special Issue #3: Internet Banking, E-Money, and Internet Gift Economies*. Available at: https://www.firstmonday.org/ojs/index.php/fm/article/view/631/552.

Benhabib, S. 1992. *Situating the Self: Gender Community and Postmodernism in Contemporary Ethics*. Routledge.

Bishop, B. 2008. *The Big Sort: Why the Clustering of Like-Minded America is Tearing Us Apart*. Mariner Books.

Castells, M. 2012. *Networks of Outrage and Hope: Social Movements in the Internet Age*. Wiley.

Dean, J. 2002. *Publicity's Secret: How Technoculture Capitalizes on Democracy*. Cornell University Press.

Dean, J. 2010. *Blog Theory: Feedback and Capture in the Circuits of Drive*. Polity.

Eyal, N. and Hoover, R. 2014. *Hooked: How to Build Habit-Forming Products*. Portfolio.

Ferguson, C. H. 1999. *High Stakes, No Prisoners*. Times Books.

Fraser, N. 1992. Rethinking the Public Sphere: A Contribution to the Critique of Actually Existing Democracy. In C. Calhoun (Ed.), *Habermas and the Public Sphere* (pp. 109–142). MIT Press.

Freund, D. M. P. 2007. *Colored Property: State Policy and White Racial Politics in Suburban America*. University of Chicago Press.

Gibson-Graham, J. K. 1996. *The End of Capitalism (As We Knew It): A Feminist Critique of Political Economy*. University of Minnesota Press.

Gillespie, T. 2010. The Politics of 'Platforms'. *New Media & Society*, 12(3), 347–364.

Gray, M. L. and Suri, S. 2019. *Ghost Work: How to Stop Silicon Valley from Building a New Global Underclass*. Houghton Mifflin Harcourt.

Griffin, S. 2015. *Broken Trust: Dysfunctional Government and Constitutional Reform*. University Press of Kansas.

Habermas, J. 1989. *The Structural Transformation of the Public Sphere: An Inquiry into a Category of Bourgeois Society*. MIT Press.

HoSang, D. M. 2011. Racial Liberalism and the Rise of the Sunbelt West: The Defeat of Fair Housing on the 1964 California Ballot. In M. Nickerson and D. Dochuk (Eds.), *Sunbelt Rising: The Politics of Space, Place, and Region* (pp. 188–213). University of Pennsylvania Press.

Jordan, J. M. 1994. *Machine-Age Ideology: Social Engineering and American Liberalism, 1911–1939*. University of North Carolina Press.

Kaplan, D. A. 2000. *The Silicon Boys and Their Valley of Dreams*. Harper Collins.

Kenney, M. 2003. The Growth and Development of the Internet in the United States. In B. Kogut (Ed.), *The Global Internet Economy* (pp. 69–108). MIT Press.

Kirk, R. and Schill, D. 2011. A Digital Agora: Citizen Participation in the 2008 Presidential Debates. *American Behavioral Scientist*, 55(3), 325–347.

Kosinski, M., Stillwell, D., and Graepel, T. 2013. Private Traits and Attributes are Predictable from Digital Records of Human Behavior. *Proceedings of the National Academy of Sciences*, 110(15), 5802–5805.

Kruse, L., Norris, D. R., and Flinchum, N. R. 2018. Social Media as a Public Sphere. *The Sociological Quarterly*, 59(1), 62–84.

Lanier, J. 2011. *You Are Not a Gadget: A Manifesto*. Vintage.

Mayer, D. and Kenney, M. 2004. Ecosystems and Acquisition Management: Understanding Cisco's Strategy. *Industry and Innovation*, 11(4), 299–326.

McStay, A. 2016. Empathic Media and Advertising: Industry, Policy, Legal and Citizen Perspectives (The Case for Intimacy). *Big Data & Society*, 3(2), 1–11.

Mouffe, C. 1993. *The Return of the Political*. Verso Press.

Noble, U. N. 2018 *Algorithms of Oppression: How Search Engines Reinforce Racism*. New York University Press.

O'Neil, C. 2017. *Weapons of Math Destruction. How Big Data Increases Inequality and Threatens Democracy*. Penguin Books.

O'Reilly, T. 2005. What is Web 2.0? *O'Reilly*, 30 September. Retrieved from: www.oreillynet.com/pub/a/oreilly/tim/news/2005/09/30/what-is-web-20 .html.

Paasonen, S. 2016. Fickle Focus: Distraction, Affect and the Production of Value in Social Media. *First Monday*, 21(10), 1–19.

Putnam, R. D. 2000. *Bowling Alone: The Collapse and Revival of American Community*. Simon & Schuster.

Rheingold, H. 1993. *The Virtual Community. Homesteading on the Electronic Frontier*. Addison-Wesley.

Rheingold, H. 2002. *Smart Mobs: The Next Social Revolution*. Perseus.

Sennett, R. 1977. *The Fall of Public Man*. Alfred Knopf.

Söderberg, J. 2008. *Hacking Capitalism: The Free and Open Software Movement*. Routledge.

Streeter, T. 2010. *The Net Effect: Romanticism, Capitalism, and the Internet*. New York University Press.

Taplin, J. 2017. *Move Fast and Break Things: How Facebook, Google, and Amazon Cornered Culture and Undermined Democracy*. Little, Brown and Company.

Turkle, S. 2017. *Alone Together: Why We Expect More from Technology and Less from Each Other*. Basic Books.

Turner, F. 2005. Where the Counterculture Met the New Economy: The WELL and the Origins of the Virtual Community. *Technology and Culture*, 46(3), 485–512.

van Dijck, J., Nieborg, D., and Poell, T. 2019. Reframing Platform Power. *Internet Policy Review*, 8(2), 1–18.

Zook, M. A. 2002. Grounded Capital: Venture Financing and the Geography of the Internet Industry, 1994–2000. *Journal of Economic Geography*, 2(2), 151–177.

Zuboff, S. 2019. *The Age of Surveillance Capitalism: The Fight for a Human Future at the New Frontier of Power*. Public Affairs.

CHAPTER 2

Platform Politics and a World Beyond Catastrophe

Ned Rossiter and Soenke Zehle

Platform Politics

Platforms pattern the grammar of this world. Across the political spectrum, from #BLM, #StopTheSteal or #GameStop, three core pillars of US society provide the institutional points of reference for the latest round of organised critique: the police, democracy and finance capital (see Stalder 2021). Rolling these distinct movements into a mashup manifesto against nihilistic fatalism is Inhabit, a distinctively North American formation cultivating attention to build a movement of the disaffected.[1] Seeking to galvanise millennials in search of a cause, Inhabit sets out 'Path B', a political tract with something for everyone: climate justice, collective care, autonomous infrastructures, planning hubs, food supply chains and networks of fight clubs recuperating a depleted masculinity ('learn to hunt, to code, to heal'). Its default platforms? Twitter, Instagram and imageboards, all infiltrated by the alt-right who seed further confusion and political disorientation into the signal of widespread alienation and despair.

Despite whatever 'platform fatigue' appears to have set in, and a growing sense of fatalism regarding the governing role played by a handful of players that continue to dominate the platform economy, no matter what the activist or

How to cite this book chapter:
Rossiter N. and Zehle, S. 2022. Platform Politics and a World Beyond Catastrophe.
In: Armano, E., Briziarelli, M., and Risi, E. (eds.), *Digital Platforms and Algorithmic Subjectivities*. Pp. 33–46. London: University of Westminster Press. DOI: https://doi.org/10.16997/book54.c. License: CC-BY-NC-ND 4.0

regulatory effort, we are convinced that the discussion about the future design of socio-technological systems has just begun. By no means is this a Silicon Valley 'problem', certainly not in any exclusive sense. The geoeconomic contest of predominantly digital platforms is also one of geopolitical variance. Alibaba and Huawei are among the chief platform and tech hegemons in the scramble for markets and the production of a new geopolitical order that goes beyond the modern territorial assertion of sovereign power by nation-states (see Lindtner 2020; Wen 2020; Zhang 2020). Certainly the world-shaping capacity of these Chinese firms depends on their complicated bind to the political and economic agendas of state authority (see Woo and Strumpf 2021). But adhering too rigidly to such a nexus diminishes the ways in which platforms hold specific technical, infrastructural and business logics that produce social relations and economic practices in ways distinct from the patterning of populations and management of the economy by national governments in partnerships with corporate actors. In other words, there is an assertive force about digital platforms able to transform the world in ways specific to their logics of operation. Political analysis of such tendencies can, if it likes, take refuge in info-political debates concerning rights, access, surveillance, privacy and so forth. These remain important battles. But we also see a need to attend to a platform politics on the brink of ecological catastrophe.

Our focus in this chapter is not on the peculiarities of these dynamics, but simply to note that the story of platforms does not unfold from Silicon Valley and out to the rest of the world. We are currently in the midst of a series of social-technological shifts underwriting a recomposition of global economies and modalities of power. Finding our bearings within these emergent coordinates requires more than a critique of the usual suspects. If platform politics orbits around the struggle for orientation, casting hope through new stories of the world, there is a tragic irony that it does so by advancing the business interests of the tech sector and surveillance industries whose data and computational infrastructures provide the architecture of connection. When culture and economy, politics and society are organised through platforms, do we lose sight of their conditions of possibility? Are the scenes of confrontation, of the political, precisely disavowed in the flat ontology of platforms, where the hegemony of standards ensures analysable user-generated data for platform economies?

In this chapter we set out some of the stakes of platform politics at the current conjuncture. Data governance issues concerning the social production of value, data rights in automated markets, data surveillance motivated by pervasive paranoia and a general ideological intolerance against off-message articulations of disaffection. These are just some of the prevailing discursive and governmental tendencies that define the horizon of our platform present. Yet there is more. Much more. We write our way through crisis to find some bearing and orientation in a world of real-time updates and automated injunctions. The machinic signalling of pervasive despair is wrought by contagion, climate and a future at once forestalled and bearing down upon us.

In ways we have come to accept as obvious, platforms are technological, socially driven and motivated by business models intent on maximum data extraction translated into stratospheric profit margins. There is a sense that critics can do little more than tinker around the edges, add local case study details, sketch out design features and describe variations in user bases and market specialisation. But that is basically it. We seek to shift the optics, to reorient scale and plot out a less immediate point of departure in framing a debate on platform politics, subjectivity, technology, economy and environment. Across these core elements of capital and life we find scenes of confrontation that manifest the political and illuminate a platform politics not reducible to the political economy of Meta, Apple, Microsoft, Amazon and Alphabet (MAMAA) and its variations. The rise of platform capitalism signals a nexus that is quite literally a far cry from what used to be 'the West', an imperial geopolitical configuration stabilised by a set of overlapping crises whose catastrophic serialisation instantiates not only the imaginary of streaming giants. More importantly, the infrastructural legacies (e.g. the SWIFT payment system) of this earlier configuration remind us that the stacks of the platform economy have geopolitical layers whose depths a mere critique of the political economy of data extractivism won't reach.[2] Indeed, the stakes are more substantial than whatever windfall might benefit the few in the next IPO hype or corporate acquisition on the geoeconomic stage of the tech sector. Our task here, as authors and readers of this collection, is to identify the contours of platform politics in the context of a world on the edge.

Planetary Perspectives

As we delineate horizons of collective action beyond pandemic politics, we begin to take stock of what has changed. The way we do democracy, for one. Rediscovering the spatial and temporal scales of our agency shrunk by lockdowns and an awkward neo-cybernetic politics of real-time governance, we are still waiting for convincing approaches to address the antagonism between decisionism and democracy that such a crisis tends to throw into relief.[3] Awkwardness prevails, in part, because the actuality of decision-making serves as a stark reminder of the vast gap between invocations of individualised data-driven and intelligent futures and the distinctly generic and low-tech responses that lack precisely the kind of differentiation such data intelligence is supposed to enable. Adding to such sobering self-exposure of states unable to wield their high-tech tools to deliver the kind of transparent and trustworthy solutions promised by narratives of public sector innovation ever since 'smart' was introduced as a feature of governance, experiences of collective and unevenly distributed struggle remind us that, no matter who gets to enter the empty stage of democracy, putting on an engaging show is the requisite theatrical trope designed to keep our faith in a fair division of labour between constituent and constituted power.[4] But things are not fair. From Belarus to Hong Kong, Myanmar or Uganda, grassroots democracy is taking a beating across the world. Throughout the Euro-American 'West', widely shared feelings of disenfranchisement aggregate wafts of righteous populism and rancid paranoia into the imaginary of a perfect storm (see National Terrorism Advisory System Bulletin 2021). Far from seeing 'the end of neoliberalism' in the arrival of state-sponsored crisis relief efforts, mobilising public debt on a scale unthinkable only a few years ago, neoliberal politics appears to have affirmed its adoption of the complexity of life as a positive promise rather than a limit to governance.[5] And as we prepare to exit not into a 'new normal' but the next iteration of crisis politics addressing the climate emergency, cutting edge public health approaches (mRNA!, tracking apps!) mesh with planetary perspectives inherited from the 1970s.

Fifty years after images of the blue planet reached us from a sky no longer beyond our reach as a human species, and NASA engineer James Lovelock suggested we embrace Gaia as the conceptual core of a neo-cybernetic imaginary matching such newly found awareness, Gaia is now part of the *mise-en-scène* of the empty stage of crisis politics. Only this time she presents herself as a massively distributed goddess of planetary health, a quasi-pantheistic collective intelligence whose capacity for self-organisation is bolstered by a growing scientific acceptance of Lynn Margulis' (1998) work on symbiogenesis.[6] A bit too soon, perhaps, advocates in the garden of Gaia celebrate the return of the political as 'critical zones' of the earth (Latour and Weibel 2020). But there might be reason for hope as a new politics of care takes shape, grounded in social-political movements, climate change and essential workers on the frontlines of crisis (Ross 2021; Morse 2021; Dowling 2021).

Regardless of whether or not one joins the chorus of Gaia as a revived neo-Enlightenment trope of salvation, the *realpolitik* of sovereign power, which is in fact far from divorced of ideological imaginaries and ethno-political horizons, is in pursuit of remaking the planet as an operating system cut across geopolitical divisions forged by infrastructural and technical protocols and standards. Here, the politics of borders are recalibrated as parametric politics constituted by data sovereignty, data security, interoperability (albeit with multiple constraints and underscored by inoperability), value extraction, population management, agri-business and finance capitalism. The standout example here is China's Belt and Road Initiative (BRI), which attracts huge swathes of business, policy, academic and news media attention (see Narins and Agnew 2020; Grant 2020). And in Europe, significant policy momentum is gathering around the European Commission's GAIA-X initiative, which seeks to build and make the case for a 'federated data infrastructure' as an 'ecosystem' that recruits states, companies and citizens into a new united geopolitical and geoeconomic front of 'digital sovereignty' able to withstand and indeed offer an alternative universe of value (economic, social, political and supposedly environmental) to its geopolitical competitors.[7] Such an agenda, driven by the hope of another iteration of the 'Brussels effect', is predicated not only on ensuring the economic and political security of a European future, but is indeed imbued with a Messianic conviction of platform solutionism on a planetary scale.[8]

The Web 3 vision of a 'creator economy' serves as a dark mirror of the soft-powerism of the Brussels effect, the 'metaverse' techno-dystopianism of a world where every act of communication is always already financialised, where becoming-finance is the new horizon of collective self-determination and where the infrastructuralism of distributed ledger systems driven by venture capital narrows the vision of the social production of value to a stateless system of temporary token-based economic empowerment, a shadow economy beyond the regulatory reach of sovereignty claiming to carve out a series of safe spaces for the economically and geopolitically disenfranchised. It is in this sense that we understand the current conjuncture as one to critically probe in terms of platform politics.

But what of forms of power not reducible to the modern idiom of the sovereign state, which is not easily fused or reconciled with the cybernetic contingencies and computational complexities of the planet as platform? What are some of the operative dimensions and social-ecological tendencies coincident at the conjuncture of a planet on the edge? Can we attribute a modality of power as a transformative force not beholden to the out-of-time routines peculiar to the sovereign state and its exercise of power? There is latent power in the everyday, power in gestures without formal consequence, expressions that are never acknowledged yet seep through and course within the social-ecological organism. We might as well give this power a name, no matter that it persists in improper ways, and call it out as a non-sovereign power (see Deseriis 2015; Wark 2013, 193).

Perhaps not surprisingly given renewed interest in the 'performative power of assembly' (Butler 2018), theatre has assumed responsibility for shifting conversations in ways that expand the conventionalised horizons of community organising.[9] Reflecting on the relationship between art and democracy, Oskar Eustis of New York's Public Theater recalls the separation in 1970s counter-culture between artistic experiments expanding our sense of the public and social justice work focusing on inequality.[10] We find similar expressions of a politics subsisting in and rubbing up against the rules of the ruling classes in the tactics and strategies of *détournement* associated with the Situationists during the same epoch, in another country across the Atlantic divide of ocean that is also a logistical medium of history and passage of connection, labour and violence in the form of the Atlantic slave trade (Gilroy 1995; Harney and Moten 2013). And, more recently, in the years closing out the twentieth century and into the twenty-first century, collective practices of political assembly, Occupy, the movement of the squares, the yellow vests and the Umbrella Movement again register the nexus of politics and performance manifest as power with the potential to resonate across time and space in ways that signal a transversal and transgenerational politics that does not submit or forget. Indeed, we might conceive such incipient power, often galvanised by the urgency and stakes of the singular event, as a form of political articulation that codes a platform politics not beholden to proprietary infrastructures of communication, even if movements increasingly organise using the infrastructural media of big tech corporations.

While we are fully aware that lumping these dynamics together makes little sense sociologically, we invoke them as indicators of a 'non-sovereign power' exercised and performed across time and space. As a banality held in common, the technical and historical seriality of connection between movements holds a political potency and imaginary that, we believe, is worth recalling in times of crisis. To be sure, the current pandemic rejuvenates the authority of the platform state and its declaration to decide. As much as the Googles, Amazons, Alibabas, Tencents, Baidus, ByteDances and all the rest go bananas with their massive accumulation of data – the fuel of automation machines – a nagging doubt will always persist and announce the inevitability of their decline and demise: the movement of people, of masses whose attention gravitates to whatever the next best media turn out to be. Underscoring this immanent deficit of commitment to any particular platform media are forms of sociality and desire that find expression through elusive gestures and the cultivation of atmospheres.[11] Such attributes are at once performative and theatrical while belonging also to public life imagined by play and performance more generally.

Infrastructural Memories of the Future

The turn to the platform as a figure of socio-technological systems design brings back core episodes from the archives of governance, both in the narrow sense of techniques of organisation and in a much broader sense of modes of relation. If infrastructure is always relational, what are the relationalities available for infrastructure design?[12] As we have written elsewhere, 'To analyse the transformation of sovereign power through the optic of infrastructure requires more than attention to infrastructural relationalities. Or rather, the relational will not suffice as the end point in thinking infrastructural arrangements within and through which economy and society, labour and life are governed. Instead, this requires attention to various registers of material constitution – from the design of infrastructures to the legal frameworks governing their operation' (Rossiter and Zehle 2017). The reflexive invocation of 'participation' may not yet have run its course as a panacea to make-things-public, but the concept has been overburdened with expectations of empowerment that have distracted from its weaknesses as a concept of fairly limited analytical reach and hence the impossibility of delivering us from the systems that structure and sustain such relationalities. Sadly, the injunction to participate more often instantiates a depoliticising directive in the form of feedback surveys, breakout groups in online meetings or joining climate change initiatives by sorting out your trash. Doing nothing is not fuel for data economies and increasingly confers a nihilistic social status equivalent to the great unwashed who bring Team Euphoria down. Not unlike the discourses of openness and making-things-visible that struggle to translate the language of the Enlightenment to an era of white-boxing intelligent systems, the language of participation has only been so successful in fighting off the subsumption of gestures into the extractivist dynamics of the platform economy.

At a time when 'you are the product' is no longer indicative of a rare awakening of critical awareness but the default design strategy of everyone and everything 'participatory', it has also become more urgent to come up with a conceptual idiom that does not simply tell us something about differences in ownership (proprietary = bad, free software = good, markets versus commons, etc.) but modes of subjectivation. Of whether, for example, the production of citizenship and consumer agency actually differs. And if so, then how? The rush of politics toward the people machines of social media suggests that we no longer care to make that distinction. Instead, we have elevated 'the market' to be our collective teacher of things relational: identity, community, story – if you need any of these, shop around.[13] At least as far as we can tell, the 'old' distinctions between publics and markets have given way to concurrent and competing dynamics of valorisation across a topology that makes such simple distinctions look naive.

Which is why, of course, this is old news. The shift toward the machinic was always tied less to an uncritical embrace of the power of distributed systems as future backbone and base infrastructure of the multitude (it was that too, and as white nationalism embraces the logics of federation we have yet to delineate the shifting boundaries between such anonymity and more progressive visions of the political). Instead, theorists invoking the political concept of the machinic were intrigued, perhaps even entranced, by the sense that affect, the corporeality of how we put first things and then stories of the world together, is what literally matters.

So what is it that is being subverted, what happened to the visions of exodus, of a power that constitutes itself through disengagement? Among the most recent flag bearers of such *degagisme*, the *gilet jaunes* were too exhausted to tell us where they wanted to go from here, only that 'here' – the world of competitive self-optimisation, of the number of unicorns as a measure of societal progress, of forms of mobility and urban development that leave those on the margin with even fewer means to move to the centre – was not a place they wanted to be. Tempting as it may be to declare yet again the failure of movements to scale and sustain in ways that demonstrate political cohesion, discipline and a strategic plan, what such undulations of insurgency demonstrate above all else is that social-political heterogeneity cannot easily be mapped onto the left-right axis of movement analysis.

At the same time, it became clear that the roundabouts where activists would gather and stage the slow down of the system as a form of critique was itself symptomatic of the difficulty of federating such micro-political initiatives. Yet these efforts did not scale on the level of organisational infrastructures, and sympathetic media enforcing the logic of representation in its search for 'spokespeople' folded events back into conventional dynamics of politics as usual. Perhaps this is too sober an assessment, potentially discounting the less than tangible 'atmospheric' effects such examples of self-organising have far beyond the event – insights into the status quo, imaginaries of change, inspirational narratives. But short-termism at the grassroots level offers no alternative to the short-termism of elites. On the contrary, it limits further the return on whatever collective investments in 'decentralisation' we may or may not want to continue to make. We do not need more peripheries, neither economic nor technological. But how do we cultivate a politics that is more futural, beyond the horizon of self-exploitation and scarcity management that may only be considered exemplary of 'resilience' if we continue to ignore how weak the infrastructures of relation have become? (see Walker and Cooper 2011; Halpern 2017).

Beyond Catastrophe as Calculation

To be sure, logics of systemic reason are always-already accompanied by catastrophe, by the laws of the accident (Virilio 2007). The sensation of nature as sublime is but a surface for carnage, destruction and the technics of contingency (see Hui 2015). In returning to the suggestion in the title of this chapter of a world beyond catastrophe, we seek to depart from a tendency in critical theory to embrace the drama of doom even when such critique presents as meta-reason transcendent from cultures of performance (catastrophe as tragic theatre). Similarly, as much as the mathematics of democracy invites tampering with the machine, accompanied by outcries of calculated interference and the manipulation of public perception, we prefer instead to probe further the conjunctural epoch in which the world transitions from carbon economies and attendant cultures of consumption to renewables and the politics of energy distribution.

As Timothy Mitchell observes, the spectrum of politics and projects surrounding renewable forms of energy 'indicate not that forms of energy determine modes of politics, but that energy is a field of technical uncertainty rather than determinism, and that the building of solutions to future energy needs is also the building of new forms of collective life' (Mitchell 2011, 238). Less an occasion to celebrate the arrival of supposedly low-impact regenerative economies, the shift underway reaffirms the power of markets to drive systemic change. Witness, for instance, the stratospheric returns on stocks in environmental futures markets over the past year. Our interest here is less on blaming the woeful condition of the planet and its fragile support of life on predatory capitalism, as if there might be other options for the taking, and instead envisaging how political intervention might engage in the design of regenerative economies. Such work is necessarily collective, bringing together the social lives of people and things with disciplines knowledgeable of quantum mechanics, environmental humanities, earth sciences, heterodox economics and systems design. Widely shared, the hope that the climate crisis will end up reconstituting the atmospheres of democratic life has already inspired a wide array of organising efforts on all levels of government – from massive public investments in 'green deals' to facilitate state-driven low-carbon neo-industrialisation to low-tech community-based solutions that build on rich traditions of self-organisation and mutual care.

In her critique of financialisation, extraction and resilience combined with 'smart' technologies that turn the planet into a 'massive medium' – a planet as platform – Orit Halpern (2017) suggests forms of futurity not prone to nihilistic submission: 'Making ourselves indebted in new ways to the many Others that occupy the earth might open to not merely a negative speculation on catastrophic futures but to forms of care, which are increasingly becoming imperative. A close examination of finance, environment and habitat might become the bedrock by which to begin envisioning and creating new futures. We cannot dream of creative destruction, since we have indeed already destroyed the world, but nor can we continue to embrace a world without futures'. How, then, to design platforms of care that address and organise differently the future-present of labour, the environment and economies not predicated on exploitation?[14] Such is the collective work of platform politics not beholden to or dependent on the monetisation of social desire that fuels the reign of the tech sector, trickling down in delayed fashion to the sad imaginaries of the state. Let us instead craft a platform politics on the edge.

Perhaps searching for new ancestors and becoming 'good' ancestors will go hand in hand here (Krznaric 2021). Collective archives of knowledge open forgotten perspectives allowing us to frame shared futures in heterogeneous ways, expanding the temporal horizon of our agency to anticipate its long-term effects on future generations. This is not to say that politics will be all fuzzy from now on as we embrace Gaian cosmopolitics. On the contrary, the environmentalisation of politics requires close attention as it reframes and reconfigures existing dynamics, introduces new tensions and gives rise to new constellations of actors. This will affect how we approach the constitution of political subjectivity. The green tent is as wide as it gets, so self-identification as an 'environmentalist' does little to help sort the field of individual, collective and institutional agency and its respective implications here. But what is already apparent is that a politics of information and infrastructure that decouples the exercise of our communicative capacity from the material contexts sustaining such agency will not lead us very far.

The new sense of articulation that comes with the cosmopolitical terrain harbours ambivalences and conflicts that may have to be renegotiated. Witness, for instance, the willingness of eco-activists to embrace nuclear power to address the climate crisis or the use of intelligent systems to reduce the resource footprint of existing infrastructures, all the while attending to the tremendous resource cost of such architectures. Such predicaments prompt us to take a systems view of how what we do affects the multiple ecologies of which we are a part, once again arguing about not only what is best for us but about the spatial and temporal scope of this collective pursuit. As localism and globalism mesh in old and new ways, the 'structures of feeling' that have helped us negotiate these tensions in the past do so again, from the narrow socialities of many populisms to a wider politics of solidarity that includes future generations.

But of course old politics of control and surveillance may reappear as the royal road to environmental governance and resource efficiency. The narrow view of markets as master allocators ('everything has its price') leads to an expansion of ecosystem accounting that does little to help us understand the cultural and social registers of ecosystem use. Proposals and activist declarations to reduce the carbon footprint of artificial intelligence are symptomatic of the now-consensual emphasis on an environmentalisation of innovation discourses and corresponding adjustments in engineering practices. But a focus on 'green IT' itself can't critically address the advance of automated decision-making or the algorithmic bias in the data used to train intelligent systems. To the extent that platform politics is here to stay, its narratives are already being transformed by a climate crisis that urges us to take a wider view, beyond the socio-technological systems built to extract value from the very processes of collective constitution, and into a wider view of collectivities for which we are still struggling to define empowering concepts of collective agency and intelligence.

Notes

[1] See https://inhabit.global.
[2] Part of our comprehension of the conjunctural is that any one moment may irrupt into another. A case in point would be the relapse into patterns of economic and geopolitical analysis that cut across whatever multipolar imaginaries have emerged since the 'end' of the Cold War. The platform economy and the foundations of an older communications, energy and military infrastructure overlap like architectonic plates shifting, sometimes violently, according to temporalities that offer sudden and surprising synchronicities.
[3] The amnesia regarding the existence of an archive of such governance experiments is stunning. Among the few cybernetics projects that continue

to attract attention is Chile's CyberSyn. See Medina (2011); see also Peters (2016). The current interest among policy makers in systemic design has, however, led to a revisiting of cybernetic frameworks of analysis. See, for example, Snowden and Rancati (2021) or the work of the OECD's Observatory of Public Sector Innovation (https://oecd-opsi.org). One of the aims of the *anticipate* research network is to retrieve such approaches into the current conversation on collective intelligence design, which really only make sense if these resonances of cybernetics are taken into account. See https://anticipate.network.

4 'The locus of power becomes an empty place. There is no need to dwell on the details of the institutional apparatus. The important point is that this apparatus prevents governments from appropriating power for their own ends, from incorporating it into themselves. The exercise of power is subject to the procedures of periodical redistributions. It represents the outcome of a controlled contest with permanent rules. This phenomenon implies an institutionalisation of conflict. The locus of power is an empty place, it cannot be occupied – it is such that no individual and no group can be consubstantial with it – and it cannot be represented. Only the mechanisms of the exercise of power are visible, or only the men, the mere mortals, who hold political authority. We would be wrong to conclude that power now resides in society on the grounds that it emanates from popular suffrage; it remains the agency by virtue of which society apprehends itself in its unity and relates to itself in time and space. But this agency is no longer referred to an unconditional pole; and in that sense, it marks a division between the inside and the outside of the social, institutes relations between those dimensions, and is tacitly recognised as being purely symbolic' (Lefort 1988, 18).

5 'Neoliberalism, as a body of theory, which in an age of liberal state interventionism articulated the need to respect complex life as the limit to governance, has therefore undergone a transformation via reflections upon the problems of actually existing neoliberalism, rearticulating complex life as the positive promise of transformative possibilities' (Chandler 2014, 63). See also the OECD's 'brain capital' initiative, https://www.oecd.org/naec/brain-capital.

6 Margulis credited as her main inspiration the work of Russian biologists like Konstantin Merezhkovsky and Boris Mikhailovich Kozo-Polyansky. See Khakhina (1992). The republication of Khakina's 1979 book in English was edited by Robert Coalson, Lynn Margulis and Mark McMenamin. Such efforts to 'set straight' the scientific record put the current rediscovery of cooperation in explorations of the human in perspective. For an overview of the state of the scientific debate, see Clark (2020).

7 GAIA-X: A Federated Data Infrastructure for Europe, https://www.data-infrastructure.eu. Accompanied by a data governance framework for the platform economy, GAIA-X is one of several initiatives in the context of the EU's first-ever strategic foresight agenda. See https://ec.europa.eu/info

/strategy/priorities-2019–2024/new-push-european-democracy/strategic
-foresight_en.

8 Analysing policy initiatives of the European Union to identify how 'market size, regulatory capacity, stringent standards, inelastic targets, and nondivisibility … are generic conditions for unilateral regulatory power, capable of explaining any jurisdiction's ability (or inability) to regulate global markets alone', Bradford finds that the EU has been particularly effective and 'has built an institutional architecture that has converted its market size into a tangible regulatory influence', driving a 'passive externalization' of many of its regulatory approaches as the European Commission has strategically stepped into the vacuum left since '[t]he WTO has become increasingly dysfunctional since the closing of the Uruguay Round in 1995' (Bradford 2020, 24–26). Wherever access to the common market matters less, however, such exercises of soft power has been significantly less effective.

9 See https://publictheater.org/programs/public-forum.

10 *New York Icon Oskar Eustis: How Theater Sustains Democracy*, PBS, 29 May 2020. https://www.pbs.org/wnet/amanpour-and-company/video/new-york-icon-oskar-eustis-how-theater-sustains-democracy.

11 This ephemeral dynamic is something British cultural studies scholar Raymond Williams (1977, 121–127) attempted to conceptually encapsulate through his elliptical yet compelling idea of a 'structure of feeling' and the philosopher Gernot Böhme (2018) explored in his reflections on atmospheres.

12 For Susan Leigh Star and Karen Ruhleder, 'infrastructure is a fundamentally relational concept' manifesting as 'organized practices' (1996, 113).

13 Jill Lepore (2020) has recently recalled the largely forgotten history of the 'people machine' built by the Simulmatics Corporation as the mother of contemporary platform corporations driven by data analytics.

14 This task of social production has gained noticeable momentum in recent years, drawing insights from earlier civil rights, anti-racism, women's and environmental social movements. Among current iterations, see Hansen and Zechner (2020).

References

Böhme, G. 2018. *The Aesthetics of Atmospheres*. Routledge.
Bradford, A. 2020. *The Brussels Effect: How the European Union Rules the World*. Oxford University Press.
Butler, J. 2018. *Notes Toward a Performative Theory of Assembly*. Harvard University Press.
Chandler, D. 2014. Beyond Neoliberalism: Resilience, the New Art of Governing Complexity. *Resilience*, 2(1), 47–63. https://doi.org/10.1080/21693293.2013.878544.

Clark, B. 2020. *Gaian Systems: Lynn Margulis, Neocybernetics, and the End of the Anthropocene*. Minnesota University Press.

Deseriis, M. 2015. *Improper Names: Collective Pseudonyms from Luddites to Anonymous*. University of Minnesota Press.

Dowling, E. 2021. *The Care Crisis: What Caused It and How Can We End It?* Verso.

Gilroy, P. 1995. *The Black Atlantic: Modernity and Double Consciousness*. Harvard University Press.

Grant, A. 2020. Crossing Khorgos: Soft Power, Security and Suspect Loyalties at the Sino-Kazakh Boundary. *Political Geography*, 76, 102070. https://doi.org/10.1016/j.polgeo.2019.102070.

Halpern, O. 2017. Hopeful Resilience. *e-flux*, 19 April. https://www.e-flux.com/architecture/accumulation/96421/hopeful-resilience.

Hansen, B. R. and Zechner, M. 2020. Careless Networks? Social Media, Care and Reproduction in the Web of Life. *spheres: Journal for Digital Cultures*, 6. https://spheres-journal.org/contribution/careless-networks-social-media-care-and-reproduction-in-the-web-of-life.

Harney, S. and Moten, F. 2013. *The Undercommons: Fugitive Planning and Black Study*. Minor Compositions.

Hui, Y. 2015. Algorithmic Catastrophe: The Revenge of Contingency. *Parrhesia: A Journal of Critical Philosophy*, 23, 122–143. https://parrhesiajournal.org.

Khakhina, L. N. 1992. *Concepts of Symbiogenesis: A Historical and Critical Study of the Research of Russian Botanists*. Yale University Press.

Krznaric, R. 2021. *The Good Ancestor: How to Think Long-Term in a Short-Term World*. WH Allen.

Latour, B. and Weibel, P. (Eds.), 2020. *Critical Zones: The Science and Politics of Landing on Earth*. MIT Press.

Lefort, C. 1988. *Democracy and Political Theory*. Trans. D. Macey. Polity Press.

Lepore, J. 2020. *If Then: How the Simulmatics Corporation Invented the Future*. W. W. Norton & Company.

Lindtner, S. M. 2020. *Prototype Nation: China and the Contested Promise of Innovation*. Princeton University Press.

Margulis, L. 1998. *Symbiotic Planet: A New Look at Evolution*. Basic Books.

Medina, E. 2011. *Cybernetic Revolutionaries: Technology and Politics in Allende's Chile*. MIT Press.

Mitchell, T. 2011. *Carbon Democracy: Political Power in the Age of Oil*. Verso.

Morse, N. 2021. *The Museum as a Space of Social Care*. Routledge.

Narins, T. P. and Agnew, J. 2020. Missing from the Map: Chinese Exceptionalism, Sovereignty Regimes and the Belt Road Initiative. *Geopolitics*, 25(5), 809–837.

National Terrorism Advisory System Bulletin. US Department of Homeland Security, 27 January 2021. https://www.dhs.gov/ntas/advisory/national-terrorism-advisory-system-bulletin-january-27-2021.

Peters, B. 2016. *How Not to Network a Nation: The Uneasy History of the Soviet Internet*. MIT Press.

Ross, A. 2021. Is Care Work Already the Future? *New Labor Forum*, 30(1), 12–18.

Rossiter, N. and Zehle, S. 2017. The Experience of Digital Objects: Toward a Speculative Entropology. *spheres: Journal for Digital Cultures*, 3. http://spheres-journal.org/the-experience-of-digital-objects-toward-a-speculative-entropology.

Snowden, D. and Rancati, A. 2021. *Managing Complexity (and Chaos) in Times of Crisis: A Field Guide for Decision Makers Inspired by the Cynefin Framework*. Publications Office of the European Union. https://ec.europa.eu/jrc/en/publication/managing-complexity-and-chaos-times-crisis-field-guide-decision-makers-inspired-cynefin-framework.

Stalder, F. 2021. Re: <nettime> GameStop Never Stops. Posting to Nettime mailing list, 5 February. https://nettime.org/Lists-Archives/nettime-l-2102/msg00025.html.

Star, S. L. and Ruhleder, K. 1996. Steps Toward an Ecology of Infrastructure: Design and Access for Large Information Spaces. *Information Systems Research*, 7(1), 111–134.

Virilio, P. 2007. *The Original Accident*. Trans. J. Rose. Polity Press.

Walker, J. and Cooper, M. 2011. Genealogies of Resilience: From Systems Ecology to the Political Economy of Crisis Adaptation. *Security Dialogue*, 14(2), 143–160.

Wark, M. 2013. *The Spectacle of Disintegration: Situationist Passages out of the 20th Century*. Verso.

Wen, Y. 2020. *The Huawei Model: The Rise of China's Technology Giant*. University of Illinois Press.

Williams, R. 1977. Dominant, Residual and Emergent. In *Marxism and Literature* (pp. 121–127). Oxford University Press.

Woo, S. and Strumpf, D. 2021. Huawei Loses Cellular-Gear Market Share Outside China. *The Wall Street Journal*, 7 March. https://www.wsj.com/articles/huawei-loses-cellular-gear-market-share-outside-china-11615118400.

Zhang, L. 2020. When Platform Capitalism Meets Petty Capitalism in China: Alibaba and an Integrated Approach to Platformization. *International Journal of Communication*, 14, 114–134. https://ijoc.org/index.php/ijoc/article/view/10935.

CHAPTER 3

Domus Capitalismi: Abstract Spaces and Domesticated Subjectivities in Times of Covid-19

Marco Briziarelli and Emiliana Armano

Introduction

The main purpose of this chapter is to investigate the relationship between digital labour and urban space production in the time of the Covid-19 pandemic, and in the broader context of a crisis of capitalism. From a theoretical and interpretative approach, our inquiry posits the pandemic's social production of space as a lens to assess the dialectics of capitalist crises, which imply both how digital spatial remedies are powered by machinic fix capital (Harvey 2003) and the contradictory positionality of domesticated subjectivities.

In our view, one of the most the significant aspects of the pandemic has been the production of *new social spaces* (Lefebvre 1991), generated by the tension between the stalling mobility of productive circuits in 'locked-down' conditions and the 'compensating' increased productivity of alternative sites under the accelerating propagation of digital connectivity and its distinctive realm, which we will define as digital abstract space. In this sense, we intend to further develop the notion of *digital abstract space* (Briziarelli and Armano 2020) in

How to cite this book chapter:
Briziarelli, M. and Armano, E. 2022. Domus Capitalismi: Abstract Spaces and Domesticated Subjectivities in Times of Covid-19. In: Armano, E., Briziarelli, M., and Risi, E. (eds.), *Digital Platforms and Algorithmic Subjectivities*. Pp. 47–61. London: University of Westminster Press. DOI: https://doi.org/10.16997/book54.d. License: CC-BY-NC-ND 4.0

order to provide a tentative answer to the following question: how have capitalist spaces changed in pandemic times? In order to both answer this question and enrich the notion of digital abstract space, we argue that the Covid-19 pandemic-induced circulatory crisis has prompted a compensatory response that can be described as (the) *digital spatial fix* (Harvey 2001; Greene and Joseph 2015), which combines measures against the crisis as well as subsumptive phenomena mainly under capitalist forms such as *digital abstract space* and machinic fix capital. We will exemplify this by examining how the private residences of many workers are being subsumed as digital abstract space (i.e. a logistical space constituted by the synergic encounter between digital platforms and subjects that operate in machinic fashion) and are shaped by multiple overlapping spheres of action, which makes them *domesticated* (Bologna and Fumagalli 1997).

In order to expound our argument, we structure the chapter as follows: after a brief introduction on the Covid-19 crisis, and its impact as a circulatory crisis of logistical and platform capitalism, we will interrogate how capitalism has responded to the crisis by creating spatial fixes in urban realms. Finally, in the third section, we discuss the reorganisation of private space in relation to the capitalist process of valorisation and the circulation of capital. We specifically focus on the diffusion of so-called 'smart/remote' work demonstrating how, during the pandemic, digital abstract space expands in co-development with the subsumption of social (re-)production, resulting in a contradictory domestication.

The Covid-19 Crisis: Value in Motion … Stalled!

The situation created by the Covid-19 viral surge since spring 2020 can be simultaneously understood as a pandemic, an epidemic and endemic. It is a pandemic because it is borderless and massive in its magnitude; an epidemic because it is also regionalised in its implications (e.g. different global regions are managing Covid-19 differently); and finally, it is an endemic as it can be framed by specific capitalist features. In our view the common thread here is the demic aspect, or the material social relations involved: as Ian thoughtfully states, 'a pandemic isn't a collection of viruses, but is a social relation among people, mediated by viruses' (Ian 2020). As far as this present reflection is concerned, we argue that much of the pandemic's significance can be assessed when confronted with predominant capitalist social relations mediated by the space of the city.

The generalised and quick spread of the disease caused an array of restrictions to the mobility of people and goods (i.e. curfews, quarantines, stay-at-home and shelter-in-place orders) in order to contain and prevent further infections. As a result, schools, universities, restaurants and other 'non-essential' businesses closed down. By April 2020, close to half of the world's population was under lockdown (euronews.com 2020). The effort to flatten the curve of contagions caused what many IMF economists defined as the Great Lockdown 2020 with a projected cumulative GDP loss of nine trillion US dollars (imf.org 2020).

There are many ways to understand this economic shut down: as an effective demand crisis, a financial crisis linked to the stock market crash of March 2020, and, last but not least, a crisis of compensatory consumerism and realisation of value. In this chapter, we frame the pandemic crisis as a force that effectively slows down the necessary motion needed by value circulation, a blockage of capital circulation in the urban environment.

In *Grundrisse* (1973), Marx distinguishes between productive consumption (e.g. essentially fixed capital) and final consumption of goods which, once consumed, exit the circuits of capital. In our view, through the spread of fear of contagion, and measures of social distancing and control, the pandemic creates circulatory slow-downs, interruptions and blockages in both areas of consumption. On the one hand, the flows within commodity chains currently required to produce relatively complex goods (i.e. manufacturing a car, IC technology or home appliances) have been disrupted as workers fell ill, were laid off or were subject to furloughs. At this level, due to flexible accumulation principles, timely logic and the tendency to avoid the formation of large inventories that could have otherwise sustained flows during lagging time, made these circuits particularly fragile. As a result, the loss of productive capacity translated into a loss of capital circulation and accumulation. On the other hand, Covid-19 restrictions impacted on final consumption, not only as populations become increasingly fiscally conservative in times of economic uncertainty, but also due to financial difficulties brought about by the pandemic, and the severe restrictions to spatial habits outside the domestic sphere (moving around, driving, going to the mall, dining out), particularly in urban spaces. Even at this level, capital circulation is vital: Harvey (2020) points out how exponential growth of capital accumulation is sustained by (relatively) instantaneous mass consumption such as tourism, spectacular cultural events and the Netflix economy. The loss at the point of final consumption translates into missing value realisation.

While issues of capital circulation and realisation possess a quintessentially global nature, we choose to concentrate on the space of the city because it simultaneously represents the social epicentre of the pandemic, and logistical activity, as well as of capital circulation and realisation.

At the Centre of Logistical and Platform Capitalism: The City

Thanks to the work of radical geographers such as Lefebvre (1991) and Harvey (1982), city spaces are privileged sites that detect and demystify both *long durée* and *episodic* kinds of transformations. In addition, over the last decade the city has become the main stage of the logistical and circulatory dimensions of contemporary capitalism (Nielson and Rossiter 2011; Huws 2006; Dyer-Witheford

2015; Cuppini, Frapporti and Pirone 2015; Grappi 2016; Andrijasevic and Sacchetto 2017; Bologna 2018).

Thus, as a complex capitalist field of study the city contributes to a perspective that pushes back against a significant over-emphasis on the moment of production in relation to the whole process of capital self-valorisation. In this sense a focus on the logistical aspects of capitalism has rectified a blind-spot in the literature by recognising the circulatory logic of capitalism as a totalising entity, 'in terms of the contradictory interaction between moments within the total process' (Marx 1990, 46). From this point of view, we look at the city as a capital landscape made of fixed and circulating capital. Following Harvey's lead (1982), we assume that the pandemic crisis consists of a 'production of spatial configuration [which] can then be treated as an "active moment" within the overall temporal dynamic of accumulation and social reproduction' (374).

Furthermore, the logistical perspective that reads capital in terms of flows (such as financial, commodities, information and workers) allows for an appreciation of other circulatory aspects of contemporary capitalism, such as its platform nature, powered by information and communication technology (ICT). Framed as circulation, the logistical and communication aspects of capitalism demonstrate the logical and historical overlapping of transportation, communication and the circulation of capital. In this sense, we concur with Manzerolle and Kjøsen (2015) in construing ICTs as particularly effective tools to overcome space/time barriers in the sphere of circulation. For example, platforms, by gathering information on users, facilitate and accelerate the circulation of capital by more effectively matching commodities with particular consumers.

Therefore, if city landscapes are currently being produced by data and algorithms alongside bricks and mortar (Graham 2020), the emerging post-pandemic capitalist paradigm, exacerbated by increased digitisation, contributes to the rise of the so-called fourth industrial revolution, based on the integration of AI, Big Data, the insertion of robotics and technological automation into the circuits of capital, all boosted by giant tech companies. As we will elaborate later in this chapter, the digitalisation process propelled by practices such as e-commerce, telecommuting, consumer demand, last-mile delivery, virtual tourism and event-going, the digitalisation of public services and smart city models are all technological changes that can be understood as a spatial fix of a specific kind, which simultaneously contains both a crisis of accumulation (which is why a fix is needed), while laying out the conditions for a surge in capital circulation as well as increasing its mobility. Furthermore, consistent with a total integral perspective of capitalism outlined above, digital media constitutes both the material conditions for capital circulation as well as the necessary apparatus to control workers via automation and surveillance, intensifying their productivity by integrating algorithms, global scale production, and social reproduction (Baldwin 2020; Casilli 2020). In other words, digital media works at the same pace as the tools of production and circulation.

The underlying assumption informing our analysis is that these circuits assume a specific social sphere, which affect both the particular subjects and their specific activities. People's subjectivities are thus both the bearer of those social forms and their agents of change. We will illustrate such a hypothesis by examining how the pandemic affects urban social space and its acceleration as logistical abstract space, as well as the process of subjectification of individuals working and interacting with digital platforms. What happens when these flows get clogged, as in current pandemic times?

Reacting against the circulatory restrictions caused by the pandemic, platform capitalism finds, in the spaces of the city, both new barriers as well as spatial fixes to cope with such barriers. For Harvey (2003), spatial fixes are temporary and contradictory solutions. In fact, *fix* means both investing in fix capital and fixing capital in place and those two aspects controvert each other. In fact, the geographical/physical anchoring of capital makes it less prone to be realised because it cannot move:

> The vast quantities of capital fixed in place act as a drag upon the capacity to realize a spatial fix elsewhere ... If capital does move out, then it leaves behind a trail of devastation and devaluation; the deindustrializations experienced in the heartlands of capitalism ... in the 1970s and 1980s are cases in point. If capital does not or cannot move ... then over-accumulated capital stands to be devalued directly through the onset of a deflationary recession or depression. (Harvey 2003, 116)

Capitalism thus overcomes space barriers by fixing infrastructures of production (such as factories, roads, power supplies) thereby reducing transport and communication costs. However, such tensions between fixity and mobility are destined to create the need for new spatial fixes because the physical fixity of capital tends to imprison capital, making it more static and unable to respond to everchanging political and economic scenarios. For this reason, Harvey describes how historically spatial fixes tend to create the conditions for further future fixes, in order to address the issues created by previous rounds of fixes.

Compared to traditional fixes, platform capitalism has generated digital fixes that operate with considerably less geographical and physical fixities. The prompt re-localisation of production during the pandemic points to such dynamicity: within a few weeks, a significant proportion of capital production was able to pass from offices to houses, by thus intensifying the pre-existing overlapping between labour and disposable time and space.

Especially exemplary are those 'domesticated' productive activities that can be performed via digital means, thus exacerbating digital labour and the creation of what we will define as digital abstract space. The transition to remote working and the expansion of gig work demonstrated how digital media infrastructures represent fix capital already in place and capable of responding effectively to the abrupt changes caused by the pandemic crisis and its consequent circulatory restrictions.

Digitalised work provides the conditions for digital spatial fixes in the sense that the digital realm is currently 'where capital seeks freedom from contemporary limits' (Greene and Joseph 2015). However, while we agree with Greene and Joseph's conception of digital space as material and not a mere representation, we also view it as possessing a distinctive ability to provide 'fixes,' as exemplified by the Covid-19 crisis. We argue that digital space relies on a combination of different kinds of capital: on the one hand, internet-based technologies necessitates capital fixed in immovable physical infrastructures such as home computers, servers, power grids, fibre and mined minerals; on the other hand, those fixes are able, comparatively more than other kind of spatialised fixes, to harness and mobilise flexible capital, i.e. people's living labour. Furthermore, those fixes do not simply harness labour capacity but also labourers' subjectivity (Armano, Murgi and Teli 2017), becoming a new and dynamic form of fixed capital (Read 2013).

This tendency to combine fixed and circulating capital was noted by Marx when he said that 'Fixed capital is "man himself"' (Marx 1973, 712): whereas machinery is understood as crystallised human intelligence, human intelligence also absorbs and 'learns' from machines. However, in the case of digital platforms, these mutual interactions between labourers and machinery seems to be qualitatively amplified. Illustrative of these interactions are the computational engines of platforms, such as algorithms, a form of fixed capital generated by social cooperation and interaction which could not exist or operate without integration – or *agencement* – (Gherardi 2016) with people.

Within platform and social media environments, fixed and variable capital are assembled together into a 'machinic environment' (Guattari 1995, 9), and working subjectivities are constituted by such a context. The combination of dynamic capital that is not simply fixed into immovable assets, the real subsumption of subjects under neoliberal forms of work ethic, flexibility and responsibilities (i.e. connected to the sudden reorganisation caused by the Covid-19 crisis), and the spatial fix from public to private, creates a general subsumptive tendency, which adds an expansion impulse to what was otherwise a contraction caused by the pandemic.

The renewed dynamicity of an otherwise less movable capital becoming machinic leads us to frame the Covid-19 crisis from a particular perspective, which demonstrates contradictions on two levels: on one level, crisis as an inner contradiction within the capitalist system; and on another level, the dialectics of crisis which can be understood as both a contractive and expansive capital circulation and accumulation. While the regressive/contractive side of crisis would suggest a connection between economic downturns and the unmaking of the conditions of subsumption (as such, subsumptive capitalist forms seem to lose their grip on society), Clover (2010) advances a persuasive insight about the intimate link between crisis and subsumption expansion in two main ways: firstly by recognising the idea of spatial fix, because such processes trigger subsumptive dynamics in order to provide fixes to the economic downturn; secondly, comparable to the example of machinic fix capital, it can actually trigger a massive expansion of that sector as exemplified by the recent spectacular growth of the gig economy.

Overall, this dynamicity of digital fixes provides a surplus value in terms of subsumption at two levels that mirrors Marx's taxonomy as expounded in *Capital* (1990): real subsumption of labourers' subjectivity, which becomes domesticated, and the formal subsumption of environments such as the private sphere of homes that were relatively free from the instrumentalisation of production. As a result, the dynamicity of machinic capital goes beyond the fix, becoming an expansive capitalist force (as opposed to a limited and temporary solution) in so much as they imply subsumption of new spaces as well as of worker subjectivity.

Digital Abstract Space

Prior to the pandemic-induced crisis, categories such as platform-powered workers of micro logistics work, such as delivering food or consumer goods, were largely considered the prototypical 'gig worker' prior to the pandemic. However, within the context of lockdowns, many knowledge workers are experiencing remote working conditions that are frequently accompanied by the precarization and intensification of work.

While 'stay at home' conditions prevent contagion, knowledge workers are becoming new operators in an emerging realm, which is colonising the private sphere: by turning our personalised, idiosyncratic living space into an effective physical and digital platform suited to Covid-19 capital. As a result, this digital realm (what we define as digital abstract space), is increasingly subsuming lives by extracting metadata to both capture and measure the value of our social relations and transforming our interpersonal communication into a linguistic machine that translates concrete meaning into abstractable information (Briziarelli 2020).

By digital abstract space, we refer to space mediated by digital technology (Briziarelli and Armano 2020), drawing on Lefebvre's notion of abstract space (1991) as a space almost entirely instrumental to capitalism. For Lefebvre, abstraction refers to space that is artificially purified (thus preventing the flow of capital circuits) and privileging quantifiable and commensurable elements rather than qualitatively distinctive ones.

Digital abstract space constitutes a conjunctural social field: a preponderant logistical venue for digital capitalism, a *hyper-industrial* capitalistic mode of production (Alquati 2000), inhabited by self-directed and self-exploited neo-liberal subjectivities that partly buy into a disingenuous narrative of 'flexibility' (Huws 2009); a highly intrusive digital connectivity ideology; and finally a protocological approach (Galloway 2004) to management that emphasises computational logic. This sense of emergency and the politics of 'essentialism' (i.e. everything is shut down except essential services) has indeed established this realm as a primary abstracting force. In fact, as the lively public debate over health vs economics demonstrates, in a capitalist society everything that is not concerned with value production-realisation can be stripped out because it is non-essential.

In the context of the digital spatial fix prompted by the circulatory/pandemic crisis, digital abstract space is generated by digital machines of different kinds (e.g. the Internet of Things, Big Data, virtual reality, AI, the cloud, robotics), which by convergence generates the capitalist social form that seems to currently insinuate into every other social form: production, consumption, sociality and social reproduction. All these different digital tools share a common propensity to shape environments in which algorithmic instructions travel across connections points enabling dialogue between the physical world, people and machines. It is indeed the systematic production of such digital environments and their effective conduciveness to capital flow that creates the conditions for these machines to act as producers of abstract space in the Lefebvrian and Marxian sense.

Accordingly, qualitatively different kind of spaces, through means of connectivity, can from the mere point of view of value production, be subsumed as digital abstract space that is able to redefine organisational and productive logics, and to reconfigure it into more commensurable sites and relations of production. Commensurability is indeed another main facet of 'abstraction.' While we have discussed abstraction as the reduction of concrete complexity into artificial essentiality, here we also point to abstraction as providing the condition of replicability and the possibility of technological automation. Finally, the same digital spatial fix that transformed traditional modes of work into remote ways of working while increasing digital abstract space shapes its agents by subsuming them as domesticated subjectivities of a kind of 'homey and cosy capitalism.' However, as we will argue in the last section of this chapter, domestication is what dynamizes traditional fixed capital into machinic capital, but not without contradictions.

Domus Capitalismi: The Contradictory Facets of Domestication

Elaborating on the considerations above in the context of digital abstract space, abstraction simultaneously describes a fetishised and impoverished space, the conditions for more effective exploitation and then suggests a future where workers are potentially replaced with machines (Briziarelli and Armano 2020). We also claim that the current unique situation allows us to both qualify and enrich our understanding of such space: digital abstract space represents the framework of social relations mediated by the digital in which machinic fix capital can move between contradictory states of abstraction and subjectifi-cation. Specific digital space produced by the Covid-19 fix must be found in the reconfiguration of space. Restrictive measures dealing with the crisis have brought about significant changes: examples include the appropriation of pub-lic space for private use, as in the case of the establishment of restaurant patios and street closures for open air dining (Trudeau and Wareham 2020); or the reconfiguration of abandoned/dormant public space, such as for mutual aid initiatives, utilising unused parking lots or converting space previously used for cars into cycle paths (Sarkin 2020).

However, in our view, the most preponderant tendency in space production consists of the acceleration of the general neoliberal tendency of privatising public space, which is accomplished by measures of partition and sanitation. Public spaces are viewed 'impure' and 'dangerous', with measures such as social distancing, mask mandates and sanitation stations attempting to impose order and control. The previous relative openness of public space now acquires inter-nal boundaries that facilitate its control via processes of segmentation and par-tition in quantifiable parcels (for example, the six foot rule in the US or the two metre rule in Europe), which operate where people congregate, such as waiting in line outside a business or a government building.

Conversely, private space becomes a refuge from contagion/human contact and freedom from state-imposed restrictions. At the same time, due to digital platforms and technology, it becomes a super-locale (Fuchs 2020) where the intimate sphere is mobilised to become a productive sphere and a new sphere of socialisation via digital connectivity. In this new productive sphere (i.e. integrating public and private) inside homes, the spatial fix manifests through a re-compression of space and time (previously decompressed by lockdown restrictions) by pushing production towards more space and more time: over-lapping and super-imposing working time/space over leisure time/space; and by compensating the disconnection from the traditional office, now deemed unsafe, with a permanent connection to a safer one. Such a digital and logisti-cal safe-zone has materialised by means of smartphones, digital platforms, the endless intrusion of advertisements on our computer screens, the never-ending buzzing of delivery trucks carrying food and consumer goods, and waste man-agement workers disposing of Amazon boxes and packaging material.

The subject at home thus pays for the privileged separation from contagion with new intrusive forms of value production and extraction that colonise their homes. Subjects experience an intensification of the pressure on individuals to combine operativity and productivity, i.e. the ability to manage and reproduce interstitial activities, to be adaptable and flexible, and to cope with high levels of transiency brought about by the pandemic (Burchi 2020; Risi 2021; Mazali, de Vita and Campanella 2021).

In this context, the worker is therefore *domesticated* twice over (Bologna and Fumagalli 1997): safe from contagion as well as subjected/controlled for smoother exploitation, while living a fundamental contradiction between an abrupt separation from a public social life now deemed dangerous, but reconnecting via digital means, one of the few sites considered to be hygienic and compliant with anti-contamination measures. Domestication then implies a paradoxical reciprocal appropriation: capitalism spills over into the worker's intimate space while the worker confronts capital within the confines of the home, thus potentially gaining tools with which to push back against it.

Bologna and Fumagalli (1997) observe that while salaried workers used to spend their active productive time in places that were owned and organised by others, now the workers' private space is subsumed under capitalist forms while, at the same time, incorporating their work into their private lives. The considerable number of humorous memes of workers caught in inappropriate attire or postures while remote working is indicative of such a paradox: on the one hand, there is a recognition of work that has infiltrated our bedrooms and caught us in our pyjamas; on the other, work that has itself become *partly* domesticated by our environment, needs and desires.

The digital spatial fix and the consequent creation of digital abstract space led to a material reconfiguration of many homes in terms of consumption and social reproduction that results in a reconfiguration of production. For example, homes mimic, on a small scale the logistical space of the city with its landscape of fixed and circulating capital: leisure and/or spare rooms become home offices. Many workers as microtaskers increased bandwidth allowances to improve remote working and schooling; entrance halls become hubs where micro-logistics workers deliver and pick up packages; the multifunctional operativity of homes is also enhanced by the creation of areas for exercise – the treadmill, the exercise bike – thus reinscribing the neoliberal preoccupation with consumption and reinforcing the notion of the individualised consumer subject (Clevenger, Rick and Bustad 2020).

The paradox of digital abstract space is that while establishing an apparent order instrumental to circulatory capitalism, it also overloads the physical environment of workers' homes by creating potential new frictions. For instance, overloaded subjects such as working mothers are experiencing an intensification of the unfair sexual division of labour inside the home (Burchi 2020) that may impact upon their productivity and general well-being. Further, the Marxian labour theory of value suggests that the magnitude of value is determined by socially necessary labour time. When capitalism is understood as a circulatory process, one could argue that digital abstract space represents a kind of socially necessary labour space; capitalism implies the subsumption of different forms of concrete labour under abstract labour (Marx 1990, 128), and most such abstraction process takes place at the level of spatialisation. Digital abstract space represents capitalism's attempt to radically de-territorialize (and re-territorialize in purely instrumental terms) the concrete physical environment. Regardless of whether a worker is at their office, in their home kitchen, in a business suit or visiting the restroom at Heathrow Airport, thanks to digital connectivity they can now provide hours of productive work.

The aforementioned memes depicting people working in pyjamas, or in the bathroom, or drinking alcohol 'on the clock' are also indicative of this double-edged re-territorialization: they represent the intrusion of work into the intimate sphere, and the intrusion of the intimate sphere into work, reflecting how the dialectic of crisis expands abstract space as well as expands the abstraction of abstract space, i.e. its potential re-concretization.

Conclusions: Inescapable Social and Spatial Tensions

The pandemic has abruptly reconfigured social space and social praxis by reformulating a utopia consistently accompanying modern media: action at a distance – the exertion of influence upon an object that does not require physical interaction. While such capability has traditionally been associated with magic or mystical magnetism, in Covid-19 times it mostly refers to a vernacular of the 'new normal'. The infrastructures required to develop contactless social practices were already in place thanks to the increasing preponderance of digital technologies in both the production and circulation of capital. In fact, the spatial fix to the crisis was so rapid that the narrative of acceptance of digital technologies as the best and safest option to enable work to continue despite the restrictions imposed by the pandemic quickly established itself as the only apparent viable solution. As a consequence, the pandemic has transformed most of our cities into living social laboratories where it is possible to experiment with the permanent integration of digital technology in every aspect of life. The city becomes the sounding board for an all *shut-in economy* (Sadowski 2020), which keeps exploiting the rhetoric of 'smart cities' coupled with 'smart working' and living in a domesticated space. As a result, social spaces are re-invented, re-territorialized, secured, distanced, eroded and re-mediated by digital connectivity.

In this chapter, we have theoretically explored the idea of a novel abstract space reconfigured in digital terms and performing as a digital spatial solution to the crisis induced by the pandemic restrictions. We used the notion of digital spatial fix to make sense of the pandemic as a circulatory crisis at the level of commodities, information and worker flows. We also used the notion of digital abstract space to describe subsumptive phenomena linked to the expansion and re-localisation of productive activities and the mobilisation of a *kind of machinic fixed capital* in which subjectivities are fundamental. The realm of digital abstract space, gestures, words and relations are not only abstracted into data but also extracted from their informational, cognitive and affective value. The agents of such space are neoliberal subjectivities that seem to be receptive enough to remote working, thus dynamizing the typical fixation on the place of assets normally generated by such a spatial fix. In fact, for example, while the number of gig workers of all kinds has dramatically increased, their employers have not provided much in terms of adaptive measures, thus relying on the typical self-responsibilisation and self-activation of neoliberal subjects. However, these subjectivities experience a contradictory situation: a tendency towards abstraction powered by digital abstract space/digital spatial fixes on the one hand, and the propensity towards the phenomenon of domestication inside their homes as the new emerging sites of production, on the other. While the former implies the alienation and deterritorialization of concrete spaces such as private space into an abstract locus of production, the latter leaves room to develop a more complex tension, a sort of re-territorialization and dis-alienation of production generated by the subsumption of private space as a space of production.

Domestication represents then the first dialectical limit of digital abstract space, which should be coupled with another: while enjoying an organic composition of capital that exploits the dynamicity of living labour in relation to constant capital, it also tends towards automatisation, thus replacing living labour with machines. If we work with the Marxian assumption that value production only derives from living labour, then digital spatial fix would find itself in a 'catch-22' situation.

Domestication leads us to keep asking questions about subsumption under digital capitalist forms, especially under the broader and possibly quintessential capitalist tendency of abstraction, and especially when universal computational language and black boxed algorithmic management become more prevalent. Are such changes inevitable? Can they be reversed? After all, part of the argument advanced here is that crises are eminently, but also unpredictably, productive: they always oscillate between destructive creation and creative destruction.

While capitalist crises represent in themselves the most deifying arguments against capital as a telos of the 'end of history', the so-called 'technological solutionism' (González and Rendueles Menéndez de Llano 2020) constitutes a powerful rhetoric that keeps threatening our ability to voice our concerns and to envision alternative uses of technology rooted in communitarian and solidarist social relations (Scholtz 2016; Teli et al. 2019). In fact, the terms of the so-called return to a post-Covid-19 normality also depend on our ability to remain vigilant of the changes that are occurring, and to keep interpreting and critiquing them.

References

Alquati, R. 2000. *Nella Società Industriale d'Oggi*. Unpublished Working Paper.
Andrijasevic, R. and Sacchetto, D. 2017. Il Just-in-Time della Vita. Reti di Produzione Globale e Compressione Spazio-Temporale alla Foxconn. *Stato e Mercato*, 3, 383–420.
Armano, E., Murgia, A., and Teli, M. 2017. *Platform Capitalism e Confini del Lavoro Negli Spazi Digitali*. Mimesis.

Baldwin, R. 2020. *Rivoluzione Globotica, Globalizzazione Robotica e Future del Lavoro*. Il Mulino.

Bologna, S. 2018. Per un Breve Panorama della Logistica dal 1970 a Oggi Intervista. Retrieved from: http://www.intotheblackbox.com/author/sergio -bologna (last accessed 24 June 2021).

Bologna, S. and Fumagalli, A. 1997. *Il Lavoro Autonomo di Seconda Generazione: Scenari del Postfordismo in Italia*. Feltrinelli.

Briziarelli, M. and Armano, E. 2020. The Social Production of Radical Space: Machinic Labour Struggles against Digital Spatial Abstractions. *Capital and Class*, 44(2), 173–189.

Briziarelli, M. 2020. Translatability, Translational Labor and Capitalist Subsumption: The Communicative Venues of Capitalism. *Democratic Communiqué*, 29(1), 46–61.

Burchi, S. 2020. *Ripartire da Casa: Lavori e Reti dallo Spazio Domestico*. Franco Angeli.

Casilli, A. 2020. *Schiavi del Clic: Perché Lavoriamo Tutti per il Nuovo Capitalismo*. Feltrinelli.

Clevenger, S., Rick, O., and Bustad, J. 2020. Critiquing Anthropocentric Media Coverage of the COVID-19 Sport 'Hiatus'. *International Journal of Sport Communication*, 13, 559–565.

Clover, J. 2010. Subsumption and Crisis. In B. Best, W. Bonefield, and C. O'Kane (Eds.), *The Sage Handbook of Frankfurt School Critical Theory*. Sage.

Cuppini, N., Frapporti, M., and Pirone, M. 2015. Logistics Struggles in the Po Valley Region: Territorial Transformations and Processes of Antagonistic Subjectivation, *South Atlantic Quarterly*, 114(1), 119–34.

Dattani, K. 2020. Rethinking Social Reproduction in the Time of COVID-19. *Journal of Australian Political Economy*, 85, 51–56.

Dyer-Witheford, N. 2015. *Cyber-Proletariat*. Pluto Press.

Fuchs, C. and Chandler, D. 2019. *Digital Objects, Digital Subjects: Interdisciplinary Perspectives on Capitalism, Labour and Politics in the Age of Big Data*. University of Westminster Press.

Fuchs, C. 2020. Everyday Life and Everyday Communication in Coronavirus Capitalism. *tripleC*, 18(1), 375–98.

Galloway, A. 2004. *Protocols: How Control Exists after De-centralization*. MIT Press.

Gherardi, S. 2016. To Start Practice Theorizing Anew: The Contribution of the Concepts *Agencement* and Formativeness. *Organization*, 23(5), 680–698.

González, A. and Rendueles Menéndez de Llano, C. 2020. Capitalismo Digital: Fragilidad Social, Explotación y Solucionismo Tecnológico. *Teknokultura: Revista de Cultura Digital y Movimientos Sociales*, 17(2), 95–101.

Grappi, G. 2016. *Logistica*. Ediesse.

Greene, D. M. and Joseph, D. 2015. The Digital Spatial Fix. *tripleC*, 13(2), 223–247.

Graham, M. 2020. Regulate, Replicate, and Resist: The Conjunctural Geographies of Platform Urbanism. *Urban Geography*, 41(3), 453–457.

Guattari, F. 1995. *Chaosophy: Texts and Interviews 1972 to 1977*. Semiotext(e).

Harvey, D. 1982. *The Limits to Capital*. Blackwell.

Harvey, D. 2001. *Spaces of Capital: Towards a Critical Geography*. Routledge.

Harvey, D. 2003. *The New Imperialism*. Oxford University Press.

Harvey, D. 2020. *Anti-capitalist Chronicles*. London: Pluto Press.

Huws, U. 2006. Fixed, Footloose, or Fractured: Work, Identity, and the Spatial Division of Labor in the Twenty-First Century City. *Monthly Review*, 57(10), 1 March.

Huws, U. 2009. Working at the Interface: Call-Centre Labour in a Global Economy. *Work Organisation, Labour & Globalisation*, 3(1), 1–18.

Ian, A. P. 2020. Ten Premises for a Pandemic. Retrieved from: https://non.copyriot.com/ten-premises-for-a-pandemic (last accessed 24 June 2021).

Lefebvre, H. 1991. *The Production of Space*. Blackwell.

Manzerolle, V. and Kjøsen, A. M. 2015. Digital Media and Capital's Logic of Acceleration. In V. Mosco and C. Fuchs (Eds.), *Marx in the Age of Digital Capitalism* (pp. 151–179). Brill.

Marx, K. 1973 [1939]. *Grundrisse: Foundations of the Critique of Political Economy*. Random House.

Marx, K. 1990 [1867]. *Capital: Volume I*. Penguin.

Mazali, T., de Vita, L., and Campanella, G. 2021. Il Lavoro Femminile 'Smart' Durante il Lockdown: Agile e Flessibile? Paper at the Conference RETI, MEDIA E CULTURE Post-Covid. Sfide, Conflitti, Disuguaglianze, Narrazioni e Immaginari a Confronto.

Nielson, B. and Rossiter, N. 2011. Still Waiting, Still Moving. In D. Bissell and G. Fuller (Eds.), *Stillness in a Mobile World* (pp. 51–67). Routledge.

Read, J. 2013. *Micro-Politics of Capital: Marx and the Pre-History of the Present*. SUNY Press.

Risi, E. and Pronzato, R. 2021, Smartworking is Not So Smart. Always-On Lives and the Dark Side of Platformization. *Work Organisation, Labour & Globalisation*, 15(1), 107–125.

Robinson, W. 2020. Global Capitalism Post-Pandemic. *Race & Class*, 62(2), 3–13.

Sadowski, J. 2020. *Too Smart: How Digital Capitalism is Extracting Data, Controlling our Lives, and Taking Over the World*. MIT Press.

Sarkin, G. 2020. Cities at the Front Line: Public Space in the Time of the COVID-19 Pandemic. *Smithgroup*. Retrieved from: https://www.smithgroup.com/perspectives/2020/cities-at-the-front-line-public-space-in-the-time-of-the-covid-19-pandemic (last accessed 24 June 2021).

Scholtz, T. 2016. Platform Cooperativism Challenging the Corporate Sharing Economy. Retrieved from: http://platformcoop.net/about (last accessed 24 June 2021).

Teli, M., Tonolli L., Di Fiore A., and D'Andrea V. 2019. *Computing and the Common: Learning from Participatory Design in the Age of Platform Capitalism*. Università degli Studi di Trento.

Trudeau, D. and Wareham, E. 2020. COVID-19 is Spurring a Reinvention of Public Space. *MinnPost*. Retrieved from: https://www.minnpost.com /community-voices/2020/08/covid-19-is-spurring-a-reinvention-of-public -space (last accessed 24 June 2021).

CHAPTER 4

Platforms in a Time of Pandemic

Niccolò Cuppini, Mattia Frapporti and Maurilio Pirone

Introduction

The recent and still ongoing Covid-19 pandemic has been described both as an extraordinary event transforming our lives and as a tipping point in a shift towards labour digitalisation. The activity of platforms has acquired more and more scholarly interest because their business has been considered as the future of work. In this chapter we will try to enlarge the perspective and place the current wave of digitalisation within a longer-term process. From this perspective we consider the pandemic as an event highlighting and accelerating some structural features of the platform economy and, more generally, of contemporary capitalism. The aim is to understand how such general tendencies have changed after, and because of, the Covid-19 outbreak.

The premise of this approach is to consider platforms as a very resilient and flexible business model. Based on algorithmic management, certain aspects of self-entrepreneurialism and the use of radical digital technologies such as smartphones (Greenfield 2017), platforms mobilise data extraction and workforce exploitation through multiple forms of territorialization. This means they do not exist in a vacuum but embed and reshape prior socio-economic conditions – such as urban specificities, omissions in labour law, gender and race inequalities – towards the commodification of social reproduction and cooperation.

How to cite this book chapter:
Cuppini, N., Frapporti, M., and Pirone, M. 2022. Platforms in a Time of Pandemic.
   In: Armano, E., Briziarelli, M., and Risi, E. (eds.), *Digital Platforms and Algorithmic
   Subjectivities*. Pp. 63–74. London: University of Westminster Press. DOI: https://
   doi.org/10.16997/book54.e. License: CC-BY-NC-ND 4.0

Obviously, there are alternative ways of distinguishing between platforms' typologies. Our aim is to concentrate on so-called lean platforms (Srnicek 2016) and geographically tethered workers (Woodcock and Graham 2020), primarily characterised by their supply of local services (i.e. ride hailing, house cleaning, etc.). Despite the positive rhetoric regarding a gig or sharing economy, we highlight how such platforms pose several challenges to other 'actors' within cities. While labour conditions under platforms are always more scrutinised for their consequences on workforce living conditions, some other elements seem to involve more than just these platform workers: for instance, urban landscapes have been radically modified by actors such as Airbnb in terms of rent increases, the expulsion of citizens and access to space. These features of platform growth have provoked a major public debate on their regulation and role, as well as generating protests we may frame in terms of class struggle and urban unionism. Recently, platform capitalism has been transformed by the Covid-19 outbreak too, and the platforms' ecosystem has had to quickly adapt to this new circumstance.

In this chapter we will consider the pandemic as a moment highlighting the resilience of platform capitalism as well as its internal differences (first section). In particular, we will consider such resilience in relation to urban transformations (second section) and labour organisation (third section), taking two platforms – respectively Airbnb and Deliveroo – as illustrative of these processes. Finally, we will summarise some of platform capitalism's features that we consider relevant in and beyond the pandemic.

Fifty Years of Changes: Toward a Post-Pandemic Transition?

Over the last fifty years we have witnessed multiple transitions, sometimes hastily called 'revolutions' (Into the Black Box 2018; Benvegnù et al. 2021). In the 1960s and early 1970s, we witnessed the *logistics revolution* when, due to the introduction of some innovative technologies, such as that of container technology (Levinson 2016), and to a changed approach in terms of transportation management (Allen 1997; Bonacich and Wilson 2008), the circulation of commodities became a new 'continent' to be explored and rendered economically valuable (Cowen 2014; Hassan 2020). Then, in the 1980s the revolution was in the field of retail: Wal-Mart became the new paradigmatic brand of the economy, roaring 'out of an isolated corner of the rural South to become the vanguard of a retail revolution that has transformed the nature of US employment, sent US manufacturing abroad, and redefined the very meaning of globalization' (Lichtenstein 2009, 4). After the neoliberal politics of Reagan and Thatcher, the global network society of the 1990s (Castells 2010) witnessed a deep change in the market with the advent of a *dotcom revolution* (Becker 2006) bringing actors such as Amazon centre stage. Eventually, after the 2008 economic crisis, *platform capitalism* (Srnicek 2016) burst onto the scene, as an unprecedented set of digital platforms 'have penetrated the heart of societies' (van Dijck, Poell and de Waal 2019, 2), quickly defining new forms of consumption as well as new groups of workers (Huws 2014). Nowadays, the Covid-19 crisis has been framed as the umpteenth revolution. Is that true? Or to frame this more precisely moving beyond a superficial approach, which changes have been brought about by the pandemic, adding to this long-term tendency towards a networked (reticular) and digital capitalism?

Covid-19 constitutes a serious threat to the global economy as containment measures imposed everywhere have limited human mobility and mitigated the flow of commodities. An economic and social system based on so-called *supply chain capitalism* (Tsing 2009) has suddenly been forced to reconsider some structural features of its mode of operation, and even for the *platform society* the pandemic was deeply shocking. On this matter we ought to make a distinction. Following José van Dijck, Thomas Poell and Martijn de Waal we can assume two types of platform: infrastructural and sectoral. The former represents 'the heart of the ecosystem upon which many other platforms and apps can be built' (van Dijck, Poell and de Waal 2019, 13). Most of these infrastructures are owned by Alphabet-Google, Facebook, Apple, Amazon and Microsoft – the so-called Big Five of the IT sector. Complementarily, sectoral platforms 'serve a particular sector or niche, such as news, transportation, food, education, health, finance, or hospitality' (ibid). Infrastructural platforms allow a digitalisation of many working activities, a general platformization of labour with many activities adopting ICT solutions. Sectoral platforms are more urban-based and transform particular activities into a supposedly entrepreneurial job. Adopting this distinction, we may highlight a first feature of the pandemic's impact: whereas infrastructural platforms expanded during and because of the Covid-19 outbreak, the situation is much more heterogenous for sectoral platforms. Put differently, we may observe a general tendency towards the digitalisation of services as being replayed during the pandemic. The use of the internet, of smartphone applications and other ICTs has seen the reorganisation of the productive process in wider and more scattered spaces, guaranteeing at the same time a high level of coordination and supervision. Some platforms represent leading players in the furnishing of digital infrastructures. Here we can consider the paradigmatic example of Amazon. Since the very start of the first pandemic wave some analysts claimed that Amazon 'will emerge stronger than ever' (Semuels 2020), bringing about the 'Amazonification of the Planet' (Merchant 2020). According to the *Financial Times*, 'lockeddown shoppers drove sales 40 per cent higher' for Jeff Bezos' company, which ended with sales of 'between $87bn and $93bn [...] up by about a third on the same quarter of 2019' for the second quarter of 2020 (Lee 2020). In contrast, the experience of sectorial platforms was very different. Those like Airbnb experienced a real shock; those like Deliveroo and other short-range logistics firms saw big increases in income. In this chapter we delve into this, outlining some insights.

This acceleration in the process of digitalisation brings us to a second hypothesis concerning the emergence of a new technical division in labour composition between so-called *smart-working* and *urban-based jobs*. On the one hand, a *housewification* of working space is observed, which means the extreme development of outsourcing, even pushed into living spaces, with an overlap between the productive and reproductive spheres (Pirone 2021); the scattered production of a reticular capitalism may individualise all these working spaces, too. On the other hand, the public spaces of cities turn into factories without walls. Platforms allow for the management of data flows, which logistically connect multiple urban places.

Both are grounded on a general push for digitalisation that favours platforms in general, and a consequent further assault on workers' rights as the status of self-employed 'independence' seems to be the newly dominant paradigm in platform capitalism. Even in 2004 the theorist Tiziana Terranova claimed that 'the expansion of the Internet has given ideological and material support to contemporary trends towards increased flexibility of the workforce, continuous reskilling, freelance work, and the diffusion of practices such as "supplementing"' (2004, 74). The pandemic could lead to a further intensification of this. However, notwithstanding that a platformization of society is all but sketched out, digital workers may still be able to play an important role in influencing or contesting such a transition, and we will try to understand how.

The pandemic also imposed a distinction between essential and non-essential productive activities – with web services and logistics deemed the former – revealing the productive hierarchies in the organisation of contemporary capitalism. Among those who were able to continue to work during lockdowns, employees in long-range logistics were immediately classed as key workers. This acknowledgement could have further consequences for some ongoing processes. Indeed, for many years now we have witnessed protests and strikes in the logistics sector. On a global level, over the last decade, circulation struggles occurred that have had a major impact on the capitalistic economy (Cuppini, Frapporti and Pirone 2015; Moody 2017; Ness and Alimahomed-Wilson 2018; Clover 2019; Dyer-Whiteford, Brenes-Ryes and Liu 2020). The Covid-19 crisis has highlighted the strategic importance of logistic workers to society, and the fragility of global value chains. As a matter of fact, although during the pandemic many container shipping companies saw increased income, showing a 'surprising resilience' (Pooler and Hale 2020), it must be noted that work intensification, a sense of precarity and health risks within the sector have led to protests and strikes (Workers Inquiry Network 2020). This could have further consequences bringing new forms of mobilisation and protest to this crucial arena of contemporary capitalism.

To conclude, the pandemic has revealed some structural features of contemporary capitalism: productive processes are based on a logistical management of (data, people and commodity) flows that require a hierarchical infrastructure of platforms. The Covid-19 outbreak does not simply illustrate a condition but operates as a transition towards a higher level of labour digitalisation that entails a further technical division of class composition according to the spaces of production. In this sense, cities constitute the main space for platform territorialization, and the pandemic has influenced the ways they will develop in the coming years, both in terms of landscape and subjectivities. We will now go on to examine this in further detail.

Is the Pandemic Shock for Airbnb a Crisis of Platform Urbanism More Broadly?

In recent years, Airbnb has deeply influenced the design of urban landscapes, urban economics and urban life (Ferreri and Romola Sanyal 2018; Gallagher 2018; Gyódi 2019; Guttentag 2013; Nieuwland and van Melik 2018; Stors and Kagermeier 2015; Wachsmuth and Weisler 2018). The 'Airification of cities' (Picascia, Romano and Teobaldi 2017) seemed, for a while, to represent an irresistible tendency towards a complete redefinition of urban dynamics. However, this platform has been one of the most severely impacted by the pandemic.

The blanket cancellations suffered by Airbnb left owners vulnerable, with no income for mortgage interest payments and local taxes, and the company plunged to almost half its value (Nhamo, Dube and Chikodzi 2020), within the broader context of the crisis of a tourism industry based on human mobility (Uğur and Akbıyık 2020; Williams 2020). The hospitality and travel industry have perhaps been the most hard-hit economic sector, with hourly paid workers facing potentially devastating hardships (Nicola et al. 2020).

While in recent years Airbnb has severely disrupted this sector, it now seems that Covid-19 has 'disrupted the disruptor'. It is the planetary dimension of this shock which made it so hard for Airbnb to find a way to relaunch its business. There has been no way out. This situation could lead to an increase in the extractive strategies of Airbnb, or it could lead to other scenarios. The shock has impacted both professional and non-professional hosts (Farmaki, Stergiou and Kaniadakis 2019). Dolnicar and Zare (2020) optimistically suggest that – following the three host type differentiations proposed in Hardy and Dolnicar (2017) – whilst the proportion of 'capitalist hosts' will decline in the future, the proportion of 'befriender and ethicist hosts' will increase, 'moving Airbnb back towards its original ethos of space sharing among ordinary citizens'. This implies that the long-term rental market came back onto the scene to help absorb shock-related risks. At the same time, hosting platforms developed other strategies to attract tourists in ways that were compatible with the restrictions imposed by the pandemic – particularly in terms of the geographic locations of listings. For instance, there was an increase in listings based in rural settings and small historical towns, in part boosted through promotions such as Airbnb's 'Italian Villages' project (Airbnb 2017).

Therefore, while many countries and municipalities were trying to regulate short-term letting to minimise negative side effects to the community (von Briel and Dolnicar 2020), it is possible to hypothesise that this dynamic could be turned upside down. To give an example, within our research we have observed that the Bologna Municipality and the University of Bologna are promoting short-term rentals to attract students to the city in order to address the urban economic losses caused by 'distance learning' on a city campus like Bologna. Rather than imposing tighter regulations on the sector, policymakers could possibly even incentivise the trading of rental space via online platforms.

Furthermore, there is a third perspective that should be taken into consideration concerning the core business of platforms like Airbnb (i.e. Big Data extraction) and its financial aspects (the company was listed on the stock exchange in 2020). Neither have been directly impacted by the pandemic, confirming their role as invariants in the development of platforms.

Even though, initially, Airbnb appeared to be a 'loser platform' during the pandemic, it is hard to sustain the argument that the company will collapse in the near future. *Airification* is not over but looks set to be extended to other territories not yet touched by platform colonisation. More importantly, our argument is that apart from the specific future of Airbnb as a company, the key point is to analyse it as a 'model', a 'rationality'. And our impression is that – as the example of Bologna shows – the platformization of the urban is a dynamic that will continue to grow. In other words, platform urbanism (van der Graaf and Ballon 2019; Mahmoudi, Levenda and Stehlin 2021) is an emerging assemblage and a way of transforming and redefining relations between institutions, markets, and urban agents, actors and populations, which is consolidating as a sort of *urban institution* (van Doorn 2020) and as a specific logic of urban development. In this sense, the uncertainties induced by the pandemic will probably increase the logistical logic of the 'just in time and to the point' (Into the Black Box 2019) use of cities, and platforms (such as Airbnb) remain the best tool for realising this logic.

The Unpeaceful Growth of Food Delivery Services

A different fate has befallen other disruptive platforms, such as Deliveroo. While Airbnb is considered meaningful for urban processes such as gentrification, food delivery platforms are often associated with another typical phenomenon linked to the digitalisation of services: the spread of forms of independent work – represented in this case by fleets of riders. It must be noted that last-mile logistics – in contrast to tourism – never stopped during the pandemic, with workers, such as food delivery riders, continuing to drive around urban spaces. Enterprises like Deliveroo gained market share almost everywhere because mobility and activity restrictions moved consumption towards digital platforms, while many restaurants searched for other potential markets.

In Italy the company reported an increase of 40% of affiliated restaurants in March 2020, and Uber Eats saw an increase of more than 55% in purchases (Chicchi et al. 2020). Last-mile logistics has been considered, in many cases, a sort of essential service for the social reproduction of the urban masses. The infrastructural role assumed by these sectoral platforms led them to a dominant position in respect to working conditions and state regulations. Nevertheless, this view of food delivery platforms as essential infrastructure did not lead to a corresponding view of delivery riders as essential workers (Chicchi et al. 2020). During the pandemic an internal migration between platforms was observed as many workers moved from services such as transportation to others such as food delivery. At the same time, due to the high demand for deliveries after the outbreak of Covid-19, Deliveroo introduced, in some major European cities including Barcelona, Paris and Bologna, a 'free login' system in order to stimulate riders to log on to the platform to offer their services at any time during the working day. Together with the loss of clear working times, riders witnessed the complete adoption of a piece-working system of payment. This system of organisation of the productive process is not only based on a tendency towards self-entrepreneurialism and valorisation of so-called human capital but moves the competition from the market to the workforce. In this case, we do not see a price decrease, but a rights decrease. Even if the growth of the food delivery market was interrupted due to the relaxing of containment measures, 'piece-working' has remained valid and become the hegemonic form of payment for almost all platforms. This lack of protections and the resulting low incomes has led to strikes and protests in the sector, despite the restrictions put in place to contain the pandemic. In this sense, riders represent not only the expansion of forms of independent work but are also at the forefront of resistance against the post-capitalist narrative of a sharing or gig economy supposedly without vertical relations of exploitation. The global labour movement of riders gained strength from the discontent around food delivery working conditions and the fear of contagion by the virus. In Latin America and Europe, protests broke out to demand wage increases, welfare and personal protective equipment (Workers Inquiry Network 2020) and culminated in the first global strike on 8 October 2020.

How to Fight the Giants

We initially reported the concept of transition to frame the Covid-19 outbreak as a moment for capitalist reorganisation based on the acceleration of some tendencies and the emergence of new challenges. It seems that generally the current pandemic will lead to a push for more automation and digitalisation, and so favour platforms. Put differently, the pandemic could reinforce a shut-in economic model with a major role for last-mile logistics and web services. In this sense, we are witnessing and experiencing the consolidating dominance of some infrastructural platforms like Amazon, and also the emergence within infrastructure of an involvement in social reproduction for some sectoral platforms. Platforms indeed demonstrate a high level of adaptability to different circumstances and, as the case of Airbnb demonstrates, are quickly modifying their services according to local conditions. Platform territorialization is a just-in-time phenomenon that is easily able to adapt to market demand and to the colonisation of new geographies. In some cases, the coronacrisis has even proved to be an opportunity to take further steps towards the imposition of more flexible and casual forms of labour organisation and payment. Nevertheless, this condition is permitted only due to a massive availability of platform workers who are, however, starting to question the forms and conditions of their labour. If platforms took advantage of the pandemic to weaken attempts at regulation, it also increased the need to search for strategies for regulating platforms themselves. We may identify several emerging strategies, each one with a particular – or more than one – subjectivity engaged. We may note the same platform workers who are organising to resist the power of the algorithm are also experimenting with new forms of unionism (Woodcock 2021), whereas others are building digital cooperatives to exercise more democratic control (Scholz 2016). If these strategies are more focused on sectoral platforms, more general perspectives regarding infrastructural platforms are gaining attention within platform society. In this instance claims are being made to either place platforms that play an essential role in society under state control (Srnicek 2016) or alternatively to share data profits and management (Morozov 2019). Far from hailing one of these as being more valid or efficient, we think they constitute different forms of engagement with platform capitalism. In this sense, the pandemic has demonstrated that, for discontented subjects, targeting vital junctures in the platform economy is the way to define a more general strategy through their articulation.

Acknowledgement

The research reported in this chapter was funded by the European Union Horizon 2020 research and innovation programme, 'Platform Labour in Urban Spaces: Fairness, Welfare, Development' (https://project-plus.eu) Grant Agreement No. 822638. The views and opinions expressed in this publication are the sole responsibility of the author(s) and do not necessarily reflect the views of the European Commission/Research Executive Agency. The PLUS project analyses the impact of four different platforms (Airbnb, Uber, Deliveroo and Helpling) in seven European cities (Barcelona, Berlin, Bologna, Lisbon, London, Paris and Tallinn). Specifically, we refer to the internal reports on the socio-historical impact of technology in the labour market (D1.3) and on the methodological tools for the qualitative research (D2.2). The section on the impact of the pandemic uses the findings from a PLUS instant report (Chicchi et al. 2020), elaborated to map local responses to the Covid-19 outbreak. Furthermore, in April/May 2020 we undertook two video inquiries – one on Airbnb and urbanism, one on Deliveroo and food delivery – to analyse platforms' reaction to Covid-19 with the collaboration of several experts, activists and workers.

The chapter is the result of an extensive cooperation between the authors. Mattia Frapporti wrote first section, Niccolò Cuppini the second and Maurilio Pirone the third. The introduction and conclusion share a common vision.

References

Airbnb. 2017. https://news.airbnb.com/airbnb-joins-ministry-of-tourism-and-anci-to-promote-small-town-italy-with-italian-villages-project.

Allen, B. 1997. The Logistics Revolution and Transportation. *Annals of the American Academy of Political and Social Science,* 553(1), 106–116.

Becker, W. H. 2006. The Dot.Com Revolution in Historical Perspective. *Entreprises et Histoire*, 43, 43–46.

Benvegnù, C., Cuppini, N., Frapporti, M., Milesi, F., and Pirone, M. (Eds.), 2021. *Capitalismo 4.0.* Meltemi.

Bonachich, E. and Wilson, J. 2008. *Getting the Goods: Ports, Labour and The Logistics Revolution.* Cornell University Press.

Castells, M. 2010. *The Rise of the Network Society.* Wiley-Blackwell.

Chicchi, F., Frapporti, M., Marrone, M., and Pirone M. (Eds.), 2020. *Covid-19 Impact on Platform Economy: A Preliminary Outlook.* AMSActa.

Clover, J. 2019. *Riot. Strike. Riot: The New Era of Uprisings.* Verso.

Cowen, D. 2014. *The Deadly Life of Logistics.* Minnesota University Press.

Cuppini, N., Frapporti, M., and Pirone, M. 2015. Logistics Struggles in the Po Valley Region: Territorial Transformations and Processes of Antagonistic Subjectivation. *South Atlantic Quarterly*, 114(1), 119–134.

Dolnicar, S. and Zare, S. 2020. COVID19 and Airbnb–Disrupting the Disruptor. *Annals of Tourism Research*, 83, 102961.

Dyer-Whiteford, N., Brenes Reyes, J., and Liu, M. 2020. Riot Logistics. In C. Benvegnù et al. (Eds.), *Capitalismo 4.0.* Meltemi.

Farmaki, A., Stergiou, D., and Kaniadakis, A. 2019. Self-Perceptions of Airbnb Hosts' Responsibility: A Moral Identity Perspective. *Journal of Sustainable Tourism.* https://doi.org/10.1080/09669582.2019.1707216.

Ferreri, M. and Sanyal, R. 2018. Platform Economies and Urban Planning: Airbnb and Regulated Deregulation in London. *Urban Studies*, 55(15), 53–68.

Gallagher, L. 2018. *The Airbnb Story: How Three Ordinary Guys Disrupted an Industry, Made Billions... and Created Plenty of Controversy.* Mariner Books.

Greenfield, A. 2017. *Radical Technologies: The Design of Everyday Life.* Verso.

Guttentag, D. 2013. Airbnb: Disruptive Innovation and the Rise of an Informal Tourism Accommodation Sector. *Current Issues in Tourism*, 18(12), 1192–1217.

Gyódi, Kristóf. 2019. Airbnb in European Cities: Business as Usual or True Sharing Economy? *Journal of Cleaner Production*, 221(1), 536–551.

Hardy, A. and Dolnicar, S. 2017. Types of Network Members. In S. Dolnicar (Ed.), *Peer-to-Peer Accommodation Networks: Pushing the Boundaries* (pp. 170–181). Goodfellow Publishers.

Hassan, R. 2020. *The Condition of Digitality: A Post-Modern Marxism for the Practice of Digital Life*. University of Westminster Press. https://doi.org/10.16997/book44.

Huws, U. 2014. *Labour in the Global Digital Economy*. Monthly Review Press.

Into the Black Box. 2018. *Critical Logistics: A Manifesto*. Available at: http://www.intotheblackbox.com/manifesto/critical-logistics-a-manifesto

Into the Black Box. (Eds.), 2019. Logistical Gazes: Spaces, Labour and Struggles in Global Capitalism. *Work Organization, Labour & Globalization*, 13(1).

Lee, D. 2020. Amazon Doubles Quarterly Profit Despite Covid-19 Costs. *Financial Times*, 30 July. Available at: https://www.ft.com/content/7a42b1d8-9ca7-4827-aaae-729fdb7637f5.

Levinson, M. 2016. *The Box: How the Shipping Container Made the World Smaller and the World Economy Bigger*. (2nd edn.) Princeton University Press.

Lichtenstein, N. 2019. *The Retail Revolution: How Wal-Mart Created a Brave New World of Business*. Picador.

Mahmoudi, D., Levenda, A. M., and Stehlin, J. G. 2021. Political Ecologies of Platform Urbanism. In M. Houdson (Eds.), *Urban Platforms and the Future City: Transformations in Infrastructure, Governance, Knowledge and Everyday Life*. Routledge.

Merchant, B. 2020. Coronavirus Is Speeding Up the Amazonification of the Planet. *OneZero*, 19 March. Available at: https://onezero.medium.com/coronavirus-is-speeding-up-the-amazonification-of-the-planet-21cb20d16372.

Moody, K. 2017. *On New Terrain: How Capital Is Reshaping the Battleground of Class War*. Haymarket Books.

Morozov, E. 2019. Digital Socialism? The Calculation Debate in the Age of Big Data. *New Left Review*, 116/117, 33–76.

Ness, E. and Alimahomed-Wilson, J. 2018. *Choke Points: Logistics Workers Disrupting the Global Supply Chain*. Pluto Press.

Nhamo, G., Dube, K., and Chikodzi, D. 2020. Impacts and Implications of COVID-19 on the Global Hotel Industry and Airbnb. In G. Nhamo, K. Dube, and D. Chikodzi. *Counting the Cost of COVID-19 on the Global Tourism Industry*. Springer.

Nicola, M. et al. 2020. The Socio-Economic Implications of the Coronavirus Pandemic (COVID-19): A Review. *International Journal of Surgery*, 78, 185–193.

Nieuwland, S. and van Melik, R. 2018. Regulating Airbnb: How Cities Deal with Perceived Negative Externalities of Short-Term Rentals. *Current Issues in Tourism*, 23(7), 811–825.

Picascia, S., Romano, A., and Teobaldi, M. 2017. The Airification of Cities: Making Sense of the Impact of Peer To Peer Short Term Letting on Urban Functions and Economy. *Proceedings of the Annual Congress of the Association of European Schools of Planning*, Lisbon, 11–14 July. SocArxiv, 25 November. https://doi.org/10.31235/osf.io/vs8w3.

Pirone, M. 2021. Pandemic Transition: Techno-Politics and Social Reproduction Struggles. *Human Geography*, 14(2), 288–291. https://doi.org/10.1177/19427786211019191.

Pooler, M. and Hale, T. 2020. Coronavirus and Globalization: The Surprising Resilience of Container Shipping. *Financial Times*, 17 September. Available at: https://www.ft.com/content/65fe4650-5d90-41bc-8025-4ac81df8a5e4.

Scholz, T. 2016. *Platform Cooperativism: Challenging the Corporate Sharing Economy*. Rosa Luxemburg Stiftung.

Semuels, A. 2020. Many Companies Won't Survive the Pandemic. Amazon Will Emerge Stronger Than Ever. *Time*, 28 July. Available at: https://time.com/5870826/amazon-coronavirus-jeff-bezos-congress.

Srnicek, N. 2016. *Platform Capitalism*. Polity Press.

Stors, N. and Kagermeier, A. 2015. Motives for Using Airbnb in Metropolitan Tourism: Why Do People Sleep in the Bed of a Stranger? *Regions Magazine*, 299(1), 17–19.

Terranova, T. 2004. *Network Culture: Politics for the Information Age*. Pluto Press.

Tsing, A. 2009. Supply Chains and the Human Condition. *Rethinking Marxism*, 21(2), 148–176.

Ugur, N. G. and Akbiyik, A. 2020. Impacts of COVID-19 on Global Tourism Industry: A Cross-Regional Comparison. *Tourism Management Perspectives*, 36, 100744. https://doi.org/10.1016/j.tmp.2020.100744.

van Dijck, J., Poell, T., and de Waal, M. 2019. *The Platform Society*. Oxford University Press.

van Doorn, N. 2020. A New Institution on the Block: On Platform Urbanism and Airbnb Citizenship. *New Media & Society*, 22(10), 1808–1826.

van der Graaf, S. and Ballon, P. 2019. Navigating Platform Urbanism. *Technological Forecasting and Social Change*, 142, 364–372.

von Briel, D. and Dolnicar, S. 2020. The Evolution of Airbnb Regulation – An International Longitudinal Investigation 2008–2020. *Annals of Tourism Research*, 87, 102983. https://doi.org/10.1016/j.annals.2020.102983.

Wachsmuth, D. and Weisler, A. 2018. Airbnb and the Rent Gap: Gentrification Through the Sharing Economy. *Environment and Planning A: Economy and Space*, 5(3), 1–24.

Williams, C. C. 2020. Impacts of the Coronavirus Pandemic on Europe's Tourism Industry: Addressing Tourism Enterprises and Workers in the Undeclared Economy. *International Journal of Tourism Research*, 23(1), 79–88.

Woodcock, J. 2021. *The Fight Against Platform Capitalism: An Inquiry into the Global Struggles of the Gig Economy*. University of Westminster Press. https://doi.org/10.16997/book51.

Woodcock, J. and Graham, M. 2020. *The Gig Economy: A Critical Introduction*. Polity Press.

Workers Inquiry Network. 2020. Struggle in a Pandemic. A Collection of Contributions on the COVID-19 Crisis. Available at: http://www.intothe blackbox.com/wp-content/uploads/2020/05/Struggle-in-a-Pandemic -FINAL.pdf.

CHAPTER 5

Black Box Power: Zones of Uncertainty in Algorithmic Management

Heiner Heiland

Introduction

Algorithms extend the agency and change the processes of social systems. This is particularly evident in the field of work, where algorithms are used to organise and control labour processes. Such algorithmic management is particularly used in platform labour. Here, platforms act as intermediaries, mediating work tasks to mostly self-employed workers, either in the form of local services (such as passenger transport), or globally distributed knowledge work (crowdwork). Such platforms are pioneers and testing grounds for new forms of controlling and coordinating the labour process. Thus, they provide a window into a possible future of work, as there are reasonable expectations that the control practices of algorithmic management embedded in platform labour will spread to other work contexts, even to areas of highly qualified work (e.g. Schweyer 2018; Sánchez-Monedro and Dencik 2019; or the 'productivity scores' in Microsoft 365).

Platform labour is a radical form of outsourcing. Workers are not employees of a company, but only have the right to use specific software, access to which can be terminated at any time. They are usually self-employed and pay for their own insurance and equipment, so platform owners have minimal to zero costs.

How to cite this book chapter:
Heiland, H. 2022. Black Box Power: Zones of Uncertainty in Algorithmic Management. In: Armano, E., Briziarelli, M., and Risi, E. (eds.), *Digital Platforms and Algorithmic Subjectivities*. Pp. 75–86. London: University of Westminster Press. DOI: https://doi.org/10.16997/book54.f. License: CC-BY-NC-ND 4.0

The workers are thus directly linked to the market and the development of the demand for their labour. Following Karl Weick, such a link between platforms and workers can be identified as a loose coupling, which 'implies the tying together of subsystems in such a fashion that neither can do without the other but neither has much control over the other' (Foster 1983, 11). Such loose coupling reduces costs and complexity for platforms, but it also increases complexity elsewhere. Since the workers are not their employees, platforms can only partially instruct them when and how to work. Nevertheless, it is essential for the success of these companies that customer demand is satisfied. Algorithmic management is crucial to meeting this challenge. Despite the formally loose coupling between platforms and self-employed workers, algorithmic management allows for the establishment of tight couplings with regard to the labour process. It allows the platform labour processes to be automated and controlled in detail.

This chapter examines algorithmic management and investigates its mechanisms. It is argued that the existing discussion is partly characterised by technological determinism, which firstly assumes comprehensive control and secondly narrows the view to technological aspects. Drawing on the organisation theory of Michel Crozier and Erhard Friedberg, the limited agency of heteronomous actors is analysed. The focus is on the opacity of algorithmic structures, which contributes decisively to the effectiveness of algorithmic management. This mechanism is identified as *black box power*, leading to an algorithmic self which monitors its actions carefully and is obedient in an anticipatory manner.

Algorithms and Algorithmic Management

Algorithms are not a new phenomenon. The term describes a calculation method by means of which decisions can be made according to a given structure – 'if A, then B'. This means that even a simple building instruction is an algorithm. As a result of increased computing capacities, the performance of algorithms used has improved significantly over the last few years, and with the ubiquity of computer-supported mediatised environments, so has their relevance. Thus, algorithms have become responsible for the coordination of numerous social activities within a short period of time. The focus within current academic literature is mostly on consumption algorithms that are used in online retail, social media or search engines. Furthermore there are work algorithms that are used 'to direct workers by *restricting* and *recommending*, evaluate workers by *recording* and *rating*, and discipline workers by *replacing* and *rewarding*' (Kellogg, Valentine and Christin 2020, 367, emphasis in original). It is not new that the use of technology in the labour process shifts 'the balance of power between capital and wage labour a significant step further in the direction of a position of extensive powerlessness for wage earners' (Schmiede

2015, 69). Previously, machines have been introduced by management and they determined specific ways of use, as did assembly lines that determined the direction and speed of the labour process. Although technological artefacts always have an 'interpretative flexibility' (Oudshoorn and Pinch 2003, 2), the technological factuality of algorithms is much more pronounced and predetermines a much narrower corridor of action for workers.

A precondition for this is datafication, that is, the standardised capture of social reality in forms that can be processed by computers. This results in a specific reproduction of social relations. Thus, for example, the evaluation systems of platforms represent a datafied objectification which allows for the processing of previously informal and socially interwoven aspects. By means of datafication, complex social relationships and individuals are dematerialised and remodelled as reduced data structures in the form of 'numerical representations' (Manovich 2001). Algorithmic calculations result in a rematerialisation that represents the 'materiality of software' (Fuller 2008). Thus 'virtuals that generate a whole variety of actuals' are created (Lash 2007, 71). This process is not objective. Just as there are no 'raw' data (Gitelman 2013), there are no objective algorithms (Beer 2017; Eubanks 2018; Kitchin 2017; O'Neil 2017). Despite this, they appear as objective mechanisms and thus lead to a 'new empiricism' (Kitchin 2014). The independence of algorithms from human decisions does not lead to the neutrality of software, but instead to invariance in the given processes. For, 'code is law', as Larry Lessig (1999) notes. Programming demands quasi-total conformity from the users and appears as non-negotiable.

In addition, algorithms are 'enigmatic technologies' (Pasquale 2015, 1) 'whose workings are mysterious' (ibid., 2). Following Burrell (2016), there are three opacities of algorithms. First, they are kept 'behind veils of trade secrecy' (Pasquale 2015, 2), because they are a key component of production in competition with rivals. Second, algorithms are not comprehensible for most people due to technical illiteracy, even if their code is transparent. And third, machine learning algorithms continue to develop independently, 'without regard for human comprehension' (Burrell 2016, 10). Algorithms are thus a formalisation of social processes whose modes of operation are opaque. As Pasquale (2015, 8) points out, the 'values and prerogatives that the encoded rules enact are hidden within black boxes' and 'authority is increasingly expressed algorithmically'. Moreover, the opacity disguises who is responsible for the decisions. Through such an 'agency laundering' (Tsamados et al. 2021, 18–19) companies can 'hide' behind algorithms, and opposition becomes more difficult.

In summary, it can be stated that algorithmic management results in a new and comprehensive form of control of the labour process which significantly restricts the autonomous agency of labour. Algorithms provide companies with a 'secondary agency' (MacKenzie 2006), so that they can enforce their interests automatically, down to the last detail and in remote locations. However, it cannot necessarily be concluded from the considerable potential of algorithmic management that this can be realised without interruption.

Zones of Uncertainty

As labour processes are usually based on cooperation between workers, they are rarely isolated but located within organisations. Organisations are structured forms of social interaction. Contrary to a one-sided analysis, according to which capital controls labour processes down to the last detail, a micropolitical perspective assumes that the valorisation of capital in companies is not simply executable and cannot be enforced without friction. The control and management of work may be planned top-down, but it is not clear whether the workers actually act accordingly in the end. According to Crozier and Friedberg (1993, 18, 39), social action in general and in organisations in particular is always a matter of power. Organisations are shaped by actors' conflicts and are a political and cultural construct (Crozier and Friedberg 1993, 111). Power and resistance are two sides of the same coin. Following Max Weber, power is defined as interaction and social relationship rather than an attribute: 'It is a balance of power from which one can get more out of than the other, but in which one is also never completely at the mercy of the other' (Crozier and Friedberg 1993, 41).

An actor's agency is based on the size of a zone of uncertainty which he 'can control through his behaviour towards his opponents' (Crozier and Friedberg 1993, 41). Control over zones of uncertainty gives actors resources of power. Central to this is therefore the 'manipulation of the predictability' of one's own behaviour and that of others (Crozier and Friedberg 1993, 41). Power belongs to whoever overlooks the actions of others and is at the same time able to make their own actions non-transparent. In organisations, actors interact in games in which they use their power resources and try to influence the rules of the game in their favour.

The management of a company is thus structurally privileged as it can oversee labour process and determine the formal rules of the game. Despite this, workers have at least limited resources of power or control over zones of uncertainty. However, this does not indicate that there is a power symmetry between companies and workers. Instead, there are relative autonomies. Weick (1976, 1) illustrates this by using the metaphor of a football game taking place on a round pitch that is inclined to one side, with several goals and several balls. Depending on the intensity of the inclination, there is a tendency for the goals to be more easily scored by one side against the other. While workers have to expend a lot of energy to win a point, the existing structures support management.

To analyse actors' agency, Crozier and Friedberg (1993, 50) identify four sources of power or types of uncertainty:

1) The knowledge of specific expertise;
2) a position that provides a privileged contact with the organisation's environment;

3) the control of channels in which information and communication are exchanged; and

4) the definition and existence of formal rules of the organisation.

These four zones of uncertainty are examined below in regard to algorithmic management.

Algorithmic Management and Zones of Uncertainty

A traditional zone of uncertainty in the labour process and a resource of power for workers is their specific production knowledge. Management coordinates the labour process and is dependent on workers for its realisation. Only workers have detailed knowledge of the various steps in the processes of the work and are therefore in a position to influence, for example, the pace or quality of work (Burawoy 1979). This aspect was central to Taylor's scientific management, which brought to light this zone of uncertainty, so that the labour process could be standardised and organised in a predictable way. One result was the restriction of workers' agency (Braverman 1974). Algorithmic management thus becomes a digital Taylorism. The need to make autonomous decisions is reduced to a minimum for platform workers: either platforms make decisions for them or they are given narrow corridors of action in which to act. Platform-mediated couriers or taxi drivers can choose their own routes, but are monitored via GPS and have to justify themselves in the case of major deviations. Furthermore, on crowdworking platforms, screenshots of workers' screens are taken at irregular intervals (Jarrahi et al. 2020).

The privileged contact workers have within the platforms' environment is also devalued by its algorithmic management establishing a zone of uncertainty. For example, the communication between crowdworkers and their clients is algorithmically monitored, and platforms can recognise, by mention of keywords such as 'PayPal' or 'email', when two parties are attempting to interact outside the platform and thus avoid commission fees (Jarrahi et al. 2020). In locally anchored platform labour (for instance that of food delivery), unobserved contacts with customers do occur, for example during the transporting of people or the cleaning of a flat. However, firstly, these are strongly regulated and mostly only organised by platforms via apps. Secondly, this zone of uncertainty is often devalued by rating systems. Customers are asked to rate workers, and this rating is taken into account, via algorithmic management techniques, in assigning further work. As a consequence, workers, rather than acting autonomously, attempt to second guess algorithmic decisions, undertaking extensive emotional work and anticipatory obedience in order not to jeopardise future work opportunities through triggering automated mediation of jobs by the platform (Chan 2019).

Further, platforms have sole control over the channels through which information and communication are exchanged. They program apps or homepages and therefore determine which information is sent to workers and how. An algorithmic decision cannot be contradicted and platforms tend to react slowly to complaints and requests from workers. For example, a manager of a crowdworking platform says: 'You cannot spend time exchanging e-mail. The time you spent looking at the e-mail costs more than what you paid them. This has to function on autopilot as an algorithmic system … and integrated with your business processes' (Irani 2015, 229–30). Moreover, interactions between workers are usually limited. While labour processes are typically characterised by cooperation between colleagues, in the case of platform labour this is taken over by algorithms, so that platform workers are isolated. They usually only have alternative and autonomous communication channels such as forums and chatrooms (Heiland 2020, 27–30).

Formal rules can also be used to devalue workers' uncertainty zones. In this respect, Friedberg explains that 'the actual role of the formal structure of an organisation is not to directly determine behaviour, but to structure the scope of behaviour for the actors' (Friedberg 1995, 151). Formal structures are 'the always provisional, precarious and problematic result of a test of power' (Friedberg 1995, 173) as they only achieve their effect when they are respected. Ignoring them or deliberate misinterpretations undermine them. It is also true for algorithmic management that its decisions only work when realised by workers. However, as mentioned above, its decisions are more binding and limit the scope of interpretation much more drastically. You cannot negotiate with code. Algorithmic bureaucracies are far more inflexible and rigid, so that the 'algorithmic cage' (Rahman 2020) they create deprives workers of power resources.

All these aspects occur in different variations and with different emphases in all forms of platform labour. In summary, it can be said that algorithmic management has created a new form of technological control that comprehensively governs the labour process and leaves only little agency to the workers. However, the discourse on algorithmic management tends towards technological determinism. Firstly, it should be noted that talk of an all-encompassing control is premature. A closer look – especially by using ethnographic analysis – shows that even under algorithmic management, workers are able, in limited ways, to act autonomously and resist forms of power (e.g. Heiland and Schaupp 2021). Secondly, although the control regimes in platform labour are technologically mediatised, their mechanisms are not solely technological. For example, platforms create internal markets in which platform workers compete for orders or shifts (Heiland 2019a; 2021a). In addition, and as discussed below, the algorithmic cage is invisible and opaque.

Black Box Power

Algorithms are black boxes. Although they determine the platform workers' daily work routine, the latter have no reliable knowledge about how they work. Platforms thus create a zone of uncertainty that is not comprehensible to the workers and is an important power resource for controlling the labour process, because 'uncertainty from the point of view of the problems is power from the point of view of the actors' (Crozier and Friedberg 1993, 13). Despite this, algorithmic decisions are rarely unexpected or irrational, as their basic objectives are usually obvious. For example, an order should go to the driver who is geographically closest to the customer. Further, platform workers are experienced in working with algorithms. They acquire this experience individually and, additionally, many workers discuss algorithm decisions and logic in lively exchanges in online chatrooms and forums (Heiland 2020, 27–30; Brinkmann and Heiland 2021).

Thus, in working with algorithms, platform workers are engaged in an individual and collective process of making sense in order to reduce uncertainty about opaque labour processes and to make its procedures predictable (e.g. Bishop 2019; Reid-Musson et al. 2020). The workers discursively and mentally reconstruct the algorithms, which allows them to understand the software. They project this ontology onto their reality and actions. A similar phenomenon is seen in computer game players, who develop a mental image of the computer model and adapt their actions to it (McGowan and McCullaugh 1995, 71). However, these reconstructions of algorithms are inevitably fragile. They only approximate actual algorithms and require – especially in the case of machine learning algorithms – constant adaptation. The reliability of expectations which the platform workers try to establish with their interpretations is therefore necessarily limited. In addition, the interpretations are often wrong. Usually, the platforms follow a 'logic of efficiency' (Friedberg 1995) rather than a 'logic of control' (Heiland and Brinkmann 2020, 135). With regard to algorithms, the main priority of platforms is the efficient design of the labour process and disciplining workers is only a secondary concern. Workers, on the other hand, often have a strong distrust of platforms and their intentions (Reid-Musson, MacEachen and Bartel 2020). For example, they wonder how the algorithms decide who gets an order when several drivers are at the same place or several workers have the same rating. They assume that platforms collect comprehensive data on the performance and compliant behaviour of workers and use it in the labour process.

The opacity of algorithms affects not only the labour process, but also the individuals themselves. In a survey, 63% of a sample of German platform-mediated food couriers reported feeling at the mercy of technology very often or often – only 10% stated that they were not aware of this feeling (Heiland 2019b, 302). Algorithmic management increases the platforms' de facto control over the labour process. At the same time, the pressure on workers to control themselves also increases. Instead of being obedient to the algorithmic specifications alone, the usually self-employed platform workers must view themselves as entrepreneurs, responsible for the creation and realisation of their own workload, which they must maximise and optimise out of self-interest. The workers thus not only have an 'invisible supervisor' through direct algorithmic control (Elliott and Long 2016, 138), but, due to uncertainty regarding the logic of algorithms, they internalise forms of control, and are self-policing, and this ensures they will conform and strive to continually improve. As known from other forms of work, workers develop an individualised sense of responsibility for their own employment and its continuation (Neff 2012, 28). Platform workers are thus not only subject to direct algorithmic power, but also to indirect and complementary *black box power*.

With the opacity of algorithmic management, platforms create a new zone of uncertainty, which are at their disposal, and at the same time devalues zones of uncertainty on the part of workers. For example, the speed of food couriers is not taken into account by algorithms, meaning that workers can influence the intensity of the labour process by utilising this knowledge. However, because of black box power, there is uncertainty among workers about this fact, and this power resource is therefore little used.

Finally, it should be emphasised that algorithmic management has a comprehensive but not an all-seeing gaze. It does not devalue all zones of insecurity and power resources of workers. Thus, they do have, to a limited extent, autonomous and sometimes resistant agencies (e.g. Heiland 2021b). Further, it is crucial for countering black box power that workers try to reconstruct the logics of algorithms based on their experiences and through communication with colleagues. It is therefore their pre-existing mistrust of precarious working conditions and the poor reputation of the platform that drives them to obedience in the first place. It is still unclear to what extent this form of control is a deliberate strategy of platforms or an unintended consequence. What is certain, however, is that, as a matter of course, they neither explain the basic logic of the algorithms to workers nor clear up obvious misunderstandings.

Conclusion

There is a long tradition of controlling labour processes via technology. Algorithms add a new chapter to this history. By means of these algorithms, control becomes automated, more detailed and applicable to new areas. It devalues zones of insecurity and thus the power resources of workers. At the same time, the analysis of algorithmic management runs the risk of one-sidedly emphasising technology as an explanation for workers' heteronomy. Next to technological control struggles over transparency and predictability have existed throughout capitalism's history. For example, in the early phase of industrial capitalism, as described by E. P. Thompson (1967), capital attempted to conceal the actual time of the day in order to conceal the working time of workers. Accordingly, the opacity of algorithms must be considered a central element:

> Uncertainty about the algorithm could lead us to misjudge their power, to overemphasise their importance, to misconceive of the algorithm as a lone detached actor, or to miss how power might actually be deployed through such technologies. (Beer 2017, 3)

Subsequently, the potential for control inherent in algorithmic management does not lie solely in the direct monitoring and steering of the labour process, but also in the opacity of the algorithms' logic – here referred to as *black box power*. Total managerial control of work is impossible and, as the analysis of zones of uncertainty shows, workers retain forms of agency despite extensive digital control. But this is limited by the opacity of the algorithms. To return to Weick's metaphor of the football game, algorithmic management not only makes the playing field even more inclined, but also hides the goals and boundaries of the game. As a result, workers have to apply their agency with uncertainty about its effectiveness. Attempts to make sense of algorithms inevitably remain precarious. Additionally, workers under algorithmic management are potentially, but not necessarily, under constant observation.

This has a direct impact on workers themselves. Their algorithmic self is one that is forced to act proactively with the constant danger of economic as well as algorithmic failure. Workers under algorithms are confronted with a market they must interpret and in which they must perform in order to maximise their profits. With algorithmic management, such neoliberal subjectivity of an entrepreneurial self (Bröckling 2015) extends to the separate steps of the labour process. Workers' individual decisions regarding an algorithm have an immediate impact on their futures – be it regarding their wages, the intensity of their work or other aspects – without them ever being completely sure of an actual causal connection between their actions and algorithmic decisions. This uncertainty, based on the opacity of digital technologies, has 'moved paranoia from the pathological to the logical' (Chun 2006, 1). The result is an algorithmic self which monitors its actions carefully and is obedient in an anticipatory manner, even where there is no direct algorithmic control.

References

Beer, D. 2017. The Social Power of Algorithms. *Information, Communication & Society*, 20(1), 1–13. https://doi.org/10.1080/1369118X.2016.1216147.

Bishop, S. 2019. Managing Visibility on YouTube Through Algorithmic Gossip. *New Media & Society*, 21(11–12), 2589–2606. https://doi.org/10.1177/1461444819854731.

Braverman, H. 1974. *Labor and Monopoly Capital: The Degradation of Work in the 20th Century*. Monthly Review Press.

Brinkmann, U. and Heiland, H. 2021. Rationalisierung statt Rationalität – Betriebliche Öffentlichkeiten zwischen Refeudalisierung und Revitalisierung. In M. Seeliger and S. Sevignani (Eds.), *Ein neuer Strukturwandel der Öffentlichkeit?* (pp. 115–136). Nomos.

Bröckling, U. 2015. *The Entrepreneurial Self: Fabricating a New Type of Subject*. Sage.

Burawoy, M. 1979. *Manufacturing Consent: Changes in the Labor Process Under Monopoly Capitalism*. University of Chicago Press.

Burrell, J. 2016. How the Machine 'Thinks': Understanding Opacity in Machine Learning Algorithms. *Big Data & Society*, 3(1), 1–12. https://doi.org/10.1177/2053951715622512.

Chan, N. K. 2019. The Rating Game: The Discipline of Uber's User-Generated Ratings. *Surveillance & Society*, 17(1/2), 183–90. https://doi.org/10.24908/ss.v17i1/2.12911.

Chun, W. H. K. 2006. *Control and Freedom: Power and Paranoia in the Age of Fiber Optics*. MIT Press.

Crozier, M. and Friedberg, F. 1993. *Die Zwänge Kollektiven Handelns: Über Macht Und Organisation*. Hain.

Elliott, C. S. and Long, G. 2016. Manufacturing Rate Busters: Computer Control and Social Relations in the Labour Process. *Work, Employment and Society*, 30(1), 135–51. https://doi.org/10.1177/0950017014564601.

Eubanks, V. 2018. *Automating Inequality: How High-Tech Tools Profile, Police, and Punish the Poor*. St. Martin's Press.

Foster, W. 1983. *Loose-coupling Revisited: A Critical View of Weick's Contribution to Educational Administration*. Victoria University Press.

Friedberg, E. 1995. *Ordnung und Macht: Dynamiken organisierten Handelns*. Campus.

Fuller, M. 2008. *Software Studies: A Lexicon*. MIT Press.

Gitelman, L. (Ed.), 2013. *Raw Data Is an Oxymoron*. MIT Press.

Heiland, H. 2019a. Reversed Solutionism: Technological and Organisational Control of Crowdwork. *PACO: Partecipazione & Conflitto*, 12(3), 640–64. https://doi.org/10.1285/i20356609v12i3p640.

Heiland, H. 2019b. Plattformarbeit Im Fokus: Ergebnisse Einer Explorativen Online-Umfrage. *WSI Mitteilungen*, 72(4), 298–304. https://doi.org/10.5771/0342-300X-2019-4-298.

Heiland, H. 2020. *Workers' Voice in Platform Labour: An Overview*. Hans-Böckler-Foundation.

Heiland, H. 2021a. Neither Timeless, nor Placeless: Control of Food Delivery Gig Work via Place-based Working Time Regimes. *Human Relations*. https://doi.org/10.1177/00187267211025283.

Heiland, H. 2021b. Controlling Space, Controlling Labour? Contested Space in Food Delivery Work. *New Technology, Work and Employment*, 36(1), 1–16. https://doi.org/10.1111/ntwe.12183.

Heiland, H. and Brinkmann, U. 2020. Liefern Am Limit: Wie Die Plattformökonomie Die Arbeitsbeziehungen Verändert. *Industrielle Beziehungen*, 27(2), 120–40. https://doi.org/10.3224/indbez.v27i2.02.

Heiland, H. and Schaupp, S. 2021. Breaking Digital Atomisation: Resistant Cultures of Solidarity in Platform-Based Courier Work. In P. Moore and J. Woodcock (Eds.), *Artificial Intelligence, Automation and Work: Making It, Faking It, Breaking It* (pp. 138–148). Bristol University Press.

Irani, L. 2015. Difference and Dependence Among Digital Workers: The Case of Amazon Mechanical Turk. *South Atlantic Quarterly*, 114(1), 225–34. https://doi.org/10.1215/00382876-2831665.

Jarrahi, M. H., Sutherland, W., Nelson, S. B., and Sawyer S. 2020. Platformic Management, Boundary Resources for Gig Work, and Worker Autonomy. *Computer Supported Cooperative Work*, 29(1–2), 153–89. https://doi.org/10.1007/s10606-019-09368-7.

Kellogg, K. C., Valentine, M. A., and Christin, A. 2020. Algorithms at Work: The New Contested Terrain of Control. *Academy of Management Annals*, 14(1), 366–410. https://doi.org/10.5465/annals.2018.0174.

Kitchin, R. 2014. Big Data, New Epistemologies and Paradigm Shifts. *Big Data & Society*, 1(1), 1–12. https://doi.org/10.1177/2053951714528481.

Kitchin, R. 2017. Thinking Critically About and Researching Algorithms. *Information, Communication & Society*, 20(1), 14–29. https://doi.org/10.1080/1369118X.2016.1154087.

Lash, S. 2007. Power After Hegemony. *Theory, Culture & Society*, 24(3), 55–78. https://doi.org/10.1177/0263276407075956.

Lessig, L. 1999. *Code and Other Laws of Cyberspace*. Basic Books.

MacKenzie, D. 2006. *An Engine, Not a Camera: How Financial Models Shape Markets*. MIT Press.

Manovich, L. 2001. *The Language of New Media*. MIT Press.

McGowan, C. and McCullaugh, J. 1995. *Entertainment in the Cyber Zone*. Random House.

Neff, G. 2012. *Venture Labor: Work and the Burden of Risk in Innovative Industries*. MIT Press.

O'Neil, C. 2017. *Weapons of Math Destruction: How Big Data Increases Inequality and Threatens Democracy*. Broadway Books.

Oudshoorn, N. and Pinch, T. 2003. Introduction. In N. Oudshoorn and T. Pinch (Eds.), *How Users Matter: The Co-Construction of Users and Technologies* (pp. 1–25). MIT Press.

Pasquale, F. 2015. *The Black Box Society: The Secret Algorithms That Control Money and Information*. Harvard University Press.

Rahman, H. A. 2020. Invisible Cages: How Opaque Control Tactics Influence Worker Behavior. *Academy of Management Annual Meeting Proceedings*, 1. Academy of Management. https://doi.org/10.5465/AMBPP.2020.20920 abstract.

Reid-Musson, E., MacEachen, E., and Bartel, E. 2020. 'Don't Take a Poo!': Worker Misbehaviour in On-demand Ride-hail Carpooling. *New Technology, Work and Employment*, 35(2), 145–61. https://doi.org/10.1111/ntwe.12159.

Sánchez-Monedro, J. and Dencik, L. 2019. The Datafication of the Workplace. Working Paper, 9 May. Data Justice Lab, Cardiff University. https://data justiceproject.net/wp-content/uploads/sites/30/2019/05/Report-The-data fication-of-the-workplace.pdf.

Schmiede, R. 2015. Abstrakte Arbeit Und Automation: Zum Verhältnis Von Industriesoziologie Und Gesellschaftstheorie. In R. Schmiede (Ed.), *Arbeit Im Informatisierten Kapitalismus: Aufsätze 1976–2015* (pp. 49–76). Nomos.

Schweyer, A. 2018. Predictive Analytics and Artificial Intelligence in People Management. Incentive Research Foundation, 27 August. https://theirf.org /research/predictive-analytics-and-artificial-intelligence-in-people-manage ment/2527.

Thompson, E. P. 1967. Time, Work-Discipline, and Industrial Capitalism. *Past and Present*, 38(1), 56–97. https://doi.org/10.1093/past/38.1.56.

Tsamados, A., Aggarwal, N., Cowls, J., Morley, J., Roberts, H., Taddeo, M., and Floridi, L. 2021. The Ethics of Algorithms: Key Problems and Solutions. *AI & Society*, 37, 215–230. https://doi.org/10.1007/s00146-021-01154-8.

Weick, K. 1976. Educational Organizations as Loosely Coupled Systems. *Administrative Science Quarterly*, 21(1), 1–19. https://doi.org/10.2307 /2391875.

CHAPTER 6

Algorithmic Management in Food Delivery Platforms: Between Digital Neo-Taylorism and Enhanced Subjectivity

Emiliana Armano, Daniela Leonardi
and Annalisa Murgia

Introduction

The emergence of platform capitalism has brought about new managerial models and practices (Srnicek 2016; Armano, Murgia and Teli 2017), as well as the control of work and data informed by digital connectivity, both of which are at the basis of so-called 'algorithmic management' (Beverungen, Beyes and Conrad 2019; Flyverbom 2019; Mumby and Plotnikof 2019). But what exactly do we mean when we speak of algorithmic management? Drawing on the case of digital food delivery platforms, this chapter proposes theoretical and interpretative hypotheses regarding the introduction of algorithmic management systems. This management model is explored in relation to both the typical model of industrial capitalism, based on direct and disciplinary control, and the managerial model typical of post-Fordism, centred instead on the subsumption of subjectivity and autonomy (Boltanski and Chiapello 1999).

How to cite this book chapter:
Armano, E., Leonardi, D., and Murgia, A. 2022. Algorithmic Management in Food Delivery Platforms: Between Digital Neo-Taylorism and Enhanced Subjectivity. In: Armano, E., Briziarelli, M., and Risi, E. (eds.), *Digital Platforms and Algorithmic Subjectivities*. Pp. 87–96. London: University of Westminster Press. DOI: https://doi.org/10.16997/book54.g. License: CC-BY-NC-ND 4.0

The first part of the chapter presents the interpretative hypothesis according-ing to which algorithmic management can, in some ways, be described as not completely new, since it includes both elements of the digital re-Taylorisation of work and the subsumption of autonomy. The second part, drawing on the results of co-research carried out with delivery riders working for food delivery platforms who took part in demonstrations in the city of Turin (Leonardi, Murgia and Armano 2020), investigates how algorithmic management is expressed and how it works in this specific context.

The conclusions highlight the redefinition of the concept of (theoretical and practical) autonomy and (direct and indirect) control on an algorithmic basis and therefore contributes to debates (see Moore, Briken and Engster 2020) which have cast light on the forms of management and self-precarization caused by digital technology.

From Direct Control of Scientific Work Organisation, Through Indirect and Introjected Control, to Algorithmic Management

As claimed by Mengay (2020), from the managerial point of view, digital transformation implies different strategies for managing forms of worker autonomy and control.

Autonomy can be described at various levels: from the broadest level concerning the aims and goals of the work carried out, to the merely organisational and operational level. It depends greatly on the type of work that people carry out, but also on management styles and strategies. A highly qualified job usually requires a high degree of decision-making autonomy – in terms of knowledge, relations, and capacity for action – while a job that requires few qualifications is more often characterised by a low degree of autonomy.

As far as control is concerned, three main forms are taken into consideration in this chapter: direct control, indirect control and algorithmic control.

Direct control is exercised by superiors and is based on the direct surveillance of performances, while machines are prevalently used to measure them. It is a typical method of the Taylorist phase of industrial capitalism, in which it is the person determining the speed of a production line who exercises control, even if mediated by measurement tools.

Indirect control is a form of domination that plays on workers' autonomy (Mengay 2020): management defines particular goals and conditions (technical supplies, goal agreements, strategic priorities, resources, etc.) and it is the responsibility of workers to define how to achieve the allotted goals by implementing a sort of 'responsible autonomy'. Indirect control requires allegiance to market imperatives, which are presented as inescapable, with workers pushed to identify with the employer's economic success and even to set their own goals, which were once defined by management themselves. Hence, management decisions evaporate behind forces considered to be objective and 'workers are thereby made responsible for the translation of their own labour power into labour output' (Ferschli 2017, 172). It is a control method typical of post-Fordism, which puts to work the subjects' very passions and desires (Armano and Murgia 2017; Bologna 2018).

The last form of control – algorithmic control – engages with both direct control and indirect and introjected control using new methods. Big Data, new sensors, integrated systems and machine learning can enable constant cycles of feedback and real-time control of labour processes. Direct control algorithms are used to inform management of decisions or automatically impose goals. But algorithmic management can be taken to a more pervasive level in the case of indirect control, when it is the worker who 'voluntarily' follows the imperatives of online reputation and 'likes'. As such, algorithmic management devices encourage alleged worker 'autonomy', but at the same time give rise to even more pervasive forms of precariousness (Wood et al. 2019; Woodcock and Graham 2019) and intervene directly in modelling identities through a similar mechanism to the interiorisation of market imperatives (Cardon 2015; Finn 2018; Zuboff 2019).

In this context, a critique of algorithmic management appears more topical than ever. An algorithm is a procedure that resolves a certain problem through a series of elementary steps. It is first of all a linguistic coding tool that enables the extension of the application of the notion of calculability. Therefore, if algorithms are linguistic coding tools, consisting of a (more or less complex) set of instructions (sequences) that the machine can carry out on the basis of a certain memory, all the worker has to do is interact (or not interact) with this digital machine. In turn, the algorithm produces tracking, in space and time, of bodies, movements and intentions, measuring with a precision that was unthinkable even a few years ago (Moore 2018).

On this basis, the theoretical hypothesis that we propose in this chapter assumes that the algorithm is activated through interaction with subjects and that, in order to be activated, it must be integrated relationally through an *active combination* with *living-human-capacity* (Alquati 1994; 2021). Specifically, the active combination connects living-human-capacity with the procedures coded in the algorithm and therefore permits the digital machine to reproduce itself. This process, to use Deleuzian terms, consists of *agencement* [assemblage] (Deleuze and Guattari 1980; Gherardi 2016) between the language and practices of the living being with the language of the digital machine. With regard to the reflections proposed by Alquati (1994; 2021), today the active combination tends to be even more pervasive and is stretching further and further, in a differentiated and diversified way, and structures different production and reproduction activities, from (increasingly digitalised) paid work to social media activities. Every time a person uses an app or platform, there is a form of active combination. In these terms, not only is active combination part of the value extraction process, but it depends on – and at the same time models – subjectivity itself. Therefore, lean digital platforms (Srnicek 2016) work through the transfer of risk from the company to the individual and the investment of his/her subjectivity, a transfer giving rise to a sort of 'precarious self-entrepreneurisation' that is also a mirror of neoliberal transformation.

Algorithmic Management in Food Delivery Platforms

The structure of food delivery platforms enables the work/activity/service supply to be regulated at any moment with corresponding consumption/fruition behaviour. What is significant is that the algorithmic control processes intervene in relation to the regulation and synchronisation of these two cycles which can be analytically distinguished and separated, even though they are functionally closely correlated.

This type of digital platform (Griesbach et al. 2019) enables the creation of a closed frame of reference inside which workers are asked to draw up their own strategies to maximise their earnings. Indeed, the food delivery platforms tend to build pre-coded environments of situations and possible action schemas, as well as routing predefined answers. Therefore, they are environments that model and restrict the possible choices of both workers and consumers, hence also conditioning their ways of thinking. To some degree, it could be said that the rules of the game are defined beforehand, unbeknownst to the players. And so, remuneration logics, order allocations and performance assessments are obscurely packaged within the algorithms that govern how platforms work. As such, workers often experience the algorithm as something that acts on their working and living conditions in an arbitrary and unfathomable manner – in not such a different way to the arbitrary authority that can be exercised by a flesh and blood manager.

What differentiates algorithmic management, according to our hypothesis, is the connection between digital algorithms and human action. The algorithm has its own internal coherence of logic and control, but the passage to operativity is not inevitable. Indeed, when an algorithm is applied to social processes, it must transform the 'numerical representations' (Manovich 2001) into a complex process of interaction with human language, social representations, subjectivities and behaviours. As a consequence, the decisive element of algorithmic management is not so much the automatised control of labour processes, but the directioning of social praxis, and above all – through *agencement* – the management of the margins of uncertainty that are implicit in them. In this context, information asymmetries are a central element of the platform's control over the work (Heiland and Brinkmann 2020; Rosenblat and Stark 2016; Rosenblat 2018; Ravenelle 2019), since the power results from the uncertainty zone that an actor can control through his/her behaviour towards a counterparty and vice versa. Therefore, in operational terms, algorithms are relevant not only due to their objective sequence, for example, the delivery allocation and order distribution program, but also due to the concealment of the data that they use, and the decision-making and manipulative processes that they implicitly carry out.

In the next section – using the results of co-research (Alquati 1993) conducted between 2016–2021 with a group of food delivery riders, who are very active in mobilising for better working conditions – we examine the processes giving shape to forms of algorithmic management and analyse both the various control methods put into practice through platforms and the answers found by workers to operate within these complex environments, as well as the attempts to challenge this management model.

Access to the Platform: Connection and Work Times

Riders access their work and begin their shift by logging into a smartphone app from their telephone. Once logged in, delivery orders are sent and assigned to them through interaction with an algorithm. Therefore, the workers must activate the app in order to be able to receive and carry out their work. After riders have provided their availability through the mobile phone app, they receive delivery requests. They are given a few seconds to accept a job, without being able to view the location details. If a rider accepts the request, the service is notified, and the rider must reach the physical site for the order to officially commence. Workers have allocated zones so the possibility of choosing or setting preferences regarding the routes they would like to receive on their app is therefore very limited. Further, companies encourage workers to use the 'auto-assignment' mode, that is, a mode in which they must accept all the orders that arrive, with no possibility of selecting them. In the words of one interviewee:

> You can substantially say to the app: accept all of the orders that arrive, or you can say: let me see all the orders that arrive and I'll tell you if I want to do them ... You get 30 seconds to choose, or maybe even less…10 seconds on the telephone. And you can say: 'yes, I want them, no, I don't want them'. If you turn off auto-assignment, you can be out and about in the city for 12–13 hours and you'll never get an order.

In this delivery acceptance and uptake mechanism, it appears clear that the algorithm has to be activated by a human act, and by a human worker capable of interacting with it in a positive manner in order to prompt a labour process. So, we have a subject who must remain available within a waiting time for the call to work, which is not his/her own time, but neither is it a time of (remunerated) performance according to business logic. It is an algorithmic management system that results in the emergence of a new conception of work time, which does not remunerate all the working hours but only time strictly defined for the delivery itself. However, such time necessarily requires additional invisible, non-obtrusive – and unpaid – worker availability, as well as listening, interpersonal and adaptive skills. These are among the most common skills in social life, but they take on vital importance in the productive context mediated by the algorithmic management of food delivery platforms. Indeed, through the connective action of *agencement*, capacities and time are connected to the language of the algorithm and made to produce value even though they are neither acknowledged nor paid. In this scenario, a new conception emerges both of the workplace and of urban space, which is reterritorialized by this experience of connectivity. Indeed, as we have seen, riders can enter and exit their workplace with just a swipe of their smartphone (Warin 2017).

Rating on the Platform: Measuring Performances and Acceptance Mechanisms

Central to algorithmic management is the order allocation and performance measurement system which is integrated with an evaluation system that assesses delivery riders' performances. After the delivery, both delivery service partners and customers make an evaluation through a system mediated by the platform. This is a complex mechanism that calls upon multiple actors. Indeed, riders are assessed by three figures: the customers receiving the delivery, the restaurants that use the platform (partners) and, finally, the company.

In this evaluation, customers consider if the rider is punctual, friendly, if the food is good and meets expectations, and if the service provided means they will want to use the platform again. In addition, the platform calculates the delivery acceptance rate, by dividing the number of accepted deliveries by the total number of requests sent to the rider. It is a mechanism that encourages availability in busier times of day, when there are more requests. Or it could be said that it is a punitive mechanism for those who do not work in the most order-intense moments. Hence, riders are compelled to maintain a high rate of delivery acceptances, which is also encouraged through occasional promotions such as 'rain bonuses' which encourages work in bad weather.

Within this framework, the evaluation system effectively results in workers accepting the highest number of deliveries possible. In general, as Ciccarelli (2019) writes:

> The ranking is a classification that serves to measure a rider's 'reputation' based on two criteria: reliability and participation. The first is measured based on a scale of 100/100, the second is expressed in a scale of 12/12. The 'evaluation' period covers two weeks when the rider carried out an activity. The algorithm sanctions riders with a loss of points in the system defined as 'reputational ranking'.

As a consequence, riders with a low average evaluation by customers and a low acceptance rate can be pushed down in the ranking and placed in the category of those who are only offered the most distant, most inconvenient and least remunerative deliveries. In practice, the mechanism is quite complex: as a rewarding logic, algorithmic management allows those with a higher score in the ranking system to view the shifts available for the next week earlier than those with the lowest scores, who can only view them at a later stage. The lower a rider's score, the less the probability of finding free shifts. As a result, s/he will be unlikely to work, which is also due to the fact that platforms deliberately 'hire' a lot more workers than are actually needed. To climb back up the ranking, riders must log on all the time, hope that a colleague will cancel at the last minute and give up their availability to cover that shift. As can be read on the Deliverance Project page:[1]

> The ranking is what chains a rider to his/her work, the long nose that reveals all the lies about fun and flexibility […] 'Work when you want' thus translates into 'work when we tell you or you won't work anymore'.

Further, interviewees mention the existence of differences between the various companies. According to one participant in the research:

> With Deliveroo we know some parameters and there's a certain punishment on the score. Instead on Just Eat the score is hidden, no one knows their score, nor the criteria it's based on.

This is why some riders opt to be hired by different platforms at the same time while trying to utilise the subtleties between the different working conditions, which are minimally in their favour. These are typical devices that push the individual to follow a sort of pre-set path, to take on risk and make their own choices on the basis of company indications imparted by the 'objective' rules of algorithmic management.

Conclusions: What's New in Algorithmic Management?

The innovation in organisational processes introduced with the phenomenon of connectivity mediated by lean platforms (Srnicek 2016) has enabled a freelance work model on a digital scale (also putting the crowd to work – see Sundararajan 2016) in which subjectivity, autonomy and risk-taking have become barycentric. The algorithms and algorithmic management are indeed changing the way in which people work in an ever-growing number of fields, with a notable jump in the period of the pandemic when the consequences of the shut-in economy were taken to the extreme (Smiley 2015), notably in the field of food delivery (Cozza et al. 2020).

The fieldwork highlighted the coexistence of two processes in the algorithmic management of food delivery platforms, which led us to develop the interpretative hypotheses presented in this chapter: a form of digital Taylorism, in itself quite evident, extended to the social sphere, and – at the same time – the request for a proactive attitude on the part of workers also typical of the culture of digital 'collaboration'. As a consequence, what effectively manages to impose control on the social actor is not just a simple piece of technology of neo-Taylorist discipline which controls, limits, tracks and directs. Indeed, what clearly emerged from the conversations with riders was firstly, the significance of the intensity of co-active interaction inherent within a digital connectivity environment, and secondly, the insistent request for availability and a proactive attitude. This shows how much the devices behind the working of the digital machine tend to perform subjectivity by propelling human capacity in a performance-based direction (Chicchi and Simone 2017). The new element that emerges with algorithmic management is therefore the formalisation of a managerial decision-making process that uses workers' perceived autonomy over the control of their labour process, which seems to be expanding as never before. By combining the terms of automation and hetero-direction (namely, the opposite of autonomy), Ekbia and Nardi (2017) coined the term *heteromation* specifically to describe the current relationship between human beings and machines, in which human operations become a mere performative appendix that depends on the algorithmic organisation of the machine. From this perspective, unlike the debate on automation revolving around the replacement and, tendentially, also the elimination of the human agent, the presupposition is therefore that human activity is still necessary. In our view, it would be a mistake to read into the labour processes that characterise platform capitalism only digital Taylorism, which Braverman, speaking about labour processes (1974), already identified as extending tendencies towards formatting, discipline and impoverishment on a digital scale. Labour processes in digital society, which in a word we could call a society of (hyper)industrialisation (Alquati 2021), are indeed less evident than those of the Fordist factory, but with further-reaching consequences than in the past. Previously, work organisations used to determine the rhythms, times and living conditions in a disciplinary manner. Now businesses intervene directly in manufacturing the neoliberal subject by putting motivations, workers' desires for autonomy and their ability to manage their own private time at stake (Zuboff 2019), thus forcing subjects into proactive behaviours and forging their very subjectivity.

Acknowledgement

The analysis was partially conducted within the 'SHARE – Seizing the Hybrid Areas of Work by Representing Self-Employment' research project (Grant Agreement no. 715950), funded by the European Research Council as part of the European Union Horizon 2020 research and innovation programme.

Note

1 Page created by the demonstrating riders: https://www.facebook.com /DeliveranceProject/about/?ref=page_internal.

References

Alquati, R. 1993. *Per Fare Conricerca*. Velleità Alternative.

Alquati, R. 1994. *Camminando per Realizzare un Sogno Comune*. Velleità Alternative.

Alquati, R. 2021 [2001]. *Sulla Riproduzione della Capacità Umana Vivente*. Derive Approdi.

Armano, A. and Murgia, A. 2017. Hybrid Areas of Work in Italy: Hypotheses to Interpret the Transformations of Precariousness and Subjectivity. In E. Armano, A. Bove, and A. Murgia (Eds.), *Mapping Precariousness, Labour Insecurity and Uncertain Livelihoods: Subjectivities and Resistance* (pp. 47–59). Routledge.

Armano, E., Murgia, A., and Teli, M. (Eds.), 2017. *Platform Capitalism e Confini del Lavoro negli Spazi Digitali*. Mimesis.

Beverungen, A., Beyes, T., and Conrad, L. 2019. The Organizational Powers of (Digital) Media. *Organization*, 26(5), 621–635.

Boltanski, L. and Chiapello, E. 1999. *Le Nouvel Esprit du Capitalisme*. Gallimard.

Bologna, S. 2018. *The Rise of the European Self-Employed Workforce*. Mimesis.

Braverman, H. 1974. *Labor and Monopoly Capital*. Monthly Review Press.

Cardon, D. 2015. *À Quoi Rêvent les Algorithmes: Nos Vies à l'Heure des Big Data*. Seuil.

Chicchi, F. and Simone, A. 2017. *La Società della Prestazione*. Ediesse.

Ciccarelli, R. 2019. Frank l'Algoritmo Antisciopero, *il manifesto*, 19 December 2019. Retrieved from: https://ilmanifesto.it/frank-lalgoritmo-anti-sciopero -la-cgil-porta-in-tribunale-deliveroo.

Cozza, M. et al. 2020. Covid-19 as a Breakdown in the Texture of Social Practices. *Gender, Work & Organization*, 28(S1), 190–208. https://doi .org/10.1111/gwao.12524.

Deleuze, G. and Guattari, F. 1980. *Mille Plateau*. Éditions de Minuit.

Ekbia, H. R. and Nardi, B. A. 2017. *Heteromation, and Other Stories of Computing and Capitalism*. MIT Press.

Ferschli, B. 2017. Capitalism without Bosses: The Nature of the Firm and Labour-Process Under Self-Management. *Momentum Quarterly*, 6(3), 167–186.

Finn, E. 2018. *Che Cosa Vogliono gli Algoritmi*. Einaudi.

Flyverbom, M. 2019. *The Digital Prism*. Cambridge University Press.

Gherardi, S. 2016. To Start Practice Theorizing Anew: The Contribution of the Concepts of Agencement and Formativeness. *Organization*, 23(5), 680–698.

Griesbach, K., Reich, A., Elliott-Negri, L., and Milkman, R. 2019. Algorithmic Control in Platform Food Delivery Work. *Socius*, 5. https://doi.org/10.1177 /2378023119870041.

Heiland, H. and Brinkmann, U. 2020. Liefern am Limit: Wie die Plattformökonomie die Arbeitsbeziehungen Verändert. *Industrielle Beziehungen*, 27(2), 120–140.

Leonardi, D., Murgia, A., and Armano, E. 2020. Piattaforme Digitali e Forme di Resistenza della Soggettività Precaria: Un'Inchiesta sul Lavoro Gratuito e la Mobilitazione dei Riders di Foodora. In E. Armano (Ed.), *Pratiche di Inchiesta e Conricerca Oggi* (pp. 29–47). Ombre Corte.

Manovich, L. 2001. *The Language of New Media*. MIT Press.

Mengay, A. 2020. Digitalization of Work and Heteronomy. *Capital & Class*, 44(2), 273–285.

Moore, P. V. 2018. *The Quantified Self in Precarity: Work, Technology and What Counts*. Routledge.

Moore, P. V., Briken, K., and Engster, F. 2020. Machines and Measure. *Capital & Class*, 44(2), 139–144. https://doi.org/10.1177/0309816820902016.

Mumby, D. and Plotnikof, M. 2019. Organizing Power and Resistance: From Coercion, to Consent, to Governmentality. In J. McDonald and R. Mitra (Eds.), *Movements in Organizational Communication Research: Current Issues and Future Directions*. Routledge.

Ravenelle, A. J. 2019. *Hustle and Gig: Struggling and Surviving in the Sharing Economy*. University of California Press.

Rosenblat, A. 2018. *Uberland: How Algorithms are Rewriting the Rules of Work*. University of California Press.

Rosenblat, A. and Stark, L. 2016. Algorithmic Labor and Information Asymmetries: A Case Study of Uber's Drivers. *International Journal of Communication*, 10, 3758- 3784.

Smiley, L. 2015. The Shut-In Economy, *Medium*, February 18. Retrieved from: https://medium.com/matter/the-shut-in-economy-ec3ec1294816.

Srnicek, N. 2016. *Platform Capitalism*. Polity Press.

Sundararajan, A. 2016. *The Sharing Economy: The End of Employment and the Rise of Crowd-Based Capitalism*. MIT Press.

Warin, R. 2017. *Dinner for One? A Report on Deliveroo Work in Brighton*. Autonomy Institute, 1 November. Available at: http://autonomy.work/wp -content/uploads/2018/08/Deliveroo-03.pdf.

Wood, A. J., Graham, M., Lehdonvirta, V., and Hjorth, I. A. 2019. Good Gig, Bad Gig: Autonomy and Algorithmic Control in the Global Gig Economy. *Work, Employment and Society*, 33(1), 56–75.

Woodcock, J. and Graham, M. 2019. *The Gig Economy*. Polity Press.

Zuboff, S. 2019. *The Age of Surveillance Capitalism: The Fight for a Human Future at the New Frontier of Power*. Public Affairs.

CHAPTER 7

Extracting Free Labour

Patrick Cingolani

Introduction

There is a de facto continuity between the uses and functions of information technologies and insecure employment. The latter became a key challenge in the second half of the twentieth century. It shed light on something of a crisis shaking up the Fordist model, starting with the central position of the factory, and also the loss of the spatial unity and separation that established it: the workforce was concentrated in a single place at a single time. Films and photographs going back as far as the end of the nineteenth century of workers leaving factories illustrate this unity of space and time through which the vast majority of employees gathered together at the same time. The segmentation and greater flexibility that companies imposed in the mid twentieth century have put this kind of unity into perspective. They have diversified working hours, particularly for part-time work, severed the legal unity of employees (for example, equality in respect of terms and conditions) on a single site, increased the number of employers (e.g. through the use of temporary employment agencies) and expanded the corporate relationship of subordination and domination beyond its physical boundaries (e.g. through sub-contracting or offshoring). Information technologies and digitization have brought about a radical change in this de-territorialization movement that would have been inconceivable until the

How to cite this book chapter:
Cingolani, P. 2022. Extracting Free Labour. In: Armano, E., Briziarelli, M., and Risi, E. (eds.), *Digital Platforms and Algorithmic Subjectivities*. Pp. 97–106. London: University of Westminster Press. DOI: https://doi.org/10.16997/book54.h. License: CC-BY-NC-ND 4.0

middle of the twentieth century, pushing it as far as the dematerialisation of the company and triggering a crisis of the conventional boundaries between work and free time, production and reproduction. By virtue of their ability to intrude, their ubiquity and invisibility, information technologies have created a revolution in the conditions of subordination and domination. Firstly, the trend to outsource, which characterised sub-contracting, has reached a level of globalisation and control that was hitherto unthinkable: performance and pro-ductivity within a company can be monitored remotely; the fragmentation of the labour process has reached the ultimate level of atomisation of the worker as a self-employed person, while taking monitoring procedures to the extreme (Berger 2005). Secondly, the crass and material means of getting around limits on working time (taking work home) or stepping up employees' time com-mitments at work (through part-time work) have been fine-tuned to under-mine boundaries between work and private life and to create opportunities for work in all places and at all times. The intrusive nature of digital technology has been used to wrest interstitial moments of work from people's daily private lives; extending the working day into the privacy of the home; making work instinctive, sometimes unbeknownst to the worker; and presenting work as a game. Within this global and comprehensive process, this chapter will focus more specifically on the debates and challenges regarding free labour, consid-ering in particular the tension between the two meanings of the term 'free', in accordance with the now canonical example which may be trivial but which speaks volumes, 'free as in beer vs. free as in speech' (Anderson 2009). The inherent ambiguity in the word 'free' does allow a better distinction between what is freely available and what is free of charge. In the movement to expand the sphere of work by undermining its boundaries, this chapter aims to com-prehend the major trends of capital development related to an ever-increasing digitisation of social relationships.

From Outsourcing to Undermining the Meanings of Work

There is therefore a continuity between digital capitalism and the outsourcing trend of the late twentieth century, as they both result in a form of capital-ism based on access (Rifkin 2001). For less than half a century, most compa-nies have given up on localised material implementation and organisation of production in a move towards remote management (Davis 2016). This means that companies have introduced a type of management which is less con-cerned with doing and more concerned with delegating: this attitude to work is essentially paradigmatic of digital capitalism. The Uber driver, the delivery rider and the Turker are all owners of their fixed assets: car, bicycle or com-puter, or indeed, they work from home. Platforms have technical (algorith-mic) and managerial control in addition to owning the digital media which organises the material conditions of production. While claiming to act as an intermediary between worker and customer, they dictate, to varying degrees, how work is monitored and manage the data generated by the labour process (Srnicek 2016). If we consider this intermediation from a labour standpoint, it firstly appears to be a clear component of a labour relation close to subordination and, incidentally, is often subject to legal classification (Uber, Deliveroo, etc.). Secondly, it is part of a triangular system, based on a two-sided or even multi-sided market rationale, leveraging one of the sides, often advertising, and offering free services to consumers (YouTube, Twitch, etc.). On one hand, the platform seems to form the foundation of a new kind of piecework (Casilli 2019). Whatever the task may be, whether skilled or unskilled, professional or otherwise, the platform's intermediation between a customer and a self-employed worker is geared towards a set piece of work for which the worker is paid (in contrast to payment by the hour, day or month). On the other hand, the platform takes advantage of its two-sided market attributes to play on the ambivalence between what is freely available and what is free of charge. The *freedom* conferred by the platform and the assistance it sometimes provides are often paid for by advertisers but also enacted through original ways of putting people to work – it is in this meaning that the *freedom to do something* appears in certain instances to be *working free of charge*, subject to appropriation and even extortion. Firstly, the exploitation logic is related to types of disciplinary checks enabled by the ability of new technologies to be intrusive. No matter how much platform capitalism constantly denies it, either through gamification or euphemism, it obligates labour. Secondly, under the guise of cooperation and a new denial of labour, including the use of amateurs or Pro-Ams, for whom the revolution was latterly heralded (Leadbeater and Miller 2004), the aim is to extract a form of non-subordinated activity or labour by any means possible. Let us analyse these two separate trends.

Most of the new piecework is related to what Nick Srnicek calls 'lean platforms' (Srnicek 2016). They operate according to the paradigmatic model discussed above. On these platforms, asset ownership is kept to a minimum while everything is outsourced: workers, fixed capital, maintenance costs, incidental expenses, training. Based on an algorithm, the platform manages and monitors the entire labour process, and this is a key criterion for the identification of various signs of subordination: monitoring (GPS), nudges, orders (obligation to accept certain rides), penalties (strikes) and deactivation (Huws et al. 2017) are aspects which concern almost all platforms of this type, from the largest (Uber, Deliveroo, Amazon Mechanical Turk, TaskRabbit) to the smallest (Foule Factory or Clic and Walk in France). Lastly, when they cannot introduce a webcam system, which monitors and tracks real-time employee behaviour, they delegate these blind spots of algorithmic management to customers and also to workers themselves. The ratings allocated to users and workers alike are, despite their apparently harmless nature, substitutes for managerial and hierarchical control. No matter how these platforms corrode the signs of labour and the relationship of subordination by hiding them under cheerful statements

('Uber's a popular new way to earn extra money by giving people ride with your own car'), or by avoiding the use of all words which evoke subordination, command and authority (starting with the use of the term *user* and avoiding the use of the verb *employ*); no matter how they promote seemingly fun competitions, such as the challenges launched by the algorithm to complete the most rides and receive a bonus; no matter how they dress up bicycle delivery as sport, a fun endeavour and a feeling of freedom in the city, they cannot really hide the signs of subordination if a worker were to take the company to court. Yet they do undermine and obscure the reality of subordination in everyday life and use. Delivery riders and drivers may 'play along' with the idea of sport and competition, as did the workers of Allied Company at the end of the 1970s (Burawoy 1979). The veil that is drawn over subordination is not only an artifice to avoid classification, but also a means of abusing the self-employed worker who has not always been familiar with heteronomical violence and who, moreover, is not always subject to an express form of financial pressure. The practice of gurus of the new economy intoning the term 'democratisation' when talking about information technologies is in this sense a prime example of how it misappropriates meanings for its own ends (Anderson 2006, 55–56). It is not democratisation but rather massification. While digital tools can play a role in democratising processes it is only under certain conditions. At other times these tools function within an asymmetrical labour relationship: we know that the platform remains in full control.

Whether they suffer and struggle, as Ken Loach's film *Sorry We Missed You* (2019) demonstrates in an exemplary manner, or whether they play, what should be understood as a metaphor within the relationship of subordination itself, is that the delivery rider, driver and Turker know that their time is constrained and subject to a commercial relationship, meaning that it will not be an end in itself. The use of disconnection appears to be a symptomatic brutality of the neoliberal undermining of the employment relationship, all the more impressive as it is trivialised in the technical act of sacking. The silence that workers face if they ever raise questions with the platform testifies to the asymmetry of the social relationship in a digital context (Huws et al. 2017). It undermines two centuries of worker movements that instituted labour protections and rights. While neocapitalism has sometimes been interpreted as a return to *formal subsumption* as it is thought to rely on the experience and expertise of a self-employed worker, the new conditions of exploitation are more complex, particularly regarding the new forms of piecework. They bring together the *formal* character of an apparent worker autonomy, related to outsourcing, and the *real* character of a process of subjection. In his formal subsumption analysis, Marx insists on an extension of the working day as a source of extracting additional time. Here, surplus labour is extracted not by extending the day but through the technical conditions of monitoring and by contracting time. The platform takes over the process used to complete the ride or the task and the algorithm is not so different to the bosses who previously punished workers for the slightest tardiness with fines and other unfair penalties. Further, as in the early days of industrial employers, contracts are often take-it-or-leave-it. Yet, we must also consider that platforms are much more subtle than the employers of the past who could only stretch out the working day and extract a surplus labour time over a twelve-hour timeframe. In a world in which the social time devoted to work has reduced significantly, platforms now know how to find avenues for micro-extortions through microtasks in the interstices of this socially available time: during the lunch hour, waiting for a train or bus, when making a purchase, and so on. This is the aim of Foule Factory and Clic and Walk in France. With the latter, companies task ClicWalkers to take photographs of their products and displays as they appear in shops, and to provide their opinion on their effectiveness, enabling companies to develop their marketing strategies. The aim of the former, as its founder claims, is to leverage 'people who like to say at midnight "I have an hour ahead of me, I'm going to do this from midnight to one"' (Barraud et al. 2018). This spinning out of tertiary working hours is one of the major disruptions of information technology. It is a genuinely new and original extraction method that is made possible by the intrusive capacities of digital tools, and also through their corrosive power over our capacity to assess work volume in everyday situations. While there has been talk of a return to the 'domestic system' (Acquier 2017) regarding platforms, and this invariably evokes work at the end of the eighteenth century or the early nineteenth century, and formal subsumption, we must consider the way in which information technologies subvert the relation of independence and the separation of the worker from the company with a view to submitting the worker to monitoring, while keeping up the illusion of a degree of freedom. The principle is in the simultaneous ability to bring together what is separate and segmented, or in other words to overcome any distance through monitoring, as we have seen.

From Subordination to Incubation

While subordination is perceptible in this first type of platform, and the feeling of exploitation is widespread, certain platforms can offer a *free* space for a free activity, which will itself be a source of profit. User-generated content becomes a source of value for the platform, not in terms of attention or audience, but of a productive or creative activity, or an invention. With his characteristic empirical clear-sightedness and business acumen, Chris Anderson noted that self-employed artists and small-scale creators of what could be called the productive universe of digital informality do not have the same interests as the major artists who defend their copyrights and intellectual property (Anderson 2006). Attention to their rights is less important than the possibility of being seen, appreciated and acknowledged, in a universe in which reputation guarantees work and payment. The theory supposes that a user is subject to multi-activity.

Before encountering the slightest success, people must be able to earn a living through another activity, another job, or from family assistance which frees up time. Someone who freely posts their work on a platform knows that this is not a means of earning a living, but they can at least build up a certain reputation, which may ultimately result in a source of income. Under such circumstances, insecurity in life or work often comes with the desire for acknowledgement and visibility, while the platform in turn financially benefits from the work of unpaid workers. The almost infinite storage options that digital technology provides causes greater insecurity for these precarious amateur contributors. Free from the cost and restrictions of stocks, the platform can let algorithms and users determine who is successful and who is not. For the latter group, the cost of their quest for reputation is insecure living conditions and unpaid labour, even at a loss. For the select few, there can be a certain degree of success, or even huge incomes. It may also be thought that this type of platform is a tremendous incubator of neoliberal norms, encouraging the internalising of an ethos of self-sacrifice and job insecurity and downplaying a competition approach which, ultimately, is a winner-takes-all model. Negotiations with advertisers for the staging of unpacking clothes or discussions between friends, the infiltration and colonisation of spontaneous behaviours by brands and their training of users, appears to be another aspect of this neoliberal school of thought.

Within this new amateur-focused model, there are also other relationships to free labour. From its emergence, the platform economy has been linked to the collaborative economy and from the outset some have viewed this less as a cooperation between peers and more as a deterioration of the previous social welfare system and the dawn of a freelance society. Many examples exist of cooperation between users, or user communities, and companies which demonstrate another side to this cooperation, but, within a capitalist system, cooperation is practiced under very specific conditions. The need for diversification and renewal may result in a crowd relationship with some companies that is very different from those of lean platforms and their neo-pieceworkers. Various activities can be an end in themselves, such as games and art. However, those who complete these skilled activities must often negotiate with the market and confront cash constraints. This is the condition under which the capitalist finds a means of trade. A fan economy emerges, not only in fashion but also in sectors where we would least expect it. The appeal and influence of certain items of the latest trend, and the pleasure of projecting an image of oneself, foster various porosities between the company and those who use its products. Brand ambassadors enjoy more favourable purchasing conditions: YouTubers are supported by the brands they promote, and the prestige of certain channels encourages volunteer work.

The example of the Danish company LEGO® is particularly interesting in this respect, in that it is related more to the universe of fun and play than that of fashion and appearance. The relationship with the famous bricks, which are used to build characters, objects and even jewellery, is not limited to children;

adults also use them, and for them play results in a blurring of the boundaries between the roles of consumer, user and producer. The Group, which is one of the most powerful companies in the world, leverages these adult users in a cooperative process in which the tension between freely available and free of charge is particularly apparent. Firstly, this is a niche market as the use of plastic bricks may be diversified according to the type of user community, and LEGO® encourages them to create their own designs. The opportunity to have free access to some of the company's tools becomes a chance for user creativity and consequently a form of crowdsourcing. Consumer-users upload their creations onto a web page, and their designs are rated by other users and may be selected by the company if they prove popular with others. Not only does the system allow LEGO® to source innovative ideas from users, but it also increases the probability of new products being successful (Antorini and Muñiz 2013). For enthusiasts, the Brickmaster Club provides a subscription to the LEGO® club magazine, which outlines projects for members to build themselves. In some cases, the company must acknowledge intellectual property rights and certain personalised kits or models clearly state the names of inventors and their rights.

The company, therefore, finds skills and expertise amongst fans and also enables cooperative social situations, which stimulates the innovative power of users, and from which it can leverage creations and recreational aspirations. More than simply free labour, which brands can extract through voluntary behaviours of their consumers and fans, this approach involves extracting the results of an experience or of a talent, which results in increments of innovation that are particularly marketable. Unlike volunteers, who give their free time and sometimes their professional skills, virtuoso amateurs lend their expertise, their insights and their innovative skills. It is both the cooperation between users, which the company encourages, and the power of invention that some of them possess, and who, while needing LEGO® to achieve their aspirations of play and pleasure, enable the company to develop their products.

The entire system is remarkable. Firstly, the management category is dilated. The company no longer enlists employees and professionals, it uses amateurs. Such management clearly has many specific features. It must manage the complex nature of profitable cooperation initiatives, but with individuals and groups who provide labour for free, and who do not offer their services for the sole intention of earning money. Crowdsourcing is not based on piece-workers' constraints, far from it. It also stems from the expertise, virtuosity and communications of users as a huge well of experience, signs and symbols. While, according to Gabriel Tarde, an invention is the intersection of different imitations which are built up in the brain, amateur clubs, groups and social situations are spaces of communication interactions in which the intelligence and expertise of players are mutually built up and incubated by LEGO® (Tarde 1902). Incidentally, the term incubation is symptomatic of digital technology, its effects, and the specific conditions under which it extracts labour. The incubation process does not involve fertilising eggs but rather oversees brood-ing them. For this form of capitalism that delegates more than it makes, incu-bating is a specific means of enlisting a workforce.

The case of *The Huffington Post* is one example of many. As long as consider-ation has not been given to the act of lending to a platform free of charge with a view to appropriating the results of a free activity, no progress will be made. One characteristic of digital technology is its almost unlimited nature, or, in other words, *that space costs practically nothing*. While storage costs are mini-mal, everyone can connect to a site and post their activity, but also all activities may be subject to free market forces: the fact that using the platform appears free does not mean that it does not register earnings. A platform's success lies in its ability to attract increasing numbers of people and to then conduct post-screening. Everyone collaborates on the platform but not everyone is remunerated as a collaborator. The market rationale, and in particular that of the advertising market, encourages those who are successful and who raise the platform's profile and value. The more general idea is to acknowledge this col-lective collaboration, not to leave it solely under the platform's arbitrary judge-ment, but to provide more fairness and transparency for all platform workers.

Conclusion: Access-based Capitalism and Its Opponents

Whereas labour no longer occupies the space and time it occupied in the Ford-ist society, but rather concerns key moments in individuals' lives, platforms tend to restructure productive systems and social landscapes. While working methods are changing, so are the conditions underpinning disputes and their means of subjectivation. Isolation, fragmentation and their consequences for the constitution of neoliberal individualism are challenged by forms of sociali-sation based on listening and reciprocity. Associations merge bringing together several types of culture or communication professional and allowing the expe-rience of the freelancer to be shared, and thus to react collectively to economic dependence. Regarding riders, collective action is more widespread in cit-ies, where the riders are occupying urban centres, which are often places of professional gatherings and exchanges (Leonardi et al. 2019). Strike action has taken on a spontaneous and radical nature that labour disputes have not seen in a long time (Cant 2020). Through self-organised cooperatives, bikers have taken hold of the platform device in order to make alternative use of it. Fol-lowing Coopcycle Federation, founded in 2017, some local platforms are now pooling their delivery software programmes, mobile applications and sales ser-vices – thus shifting intermediation systems from an asymmetrical instrument to a reciprocal one. The old idea of an appropriation of the means of production seems to rise up from the past. It suggests public control of private structures, which are increasingly the intermediaries of our daily lives. During the pan-demic, some biker associations used platforms for social purposes, delivering food packages to the elderly or isolated. The 'lean' nature of work platforms (Srnicek 2016) encourages workers to subvert these structures, within which workers are, moreover, already taking in hand the means of their own work (Cingolani 2021). To turn the device around and move it from a capitalist to a cooperative framework, it is simply necessary to bring together the producer and the consumer.

Against a backdrop of global imbalances, segmentation and opacity due to offshore arrangements, the increasingly informed nature of consumers has had an impact on some companies' offending and illegal practices. Even though it is still insufficient, we have seen them apply their full weight against firms who partake in child labour or who expose their employees in developing countries to health risks (Cingolani 2018). Outsourcing, and the lack of transparency that it provides for capitalism, fosters divorce between consumers and workers and maintains competition among them by making low cost remuneration the condition of a cheap service. It is time for the consumer to stop consenting to market logics and to recognise the need to reject immediate satisfaction in order to have a voice within companies, alongside workers. The stakes seem higher as companies connect citizens via major information and communication platforms. Google, Facebook and their subsidiaries have exploited, for their own benefit, structures that could have been designed as commons or public property.

We are now at a turning point in which deregulation is related to a conventional situation whereby new labour relations, shaken up by the neoliberal disruption of platforms, have not yet acquired sufficient weight to protest against and to neutralise the effects of social imbalances. If there are further attempts to take advantage of this digital precariat, and to abuse the cooperative creativity of amateurs, semi-professionals or professionals by making them work for little or for 'free', people and crowds have the means to demand recognition of their common activity (Wark 2013). Unlike the crowds that conservative theorists fantasised about at the start of the twentieth century, the network-based crowds of the twenty-first century are increasingly competent and knowledgeable. As the offsetting of labour suggests, criticism and protests may no longer stem from institutional structures coming from the company alone, or even conventional institutions of labour negotiations and disputes, but rather from specific or hybrid forms of organisation and mobilisation of these pluri-active multitudes who are increasingly visible at the turn of the twenty-first century.

References

Acquier, A. 2017. Retour Vers le Futur? Le Capitalisme de Plate–Forme ou le Retour du « Domestic System ». *Libellio d'Aegis*, 13(1), 87–100.

Anderson, C. 2006. *The Long Tail: Why the Future of Business Is Selling Less of More*. Hyperion.

Anderson, C. 2009. *Free: The Future of a Radical Price*. Hyperion.

Antorini, Y. M. and Muñiz A. M. 2013. The Benefits and Challenges of Collaborating with User Communities. *Research-Technology Management*, 56(3), 21–28.

Barraud, P. and Sigalo Santos, L. 2018. Et Pour Quelques Euros de Plus: Le Crowdsourcing de Micro-Tâches, et la Marchandisation du Temps. *Réseaux*, 212(6), 51–84.

Berger, S. 2005. *How We Compete: What Companies Around the World Are Doing to Make It in Today's Global Economy*. Currency Doubleday.

Burawoy, M. 1979. *Manufacturing Consent: Changes in the Labor Process under Monopoly Capitalism*. University of Chicago Press.

Cant, C. 2020. *Riding for Deliveroo – Resistance in the New Economy*. Polity Press.

Casilli, A. 2019. *En Attendant les Robots: Enquête sur le Travail du Clic*. Seuil.

Cingolani, P. 2018. Le « Salariés Autonome » et la Solidarité des Employeurs dans l'Obligation Juridiques. *Droit Social*, 3, 246–249.

Cingolani, P. 2021. *La Colonisation du Quotidien: Dans les Laboratoires du Capitalisme de Plateforme*. Amsterdam Editions.

Davis, S. 2016. *The Vanishing American Corporation: Navigating the Hazards of a New Economy*. Barrett-Kohler Publishers.

Huws, U., Spencer, N., Syrdal, D., and Holtz, K. 2017. *Work in the European Gig Economy*. Foundation for European Progressive Studies.

Leadbeater, C. and Miller, P. 2004. *The Pro-Am Revolution – How Enthusiasts are Changing our Economy and Society*. Demos.

Leonardi, D., Murgia, A., Briziarelli, M., and Armano, E. 2019. The Ambivalence of Logistical Connectivity: A Co-Research with Foodora Riders. *Work Organisation, Labour & Globalisation*, 13(1), 155–171.

Rifkin, J. 2001. *The Age of Access: The New Culture of Hypercapitalism*. Tarcher-Perigee.

Srnicek, N. 2016. *Platform Capitalism*. Polity Press.

Tarde, G. 1902. *L'Invention Considérée comme le Moteur de l'Evolution Sociale*. V. Giard et E. Brière.

Wark, M. 2013. Considerations on a Hacker Manifesto. In T. Scholz (Ed.), *Digital Labor: The Internet as Playground and Factory* (pp. 91–97). Routledge.

CHAPTER 8

On Value and Labour in the Age of Platforms

Andrea Miconi

On Platform Economy

This chapter analyses the most widely credited hypotheses on platform economy – those of Tarleton Gillespie, Nick Srnicek, José van Dijck, Thomas Poell and Martijn de Waal and Shoshona Zuboff – and its ability to shape work forces and social subjectivities. Even though the *platformization* discourse is widespread, we focus on the main attempts to define a general theory.

Gillespie focuses on the rise of platforms as intermediaries and on the responsibility of the companies in control of them. Hence, the 'platform' is a new agency taking on the functions of previous gatekeepers – aggregators or search engines – with the same goal of providing users with a 'safe harbour' in the open sea of the web. Gillespie (2010, 349) rightly notes that the term 'platform' did not appear out of nowhere and that it was knowingly chosen to put an emphasis on the alleged neutrality of the new mediators. The neutral façade of platforms depicted by influential stakeholders – or by those Dean (2010) would call 'displaced mediators' (26–29) – was purposely designed to make the internal tensions intrinsic to platforms' service opaque – that is the tensions between amateur and professional content, between moderation and neutrality

How to cite this book chapter:
Miconi, A. 2022. On Value and Labour in the Age of Platforms. In: Armano, E., Briziarelli, M., and Risi, E. (eds.), *Digital Platforms and Algorithmic Subjectivities*. Pp. 107–119. London: University of Westminster Press. DOI: https://doi.org /10.16997/book54.i. License: CC-BY-NC-ND 4.0

and between self-branding and community. Gillespie (2017) describes platforms as the following:

> I mean sites and services that host public expression, store it on and
> serve it up from the cloud, organize access to it through search and
> recommendation [...] This includes Facebook, YouTube, Twitter, Tum-
> blr, Pinterest, Google+, Instagram, and Snapchat [...] but also Google
> Search and Bing, Apple App Store and Google Play, Medium and Blog-
> ger, Foursquare and Nextdoor, Tinder and Grindr, Etsy and Kickstarter,
> Whisper and Yik Yak. (255)

Gillespie (2018) equates platforms to social media, and here lies the difference with other interpretations, as he distinguishes between two categories.
On the one hand, we have social media, which connects people to each other
and offers customised recommendations with the goal of keeping users on
the platform and collecting their data. On the other hand, we have 'marketplace services', which 'present themselves as social media platforms' while
being based on different business models (Gillespie 2018, 41–43). The core
mission of platforms is to provide a mediation by means of content moderation; therefore, other services that 'do not nearly fit the definition of platform'
and still perform 'some tasks of content moderation' should be properly clus-
tered in 'a second set' that contains TripAdvisor, Airbnb and Uber (Gillespie
2018, 18).

Gillespie's (2018) final elaboration further narrows the definition by shed-
ding light on content moderation, which takes place in three different environments: editorial review, community flagging by users and algorithmic
automatic detection. As the first category shows, Gillespie (2018, 114–117,
120–124) is well aware that computer-mediated communication (CMC),
for instance the removal of illegal posts or pornographic images, requires
human work, and this crowdsourcing is used by companies to hire low-
waged collaborators. Nonetheless, he is less interested in the division of
labour than in the overall function played by the platforms. The ultimate
definition of platforms provided by Gillespie (2018, 18–21) tends to include
services that:

a) host, organise, and circulate users' shared content or social interactions for
them,
b) require others – rather than platforms themselves – to produce or commission content,
c) are built on an infrastructure, beneath that circulation of information, for
processing data for customer service, advertising, and profit,
d) platforms do, and must, moderate the content and activity of users, using
some logistics of detection, review and enforcement.

There are two aspects of Gillespie's (2018) contribution that need to be considered, specifically that the definition of platform is restricted to social platforms, which mainly work through user-generated content (UGC) moderation, and that more attention is paid to their social function than to the human effort underpinning them. Gillespie argues that, 'moderation is, in many ways, the commodity that platforms offer' (13). This may be true, but it would still require a deeper understanding of the human labour involved. The blindspot of his analysis is therefore the *value* issue, which is understandable given the priorities of the author, but a further investigation remains necessary.

In contrast, Srnicek's (2016) analysis presents itself as an inquiry into the economic side of platform society, starting with the very title of his book. He can be credited with tracing the first application of 'platform' discourse back to business language. Like Gillespie (2010), Srnicek detects the bias of the word itself, which was intentionally chosen by influential players and used to prepare the ground for a new market. This may be a positive and necessary illusion for a debate that often mistakes many-to-many communication for grassroots participation and two-sided platforms for bottom-up phenomena.

In Srnicek's (2016) work, the platform is the operational answer to global capitalism's crisis, just as Castells (1996) connected the origin of network society to the restructuring of industrial economies after the 1973 downturn. Twenty-first century capitalism eventually adopted a new solution due to the discovery of 'a particular kind of raw material: data' (Srnicek 2016, 39). Platforms arise from the internal company's need to collect and analyse data (Zuboff 2019). Therefore, platformization takes place in all fields of economics, leading to five different versions of platforms: *advertising* platforms, such as Google and Facebook; *cloud* platforms, which own the hardware or software for business; *industrial* platforms, which build hardware and software; *product* platforms, such as Spotify, whose business model is based on fees or rent; and *lean* platforms, such as Uber, which reduce their asset to the minimum and offer their space to buyers and sellers (2017, 28–45). One may become aware of an extensive generalisation of the platformization idea, which is typical of the hype of a concept. As for Srnicek's (2016) definition of platforms, unlike Gillespie's (2017), it is based on economic value:

> at the most general level, platforms are digital infrastructures that enable two or more groups to interact. They therefore position themselves as intermediaries that bring together different users: customers, advertisers, service providers, producers, suppliers, and even physical objects. (25)

Srnicek (2016) frames the origins of platform economy within the history of capitalism by considering its *disruptive*, constant look for new markets to exploit. Nonetheless, any similarities of Srnicek's view to a Marxist-based analysis are superficial as he willingly underestimates the role of labour in the digital economy by arguing that 'revenue is generated through the extraction of data from users' activities online' rather than through the appropriation of unwaged labour (31). His work is part of a broader tendency to consider data as the main – if not the sole – source of value for digital capitalism.

The underestimation of labour also leads Srnicek (2016) to interpret digital disruption as the result of purely intra-capitalist competition. Therefore, the adoption of the platform model makes the difference in competition between companies, where it can explain the survival of some and the fall of others. In this respect, his analysis of the labour market results in a singular consideration:

> not all – and not even most – of our social interactions are co-opted into a system of profit generation. In fact one of the reasons why companies must compete to build platforms is that most of our social interactions do not enter into a valorisation process. If all of our actions were already captured within capitalist valorisation, it is hard to see why there would be a need to build the extractive apparatus of platforms. (Srnicek 2016, 30)

This is hardly conclusive as according to Marx (1867, 359–360), subsumption is a never-ending process and the transition from absolute to relative surplus value is never complete and constantly takes place in different job markets. Capitalism is driven by the production of value, however, which is the appropriation of people's time by companies. Indeed, Marxist thought has been split into two different interpretations of the origin of conflict. In traditional versions, history is propelled by capital and workers subsequently fight back by forming their unions, whereas according to Italian *operaismo* theory (Tronto 2019), history is rather propelled by social evolution – from *mass* to social *class* to *multitude* – and capital organises itself following these transformations with the purpose of regulating it (Negri and Hardt 2004).

In any case, the history of capital *is linked to that of labour*, which is not the case for Srnicek (2016). Although other interpretations of capitalism are possible, such interpretations should be acknowledged – something Srnicek did not do when quoting *Capital* and when considering competition as the main force behind modern capitalism. To some extent, Srnicek shares Gillespie's (2017) unclear position on the agency/structure issue, with the emphasis on economic enterprise blinding them both when it comes to the appearance of neoliberal subjectivity.

Van Dijck et al. (2018) are positioned in the middle as they look at the technological, social and economic aspects of the process. At first glance, their book reflects the historical moment when the web was carried along by centralisation tendencies (Helmond 2015) with the most popular sites becoming platforms and invading the network's ecosystem. Here is the 'ecological' idea of platforms as the sum total of human activities, but where no reference is made to McLuhan's theory, which seems to fit the case.

In all likelihood, the idea derives from the merging of social media studies, namely van Dijck and Poell's (2013) tetrad, with the contiguous field of 'infrastructural studies' (Plantin, Lagoze and Edwards 2016). Platforms are not simply used by people or companies, they are closed systems in which economic and political processes increasingly take place. An affinity emerges here with Castells' (1993, 136) idea of a 'space of flows' as the topological pattern of the global economy. The main difference is that Castells took into account the relationship between network society and other frameworks, such as post-industrialism and post-Fordism, while the macro-text of platform society, with the partial exception of Srnicek and Zuboff, reveals a lack of contextualisation in the analysis of the contemporary world.

Here, a problem emerges, which has to do with social subjectivity and the unclear hierarchy between different players and with the tension between structure and agency. Platform economy is overdetermined by the power of platforms' owners, while its future will be shaped by the decisions we will take (Kenney and Zysman 2016), which is not useful until one clearly sketches the lines of social conflict. The open conclusion of van Dijck et al. (2018, 144–154) leaves us with a similar assumption: the future is still to be written and platforms are a space for citizens to step in and contribute to the shaping of a sustainable innovation. Here, van Dijck et al. (2018, 55–56) do not adopt a position regarding the structure/agency issue. They observe that platformization brought about both enabling and disabling effects and favoured both people's empowerment and disempowerment. This is a sort of paradox. On one hand, the concept of platforms is *reified* by the idea of the free space of the web being colonised by monopolists. On the other, emphasis is put on *agency*, as if users are vested with the power of reprogramming the networks.

This is the same trajectory as that of Castells' (1996) theory, which was originally based on the 'pre-eminence of social morphology over social action' (469), and even on the 'schizophrenia between structure and meaning' (3), while his later work (2009; 2012) suddenly prioritises agency over structure in the name of the so-called insurgent politics. The more the web becomes a closed system, the more Internet Studies take the side of *agency*, a choice that has the effect, if not the intention, of taking attention away from the consolidation of monopolies and from the narrowing of space for social action (Dean 2016, 73). In a similar vein, Zuboff's call for a collective mobilisation can hardly be understood (influenced by behaviourist psychologist B. F. Skinner) in the light of her interpretation of digital manipulation.

Regarding the definition of platforms, according to van Dijck et al. (2018), they are made of four elements and vitalised by three kinds of processes. The four elements have to do with platforms being fed by data, organised by algorithms, framed by 'ownership relations driven by business models' and ruled 'through user agreements' (van Dijck 2018, 9–12). The three processes can be defined as datafication, commodification and selection. Platforms store personal data, translate them into economic value and use them to customise information. This led to van Dijck et al. making a distinction between 'infra-structural platforms' – the Big Five: Google/Alphabet, Meta, Apple, Amazon and Microsoft – and 'sectoral platforms', such as Airbnb and Uber. The latter provide specific services and are unable to survive without the foundations provided by the former.

While van Dijck et al. (2018) offer a detailed investigation of some sectoral platforms and a thorough analysis of a variety of data mining practices (Plantin 2019), here we deal with a broader theoretical assumption. By commodification, van Dijck et al. mean the conversion of 'online *and* offline objects, activities, emotions and ideas into tradable commodities' (37), a definition that is very close to the Marxist one. This notwithstanding, their technical definition of platforms describes them as 'multi-sided markets' that can include audiences, advertisers, providers and all other players (van Dijck 2018, 59). As an evolution of network economy theories, the multi-sided market model deals with *individuals* rather than social classes, which is a symptom of a bigger problem. The concept of commodification, which is not the same as *commoditisation*, implies a specific notion of *value*. This is not compatible with the multi-sided model, which replaces value extraction with marginal costs. It also implies the underestimation of exchange-value dynamics, which are discussed in the next section.

Critical Theory and Platform Society

When reflecting on platform economy, three main problems can be detected. Gillespie (2018) has a tendency to ignore labour issues, Srnicek (2016) prioritises data extraction over other forms of value production and van Dijck et al. (2018) fail to address the incongruence between the notion of a multi-sided market and that of commodification. We discuss these three issues in this order.

To some extent, Gillespie's (2018) definition is the least controversial from the perspective of critical theory as it mostly focuses on non-economic aspects. Nonetheless, Gillespie has the ability to reflect on the 'hidden labor behind content moderation' (9), along with the conditions of crowdsourcing, the precariousness of the labour conditions in IT factories (83, 122–123) and the pyramid of CMC contributors, from waged to unwaged (116). His work, as well as research by Roberts (2016), lifts the curtain on various invisible activities and reminds us that far from replacing human labour, digital platforms still require it. Casilli (2019, 208–212) describes the tendency of digital capital to hide the contribution of human work, which takes post-Fordist externalisation strategies to their limits, and conceal it beneath the image of artificial intelligence and robotisation – so-called 'fauxtamation' (Taylor 2018).

Conversely, the main thing missing in Gillespie's (2018) analysis is the connection between *labour* and *value*, which would require a shift from an integrated view of the functions carried out by the platforms to the idea of conflict taking place *within* the platforms. Kenney, Rouvinen and Zysman (2020) provide a rejoinder to this claim by proposing a taxonomy of platforms' economic capabilities and forms of value production. In the case of 'platform-mediated content creation', which is the closest to Gillespie's, there are three possible forms of value: data extraction, building of websites and content creation in the strictest sense. In 'platform-mediated work', we can find direct forms of work for the platforms, as well as the wide range of gig professions. The 'platform firm' sector is organised around a classical hierarchy of high-income creative professionals and low-waged freelance contributors. In all cases, platformization of work becomes one with its *taskification*, a tendency that Amazon Mechanical Turk is stressing to its limits.

In both Kenney, Rouvinen and Zysman (2020) and Gillespie (2018), no reference is made to the labour–value dyad, which might seem to be a neutral assumption that also engenders well-defined consequences. The idea of platforms as multi-sided markets, where offer and demand meet, is one of those slippery ideas that are freighted with more than what they literally mean. A corollary of the multi-sided theory is that the market is the confluence between companies and workers, where decisive processes happen and balances and counterbalances are in equilibrium but where things would radically change with the introduction of value as a main variable.

Srnicek (2016) is in good company as his idea of Big Data marking a turning point is diffused and comes in different versions. According to Mayer-Schönberger and Cukier (2013), digital capital is replacing value production with the intrinsic value of raw information, so that 'value will be in data itself' (134). They argue that the economy is no longer regulated by money due to the transition from 'money-rich markets' to 'data-rich' markets.

> With the market economy advancing with the help of data, we may no longer label the future 'capitalist' in the sense of power concentrated by the holders of money. Ironically perhaps, as data-driven markets devalue the role for money, they prove Karl Marx wrong, not Adam Smith. (Mayer-Schönberger and Ramge 2018, 143)

Mayer-Schönberger and Ramge (2018) perfectly define the problem we have already detected. According to Marx (1867), capitalism has little to do with the 'power concentrated by the holders of money', its main goal is the extraction of value to be subsequently converted into money. It is a common mistake to declassify the concept of value in terms of a monetary unit that materialises as its final objectivation. Data collecting is the ultimate form of value appropriation, and its transformation into actual revenue is the last manifestation of a classical mechanism. By directly trading people's *time*, the web economy has not overturned capitalism, instead it is revealing its genuine nature. According to Marx, 'Capitalist production is not merely the production of commodities', 'it is essentially the production of surplus-value' (1867, 359).

Couldry and Mejias (2019) developed a similar idea in terms of 'data coloni-alism'. They consider data exploitation within the frame of capitalist exploita-tion, while also accentuating the innovative tracts of algorithmic dispossession, and define our present as a colonial era due to the discovery of a new raw mate-rial. Much like geographical explorations opened the way for modern capital-ism by providing the Western world with resources and staple goods, the accu-mulation of data has enabled digital capitalism to appropriate human life itself. The first problem with this description is in the comparison of historical and digital colonialism as this no longer functions when one considers that data, *unlike* the natural resources of the sixteenth and seventeenth centuries, are not raw material to be collected. Data are created by means of both direct and indi-rect human labour; usually by machines *built by human work* and *incorporating that work*, according to a typical Marxist concept. This is also the problem with Srnicek's (2016) idea that value is based on data rather than on labour. A similar misunderstanding can be found in van Dijck et al.'s (2018) idea of datafica-tion as a typical feature of platforms if one keeps in mind that data are a main resource for some of these platforms, such as Facebook, an indirect source of value for others, for example Amazon, and not even part of the core business of others, such as Apple or Microsoft, which are industrial companies in the traditional sense. According to Marx (1864), different forms of value produc-tion *are integrated with each other*, given that a commodity incorporates the quantum of labour needed for its production. Therefore, data *do not replace* human labour as they are the last link in a longer value chain.

The main objection by Srnicek (2016), among others, is that unwaged labour performed by web users is not intended as a form of labour as it takes place outside of the context of a 'production process oriented towards exchange' (30). Srnicek aptly notes that digital capitalism is based on many other value sources, but I think he misses the point when replacing labour with data. User-generated content can be framed in terms of labour/value as they arise from a specific production relationship – the separation between human activities, such as posting a video or liking a picture, and the control of the technical means nec-essary for these activities. Therefore, the client/server hierarchy is the ultimate version of the fundamental process Marx (1867) referred to as 'primitive accu-mulation' (508), the split between labour as human effort and the material con-ditions necessary for its realisation.

Van Dijck et al. (2018), for their part, do not pay proper attention to labour issues, not even when they are directly engendered by platformization, as in the gig economy. Their definition of platforms brings together different forms of labour with no distinction between well-paid and low-paid and waged and unwaged tasks. Furthermore, a contradiction takes place due to the concept of commodification clashing with the multi-sided model. As discussed previ-ously, van Dijck et al. interpret commodification in a Marxist way, which deals with the extraction of vital resources on the part of capital. On the contrary, the multi-sided economic model is all about coordination between parts, and platforms serve the interests of all players. In other words, 'provide participants with the ability to search over participants on the other side and the opportunity to consummate matches' (Evans et al. 2011, 5). Here, platforms' owners mostly act as regulators, and in so doing, they make the meeting of different social groups and complementors possible (Boudreau and Hagiu 2009, 164–166). In multi-sided markets, marginal costs make the difference, but is this still the case under the rules of commodification theory?

In actuality, Marx is clear about value being extracted *before* the market stage, when labour time is appropriated by capital. This is precisely what the notion of *value* refers to, so that:

> the result is not altered by introducing money, as a medium of circulation, between the commodities, and making the sale and the purchase two distinct acts. The value of a commodity is expressed in its price before it goes into circulation, and is therefore a precedent condition of circulation, not its result. (Marx 1867, 112)

The value of a commodity is a measure of the amount of socially needed work, the objectification of human time requested by its production. What owners control is the exchange-value made by 'incorporated social labour' through a series of transitions, and the same happens in *digital* transitions (Fuchs 2012). All these state transitions change the *form* of value, while not engendering any 'change in the magnitude of the value' itself (Marx 1867, 112). Therefore, value production takes place 'in the background' (Marx 1867, 115) before the circulation and before the conversion of value into money and that of money into a specific prize. That is commodification according to Marx (1867), and from this perspective, marginal costs do not make any real difference as value is extracted before players meet on the market.

In this respect, Zuboff (2019) is on the opposite side of the spectrum as she focuses on the close connection between surveillance and exploitation (Allmer 2015; Sevignani 2016). From her perspective, the 'Big Other' is even expropriating human rights and shaping a new social order that is based on people being captured as raw material rather than a workforce in the traditional sense. Zuboff (2019) also takes into account the whole arsenal of digital capitalism – automation, job surveillance, the quantified self and targeted advertising – and traces back the new accumulation regime to the rise of Google, whose impact 'was just as dramatic as Ford's' (87). Zuboff provides a precious overview of the history of platformization but falls short when identifying the corresponding forms of social subjectivity. With capitalism appropriating human 'voices, personalities, and emotions', which is hardly a new argument, we would witness the rise of a 'behavioural surplus' (Zuboff 2019, 8). Nonetheless, the conversion of 'behavioural data' into 'means of behavioural modification' – a problem close to Marx's *transformation* – is more a tendency than it is a provable form of 'mass behaviour modification' (ibid., 8).

Zuboff (2019) purposefully uses an old Pavolovian paradigm like B. F. Skinner's to define the contemporary reinvestment cycle: as the market mostly trades in consumers' acts, big companies take advantage of their ability to 'predict or influence' people's future behaviour. It should be noted, however, that *predicting* and *influencing* behaviour are different tasks. The former has to do with Big Data articulating the repetitive patterns of everyday life (Barabási 2010), while the latter requires a more advanced analysis than Skinner's simplistic psychology.

Conclusion

As often happens to arguments reaching a peak in interest platform theory needs to be thoroughly discussed. In the hype cycle, the platformization concept is sometimes used to relabel traditional processes with no significant increase in knowledge. According to van Dijk's (1999a, 242; 1999b) critique of Castells' theory, this runs the risk of somehow *reifying* platform as a universal keyword. Castells' theory shows his propensity towards the reification of the network as a protagonist of human history. With the same category applying to both Apple and WhatsApp, for example, *two platforms that have little in common*, the discourse about platformization eventually comes across the same problem.

In some situations, there is the risk of reifying the network, as stated previously, and reifying platforms, when one considers that the same category also covers geopolitical and governmental issues (van Dijck et al. 2018, 160–161, 163–166) and is expected to account for all forms of commodification and surveillance (Zuboff 2019). There is also a more subtle consequence of this emphasis on platforms: the common definition of a multi-sided market becomes *equidistant* between the extremes of critical and marketing-driven theories. Being equidistant is useful in many aspects of life, and it may sound like a good rhetorical adjustment, but is it any good when it comes to scientific knowledge? Weber (1949) wrote that:

> We must oppose to the utmost the widespread view that scientific 'objectivity' is achieved by weighing the various evaluations against one another and making a 'statesman-like' compromise among them. Not only is the 'middle way' just as undemonstrable scientifically (with the means of the empirical sciences) as the 'most extreme' evaluations; rather, in the sphere of evaluations, it is the least unequivocal. (10)

Weber's statement fits the platform paradigm, which avoids taking a position on decisive issues, such as labour/value and agency/structure, and borrows concepts from both marketing and critical theory.

In the end, it is worth recalling that we did not take into account all facets of the platformization process, such as the design of platforms (de Reuver, Sorensen and Basole 2018; Lovink 2019) or the different market segments affected by the process (Wilken 2014). We rather adopted a perspective based on the concepts of value and neoliberal subjectivity. By applying the category of labour/value, we came across three main problems: the underrated role of human work, the over-estimation of data mining and the irreconcilability of the concept of commodification and the multi-sided model. One may argue that other interpretations of capitalism are possible, *and actually they are*, in the macro-text of platforms theory, although these interpretations are never declared or explicitly put into action. On the contrary, Marxist formulas are widely used, resulting in a sort of stylistic appropriation of some of the main motifs of Marxist theory. For the platform society to become a new paradigm, a more substantial confrontation with critical theory is needed.

Note

This chapter is an outcome of research funded by the European Commission in the Horizon 2020 framework: research project EUMEPLAT- European Media Platforms: Assessing Positive and Negative Externalities for European Culture, 2021–2024, Grant Agreement number 101004488.

References

Allmer, T. 2015. *Critical Theory and Social Media: Between Emancipation and Commodification*. Routledge.

Barabás, A.-L. 2010. *Bursts: The Hidden Patterns Behind Everything We Do, from E-Mail To Bloody Crusades*. Penguin.

Boudreau, K. and Hagiu, A. 2009. Platform Rules: Multi-sided Markets as Regulators. In A. Gawer (Ed.), *Platforms, Markets and Innovation* (pp. 163–189). Edward Elgar.

Casilli, A. 2019. *En attendant les robots: Enquête sur le travail du clic*. Seuil.

Castells, M. 1993. Cities, the Information Society and the Global Economy. In N. Brenner and R. Keil (Eds.), *The Global Cities Reader* (pp. 135–136). Routledge.

Castells, M. 1996. *The Rise of the Network Society*. Blackwell.

Castells, M. 2009. *Communication Power*. Oxford University Press.

Castells, M. 2012. *Networks of Outrage and Hope: Social Movements in the Internet Age*. Polity.

Couldry, J. and Mejias, U. 2019. *The Costs of Connection. How Data is Colonizing Human Life and Appropriating it for Capitalism*. Stanford University Press.

Dean, J. 2010. *Blog Theory: Feedback and Capture in the Circuits of Drive*. Polity Press.

Dean, J. 2016. *Crowds and Party*. Verso.

De Reuver, M., Sorensen, C., and Basole, M. H. 2018. The Digital Platform: A Research Agenda. *Journal of Information Technology*, 33(2), 124–135.

Evans, D. S. et al. 2011. *Platform Economics: Essays on Multi-sided Businesses*. Available at: https://www.researchgate.net/publication/228215476_Platform _Economics_Essays_on_Multi-Sided_Businesses.

Fuchs, C. 2012. With or Without Marx? With or Without Capitalism? A Rejoinder to Adam Arvidsson and Eleanor Colleoni. *tripleC*, 10(2), 633–645.

Gillespie, T. 2010. The Politics of Platforms. *New Media & Society*, 12(3), 347–364.

Gillespie, T. 2017. Regulations of and by Platforms. In J. Burgess, T. Poell, and A. Marwick (Eds.), *Sage Handbook of Social Media*. Sage.

Gillespie, T. 2018. *Custodians of the Internet: Platforms, Content Moderation, and the Hidden Decisions that Shape Social Media*. Yale University Press.

Helmond, A. 2015. The Platformization of the Web: Making Web Data Platform Ready. *Social Media + Society*, 1(2). https://doi.org/10.1177/2056 305115603080.

Kenney, M., Rouvinen, P., and Zysman, J. 2020. Employment, Work, and Value Creation in the Era of Digital Platforms. In S. Poutanen, A. Kovalainen, and P. Rouvinen (Eds.), *Digital Work and the Platform Economy; Understanding Tasks, Skills and Capabilities in the New Era*. Routledge.

Kenney, M. and Zysman, J. 2016. The Rise of the Platform Economy. *Issues in Science and Technology*, 32(3), 61.

Lovink, G. 2019. *Sad by Design: On Platform Nihilism*. Pluto Press.

Marx, K. 1864. The Process of Production of Capital. Draft chapter 6, *Capital* (B. Fowkes, Trans). https://www.marxists.org/archive/marx/works/1864 /economic/index.htm.

Marx, K. 1867. *Capital: Critique of Political Economy. Volume I*. Based on the 1887 English Edition, proofed by A. Blunden and C. Clayton (2008), M. Harris (2010) and D. Allison (2015). Available at: https://www.marxists .org/archive/marx/works/download/pdf/Capital-Volume-I.pdf.

Mayer-Schönberger, V. and Cukier, K. 2013. *Big Data: A Revolution That Will Transform How We Live, Work And Think*. John Murray.

Mayer-Schönberger, V. and Ramge, T. 2018. *Reinventing Capitalism in the Age of Big Data*. John Murray.

Negri, A. and Hardt, M. 2004. *Multitude: War and Democracy in the Age of Empire*. Penguin.

Plantin, J.-C. 2019. Review Essay: The Platform Society: Public Values in a Connective World. *Media, Culture & Society*, 41(2), 252–257.

Plantin, J.-C., Lagoze, C., and Edwards, P. N. 2016. Infrastructural Studies Meet Platform Studies in the Age of Google and Facebook. *New Media & Society*, 20(1), 293–310.

Roberts, S. T. 2016. Commercial Content Moderation: Digital Laborers' Dirty Work. Available at: http://ir.lib.uwo.ca/cgi/viewcontent.cgi?article=1012& context=commpub.

Sevignani, S. 2016. *Privacy and Capitalism in the Age of Social Media.* Routledge.

Srnicek, N. 2016. *Platform Capitalism.* Polity Press.

Taylor, A. 2018. The Automation Charade. *Logic,* 1 August. Available at: https:// logicmag.io/failure/the-automation-charade.

Tronto, M. 2019 [1966]. *Workers and Capital* (D. Broder, Trans). Verso.

van Dijck, J. and Poell, T. 2013. Understanding Social Media Logic. *Media and Communication,* 1(1), 2–14.

van Dijck, J., Poell, T., and de Waal, M. 2018. *The Platform Society: Public Values in a Connective World.* Oxford University Press.

van Dijk, J. 1999a. *The Network Society: Social Aspects of New Media.* Sage.

van Dijk, J. 1999b. The One-Dimensional Network Society of Manuel Castells. *New Media & Society,* 1(1), 127-138.

Weber, M. 1949 [1904]. *The Methodology of Social Sciences.* The Free Press.

Wilken, R. 2014. Places Nearby: Facebook as A Location-Based Social Media Platform. *New Media & Society,* 16(7), 1087–1103.

Zuboff, S. 2019. *The Age of Surveillance Capitalism: The Fight for a Human Future at the New Frontier of Power.* Public Affairs.

PART II

Case Studies

CHAPTER 9

The Digital Traces of Crypto-Finance

Alberto Cossu

Introduction: Cryptocurrencies and Internet Cultures

The last three decades in the history of the internet could be ideally divided into three main phases. The first was the 1990s, which saw the emergence of a libertarian/utopian declination of the potentialities to create a new space where people could build knowledge (for example through hyperlinks) and ultimately reclaim the 'net' as an alternative space where the rules of the 'outside' world would not/could not apply. This is exemplified by the infamous 'declaration of independence of cyberspace' (Barlow 1996). In the following years, the second phase is most notably described by the rise of the 'collaborative' internet, so-called 'Web 2.0' (O'Reilly 2007), largely based on dynamic internet protocols that allowed and incentivised the production of content by users into increasingly organised archives: from early blogging, online encyclopaedias and, finally, social media. They allowed users to overcome the technical barriers underlying the creation of autonomous websites, siphoning user activity into ever larger conglomerates (Helmond 2015). This leads us to the third phase, during which tech enterprises who had survived the dotcom bubble in the late 1990s (notably Google and Amazon), along with new ones (Facebook), dominate the market and have led academics, public bodies (e.g. the US Senate and the EU Commission) and public opinion to question the legitimacy of such levels of concentration and surveillance. The debate is centred around

How to cite this book chapter:
Cossu, A. 2022. The Digital Traces of Crypto-Finance. In: Armano, E., Briziarelli, M., and Risi, E. (eds.), *Digital Platforms and Algorithmic Subjectivities*. Pp. 123–134. London: University of Westminster Press. DOI: https://doi.org/10.16997/book54.j. License: CC-BY-NC-ND 4.0

massive processes of data harvesting and data analysis along with commercial and political exploitation of that data. These debates have evolved around keywords such as: datafication, quantification, data surveillance and surveillance capitalism.

We have now grown accustomed to the idea that almost every action that we perform is tracked, monitored, evaluated, stored, sold. Although many of these platforms are freely accessible this obfuscates the fact that their functioning requires extensive human, computational, natural and economic resources – this in turn has contributed to the well-founded suspicion that, since commodities cannot really be 'free' then it must be users and their activities that are themselves the product in this value creation process. But this should not lead us to simplistic conclusions, as we know that the value of a company like Facebook is not based on the sum of the value of the individual data it has stored but rather on promises of growth it can successfully deliver to its shareholders (Arvidsson 2016).

Furthermore, datafication has now reached almost every aspect of our lives, including the most intimate domains of sexuality, dating and health. In fact, as the literature has shown, there are concerns over the Chinese takeover of the gay dating app Grindr (Myles 2020), as it includes information about millions of individuals' sexuality that could be used to publicly discriminate.[1]

Crypto-Ideologies

In this context, how should we understand the rise of crypto-finance? At first glance, we can say it displays traits of the first-wave internet, a utopian scenario in which communities of hackers, techies and believers in the value of freedom and autonomy created new protocols, indeed new forms of social organisation, where they could create their own rules, their own worlds and, ultimately, their own finance. The start date is canonically understood as being 3 January 2009, when an anonymous inventor – Satoshi Nakamoto, a pseudonym behind which, it is speculated, is a team of people – published on the web the first version of Bitcoin code, the first and most high-profile cryptocurrency. It is based on cryptography, decentralised and anonymous exchanges and a distributed record of transactions (ledger). Most importantly it emancipates the creation of money from central institutions, reclaiming a very similar sense of autonomy to that of the first phase of cyberspace. In fact, the understanding of cryptography as a medium through which to achieve autonomy from institutionalised social worlds comes from Wei Dai, and is based on his work during the 1990s on the mailing list subculture of 'Cypherpunks'.[2]

These processes were happening as similar changes were radically transforming finance itself. Even if the first transatlantic bank transfer mediated by wires had happened back in 1919, in the 1980s and 1990s trading floors in stock exchanges were still largely based on dense human interaction, where middlemen and other organisations remained the fundamental engine for the coordination of financial markets. As a recent book on the subject brilliantly summarises regarding the current situation:

> Trading floors have disappeared, replaced by what anthropologist Ellen Hertz (1998) calls a 'community of effects' built through computers, screens, and cables scattered across inconspicuous locations throughout the world and where actions are not the result of a distinct collective intention but of the exercise of countless individual wills. In present-day financial markets, the logic is not one of coordinating interpersonal interactions but of managing the punctuated electronic signals that encode the orders from masses of anonymous investors. (Pardo Guerra 2019, 3)

The anonymous masses of 'official' finance closely resembles the amateur ones that animate the community of cryptocurrency investors that has emerged since the early 2010s. Initially confined to an inner circle of early adopters, investing in currencies such as Bitcoin became a significantly more popular activity thanks to a combination of factors, including the massive gains in the value of Bitcoin,[3] the creation of autonomous exchanges (for example, Bittrex, Binance etc.) and the accessibility of conversion points that allow for the easy exchange of *fiat* currencies into cryptocurrencies thanks to the mediation of major credit cards' circuits. Finally, Bitcoin ended up becoming a mythology in itself led by a fascination with alternative financial systems, especially if we consider how it thrived in the aftermath of the major 2007–8 financial crisis and the austerity politics that ensued. This has intensified the political appeal to an audience of tech-loving millennials (OECD 2019). However, we are aware that this mythology, like all mythologies, often hides a part of the truth in its promise of liberation and emancipation, so that, even if cryptocurrencies clearly signal a rupture and a political design based on liberation from the constraints of states and centralised markets:

> The currency has generated a thriving community around its political ideals, relies on a high degree of social organization in order to be produced, has a discernible social structure, and is characterized by asymmetries of wealth and power that are not dissimilar from the mainstream financial system. (Dodd 2018, 35)

What differs is that cryptocurrency projects harbour a promise of radical change, coupled with an intention towards 'social good' (Bandinelli 2020), viewing the current establishment as a vestige of the past – outdated and redundant. In this sense the appeal of traditional finance as possibly entailing similar results is ideologically inconceivable, although there are currently several popular apps which, in bridging alternative financial markets (Shrikanth 2020) can also concentrate on a seamless trading of official stocks listed on exchanges such as the New York or London Stock Exchanges. We understand this recent evolution as a possibility created by the alternative financial sector itself, at least in making it plausible or ethically sound to invest and speculate in assets. What is also noteworthy is how the appeal of investing in cryptocurrencies soared during the first lockdown months of 2020. During this period record levels of investors registered and transacted on these exchanges (Shrikanth 2020) while academics debated the hypothesis of whether crypto-assets could be perceived as 'safe havens' (Conlon, Corbet and McGee 2020) for investors during the Covid-19 pandemic. This also calls for a renewed understanding of each generation's approach to finance. Recent demographic inquiries led by industry players in crypto-finance give us a clearer picture of who these investors are. In particular, data coming from the UK and the US (Gemini 2021b) provides us with some very pertinent insights. In the first place, investing in crypto is an activity involving several generations, and not only those in their twenties – the memetic, Reddit-intensive Gen-Z who might be overrepresented if one pays attention to online posting only. Current crypto-investors in the US are on average 38 years old, with 75% being equally distributed between two age brackets: 25–34 (37%) and 35–44 (17%). The income of crypto-investors in the US is on average $111,000 (Gemini 2021b), and is significantly higher than the median income of American citizens of $69,000 (United States Census Bureau 2021). The age distribution for prospective investors – those who are at the moment only curious about crypto – is more balanced across multiple age cohorts, including 27% of North Americans aged between 45–54, and 22% between 55–56. What is also notable is the gender breakdown, skewed to men for current investors (74% male, 25% female), with those who are only curious being mostly female (53%). In the UK the picture is more precise (Gemini 2021a), based on a survey conducted on a sample of 2,000 individuals, 13.5% of whom currently invest or have invested in crypto in the past. The composition is more diverse across all areas, from gender to income and education. The typical investor here is more likely to be aged 18–44, split more evenly between genders (41% female, 56% male), is more likely to be in a relationship, less likely to own their own home and, interestingly, more likely to have children or dependents at home. This is coupled with an investing activity that, in terms of household yearly income, starts at £20,000, which is below the national (mean) average. Given crypto-investing starts at incomes below mean income levels, it might constitute their prime or sole form of investing, therefore exposing investors to considerable risk because of the high volatility of crypto-assets. To conclude this demographic snapshot, the same reports reveal that normally investors have a rather safe orientation, investing and holding a position for weeks or months, as opposed to the narrative we find on social media that overrepresents overly aggressive and speculative attitudes based on intense day trading activities.

In this context, I will now attempt to pin down the abstract processes that define this new approach to finance. In the first place, we can identify a process of datafication that we can comprehend as a base rhythm, the sound of machines storing everything that we do, that we value, that we like online. Secondly, based at this material level, we have cultures and ideologies that struggle for either hegemony or counter-hegemony, the latter exploiting the same financial mechanisms but rooted in a digital culture that provides an alterity. Thirdly, the positionality of a new generation of investors, and more specifically those investors who have been capable of shaping a counter-cultural narrative mostly on social media, should be assessed as being *passive* data producers and active data users that utilise a vast array of data types to participate in the creation of alternative financial value. In this chapter, focusing on data and data-related processes (specifically processes of data analysis but also processes of financial literacy crucially mediated by digital technologies), I aim to dissect the political and cultural entanglement that defines the peculiar positionality of a cryptocurrency investor as data-subject. By doing so, I try to illuminate the ambiguities and the possibilities of emancipation through digital technologies.

The Wisdom of Digital Crowds?

Digital media's role in the social life of cryptocurrencies can scarcely be underestimated. To a certain extent, the foundational ideas of cryptocurrencies are digitally native.[4] I will explore the different roles digital media plays, not just in educating investors, but in attracting them to cryptocurrencies over other types of investment. In the first place, digital media enabled the creation of an ethos that distinguishes between old/bad traditional finance and the new 'saviour' nature of cryptocurrency. This is relevant because it was not that online banking services, which have been available since at least the early 2000s, were not usable earlier, but what was missing was the cultural element that made this possibility appealing. A further distinction is made between small and large investors. In their online chats, Bitcoin investors often refer to large investors as *whales*,[5] not without a tone of mockery and mild deprecation, and they are perceived as responsible for the price fluctuations that hinder the strategies and profits of the many 'small fish' – however, as we noted earlier, these same wild fluctuations also contribute to generating interest. This reveals an attribution of a positive value to the fact of having a small amount of resources, as if the quantity of capital invested was able to legitimise and differentiate the will (and the right) to profit between the two groups. In fact, it is known that cryptocurrencies are not immune to the interference of large private investors, and they are not alien to the intervention of sovereign funds as countries such as Russia and China (Peng 2020), amongst many others, started investing in this lucrative and highly volatile market years ago.

Digital media is responsible for the circulation of key information on where and how to invest. There are countless online outlets that provide precisely this kind of content: forums, Telegram chats, Discord channels, official blogs, podcasts, etc. An important difference lies in the fact that one large part of the context is produced by users themselves, while the official, established financial press also now covers, on a daily basis, an analysis of crypto-assets. In the domain of user-generated content the same 'laws' of popularity apply that academic studies of new media have long identified (Abidin 2018). We can find many popular crypto 'influencers' that – often in explicit partnerships – evaluate the market, provide fundamental analysis and ultimately evaluate the potential of a given asset to be profitable. This reveals an aspect of performativity in the creation of value, as it is often the same hype produced by the influencer (by virtue of being trusted by their followers) that results in 'making' the investment profitable. Influencers can have tens of thousands of followers, and their activities include sharing their own daily investment plans on Twitter, or predicting future market directions based on a live analysis.

Another key aspect of educating this new generation of investors is the widespread and free access to financial literacy. On platforms such as YouTube some channels have now become alternatives to formal training and university degrees on these subjects, allowing prospective investors to learn the foundations of trading, of market analysis, trends etc. A common view is that sixty hours of training is needed to start to grasp the foundations of trading. Practices of becoming literate in any subject thanks to the internet should not be particularly surprising in the 2020s. However, it is relevant that a new class of investors, a new subjectivity, a sense of collective belonging is created in the realm of finance, possibly signalling a specific generational set of desires, aspirations and ideals. In fact, the creation of an infrastructure for decentralised trading is based on a will that it is also political. However, it does so by mimicking the same artefacts, techniques, screens and indicators of traditional finance. In fact, there is a massive reappropriation of techniques that were developed for traditional finance. Exploiting existing knowledge, merging it with a utopian ideal of liberation from 'central institutions', signals a process akin to that of a 'world creation' or myth (Dodd 2018).

The evolution of cryptocurrencies has led to the creation of an entire new industry that spans from the creation of crypto-exchanges to Big Data approaches to investing which amateur investors can deploy. Many of these exchanges are, in fact, based on APIs (Application Program Interfaces) that allow for a constant 'dialogue' between investors and the market, leading to the rise of intermediary services. One such example is '3Commas' (3Commas n.d.), a platform that allows users to encode their own strategies using bots that can be deployed automatically if certain triggers are activated. Another example is platforms that offer Big Data social analytics to guide investors, e.g. 'Santiment' (Santiment n.d.), a digital start-up that aggregates social and financial data.

The implicit link between these two services is that it is possible that analysing what is said about a certain cryptocurrency online can ultimately influence its value. Tracking the number of online posts that discuss a currency, or the level of coding activity on GitHub, analysing the overall 'sentiment' of a currency in a given moment – this data is the aggregation of the same users' digital actions.

This current setting is possibly explained by reviving a theory of collective/connective intelligence (Levy 1997), by which a greater knowledge is achievable via online coordination and may be understood as a means to guide investors' actions and turn uncertainty into calculable risk (Knight 2006). Similarly, economics scholars have explored the possibility that crypto-finance could actually prove the theory that posits a 'wisdom of crowds' (Lee, Li and Shin 2019) to be true: by being able to collectively evaluate and communicate among themselves crowds might be able to achieve above average results. However, the availability of such insights openly shared for free (or behind reasonable paywalls) might make it seem as if they were non-rivalrous goods – a sort of digital commons (Wittel 2013) – but this is far from reality. In fact, the internal financial mechanisms that the crypto-world mimics and borrows from traditional finance invariably replicates it along with the same mechanisms of exclusion and tiered or preferential access to valuable information.

What Kind of Subjects are the Digital Subjects of Crypto-Finance?

How do algorithmic processes see us? It they could see us, sense us, we would probably be akin to a galaxy of data points, a representation of all our actions that are subjected to digital tracking (Lupton 2020). In a transhumanist vein, we might also consider the co-substantial relationship we entertain with these data points: they are somehow connected to us, and they act on us for the knowledge that they store about us and that can be resurfaced in precise moments (e.g. when an algorithm suggests something to us to which we can respond). We could ascribe this relationship to a sort of filiation that originates in the primary human subject, or in a way that allows for a circularity to be possible between human and non-human agents (see Stiegler's concept of *exosome* (2018)). It is telling, in this respect, to examine a key article in the General Data Protection Regulation (GDPR), article 4(1) (emphasis added):

> 'Personal data' means any information relating to an identified or identifiable natural person ('data subject'); an identifiable natural person is one *who can be identified*, directly or indirectly, in particular by reference to an identifier such as a name, *an identification number, location data, an online identifier* or to one or more factors specific to the physical, physiological, genetic, mental, economic, cultural or social identity of that natural person.

This makes very tangible the idea that we can now be legally identified by some of our own data points, as indices, as traces of us. We belong to that data as the data, partially, belongs to us. What does this say about our condition? And what does it say about the aspirations, hopes and efforts of this new generation of investors to create value and profit from their digital activities that are exploited and self-exploited? On the one hand, there is an empowerment spiral; on the other, there is the inevitable implication in an exploitative system.

Investors, however, beyond having a certain relationship with their own 'data points' and the use of aggregated data of other investors, are subjected to a foundational layer of data tracking and exploitation that falls outside the possibility of full ownership. This is the type of data processed by the profiling algorithms of major platforms on which the socialisation and popularisation of finance happens: YouTube, Reddit and other major platforms retain valuable information about their own activity. This appears to be the hard limit for a possibility of a 'full' ownership of our own data.

Investing in these cryptocurrencies is not safe – as it never is for any kind of financial investment. However, reliable survey data (OECD 2019) tells us that cryptos have guaranteed a possibility of immediate profit for most investors. This indicates the relative success of a method of financial value extraction invented by utopian coders and adopted *en masse* by a new generation of financial investors. This also allows us to provisionally assert that, above the foundational layer of data exploitation that we are all subjected to, it is possible to create a parasitic layer that allows investors to exploit tactically, ultimately providing an economic benefit for them. We are data subjects, and as such we are constantly subjected to forces, but at the same time there are possibilities for the creation of new worlds and institutions that allow new ideas and social formations to exert a counter-power. A part of it is the fact that our society works based on specialised sub-systems that gain instrumental advantages by keeping control within their boundaries, as in the case of traditional finance. In a realpolitik power analysis, the new crypto-scene needs a world that it has created and that it rules technically and culturally.

Overall, the balance of these two forces of datafication and reappropriation of finance by means of code points towards a peculiar form of political critique, one that is enmeshed in and moulded following the same models of extraction. If the Italian autonomist theorists of the 1970s predicated the juxtaposition of being 'within' the system and 'against' the system to be effective in the counter struggle, it is plausible to think that now being 'against' also means being at a meta level above the fiction of capitalism to see its workings behind the curtain in order to learn capitalism's strategies and replicate them in hopefully largely autonomous worlds. This is a possible line of development for a critique that can disentangle and bring us back to the taboo of the machinic colonisation of the subject: as a primitive financial colonisation that dates back 150 years, that is now mimicked, appropriated and re-encoded in this new financial wave led by amateur investors and emerging technological leaders. To this we should also add the anthropological implications of the alienated relationship between ourselves and our data traces. Somehow the dynamics inherent in data traces speak of our corrupted condition – colonised by financial and technical systems – while at the same time they inevitably chain us to this new capitalist spirit of the time.

Conclusion

In this chapter I have tried to present some lines of investigation that pertain to a wider-ranging research agenda I have been developing on cryptocurrencies, including an evaluation of the case for a democratisation of finance via cryptocurrencies. There are many ambiguities that affect this financial emancipatory project on both a systemic and subjective level. I believe that in this respect it is also productive to think along the lines of recent debates on connection/disconnection. As Natale and Treré have said, 'engagement with digital technologies is instrumental to develop critique and resistance against the paradoxes of digital societies' (Natale and Treré 2020, 630), therefore positing that the possibility of escape from a seemingly corrupted world does not end just by furthering a progressive agenda. In this sense, it is about evaluating politically if devising such a critical yet exploitative practice as crypto-investing in the search of a new form of (passive) income, or supporting a wave of change embodied by the crypto-scene, can constitute a positive force in society. The range of positions here is infinitely varied, as we know from activism narratives that show that aligning one's private consumption and lifestyle to a public persona is often afflicted by a noticeable cleavage between the two. I believe that if we follow Tania Bucher's insights on the digital condition we can see that there is 'nothing to disconnect from in the digital world' (Bucher 2020). However, clearly more can be done to assert more equitable conditions faced with the massive exploitation and self-exploitation of data. We may witness an extensive academic exploration of decentralised architectures and protocols and their underlying ideologies. My intention here is to underline what I believe is a dire need to assess the cultural production of the digital publics of crypto-finance in several aspects: the creation of a distinctive crypto-ethos and the socialisation of new financial practices, largely undertaken in a peer-to-peer mode. This agenda is highly important as this crypto-scene has proved capable of penetrating the public sphere and influencing mainstream discourses on economics. Furthermore, a fuller agenda should certainly include the vast ecology of cryptocurrencies, taking into account not just retail investors or social media posters but also the coders that ultimately create new architectures and who often embed a distinctive ethical and financial form in their operations. Lastly, an updated agenda should reflect the typical modern capitalist dynamic for which the disruption of a new technology (e.g. blockchain, peer-to-peer, trustless) is often regulated by states, as is happening right now. The UK has recently prohibited their own citizens from investing via Binance, one of the largest trading platforms. Yet at the same time, these innovations have led many to start thinking again about the foundations of money, as something that is always, inherently, a social process.

Notes

1. Here I suggest some key texts on critical approaches to platform society that have recently appeared on this subject: *Platform Society* by van Dijck, Poell and de Waal (2018*), Surveillance Capitalism* by Shoshana Zuboff (2019) and *The Costs of Connection* by Nick Couldry and Ulises Meijas (2019).
2. For example, b-money in 1998. See http://www.weidai.com/bmoney.txt, '… a scheme for a group of untraceable digital pseudonyms to pay each other with money and to enforce contracts amongst themselves without outside help'.
3. Bitcoin prices rose in 75 days from $5,000 to $19,783, from 1 October to 17 December 2017, and from $3,500 in March 2020 to the same heights in December 2020; this also accounts for the extreme volatility of its value which both deters and appeals to speculators.
4. Their roots, however, also lie in an economic thinking that spans beyond internet history and looks back at neoclassical economy, anarcho-capitalism as well as mutualism. On this see Swartz (2018) and Dodd (2018).
5. Bitcoin whales are the big investors. This is due to the concentration of shareholders' portfolios. At the time of writing, three Bitcoin addresses own nearly 8% of all Bitcoins (equivalent to $396 million), while the first 100 wallets hold 31% ($1.7 billion).

References

3Commas. n.d. Monetize your crypto portfolio (home page). 3commas.io (last accessed 12 April 2022).

Abidin, C. 2018. *Internet Celebrity: Understanding Fame Online*. Emerald Publishing.

Arvidsson, A. 2016. Facebook and Finance: On the Social Logic of the Derivative. *Theory, Culture & Society*, 33(6), 3–23. https://doi.org/10.1177/026327 6416658104.

Bandinelli, C. 2020. *Social Entrepreneurship and Neoliberalism: Making Money While Doing Good*. Rowman and Littlefield.

Barlow, J. P. 1996. A Declaration of the Independence of Cyberspace, *Electronic Frontier Foundation*, 8 February. Retrieved from: https://www.eff.org/it /cyberspace-independence (last accessed: 10 December 2020).

Bucher, T. 2020. Nothing to Disconnect From? Being Singular Plural in an Age of Machine Learning. *Media, Culture & Society*, 42(4), 610–617. https://doi .org/10.1177/0163443720914028.

Conlon, T., Corbet, S., and McGee J. R. 2020. Are Cryptocurrencies a Safe Haven for Equity Markets? An International Perspective from the COVID-19 Pandemic, *Research in International Business and Finance*, 54. https://doi .org/10.1016/j.ribaf.2020.101248.

Couldry, N. and Meijas, U. 2019. *The Costs of Connection: How Data Is Colonizing Human Life and Appropriating It for Capitalism*. Stanford University Press.

Dodd, N. 2018. The Social Life of Bitcoin. *Theory, Culture & Society*, 35(3), 35–56. https://doi.org/10.1177/0263276417746464.

Gemini. 2021a. State of Crypto in the UK 2021. Available at: https://www .gemini.com/state-of-uk-crypto (last accessed 8 July 2021).

Gemini. 2021b. State of Crypto in the US 2021. Available at: https://www.gemini .com/state-of-us-crypto (last accessed 8 July 2021).

Helmond, A. 2015. The Platformization of the Web: Making Web Data Platform Ready. *Social Media + Society*. https://doi.org/10.1177/2056305115603080.

Hertz, E. 1998. *The Trading Crowd: An Ethnography of the Shanghai Stock Market*. Cambridge University Press.

Knight, F. 2006. [1921]. *Risk, Uncertainty and Profit*. Dover Publications.

Lee, J., Li, T., and Shin, D. 2019. The Wisdom of Crowds in FinTech: Evidence from Initial Coin Offerings. Retrieved from SSRN: https://ssrn.com/abstract =3195877 (last accessed: 10 December 2020).

Levy, P. 1997. *Collective Intelligence: Mankind's Emerging World in Cyberspace*. Perseus Books.

Lupton, D. 2020. Not the Real Me: Social Imaginaries of Personal Data Profiling. *Cultural Sociology*, 15(1), 3–21. https://doi.org/10.1177/1749975520939779.

Myles, D. 2020. Les rencontres amoureuses et sexuelles au temps des algorithmes: Une analyse comparative de Grindr et Tinder. In C. Piazzesi, M. Blais, J. Lavigne, and C. Lavoie Mongrain (Eds.), *Intimités et sexualités contemporaines: changements sociaux, transformations des pratiques et des representations*. Presses de l'Université de Montréal.

Natale, S. and Treré, E. 2020 Vinyl Won't Save Us: Reframing Disconnection as Engagement. *Media, Culture & Society*, 42(4), 626–633. https://doi .org/10.1177/0163443720914027.

OECD [Organisation for Economic Co-operation and Development]. 2019. *Consumer Insights Survey on Cryptoassets*. Available at: https://www.oecd .org/financial/education/consumer-insights-survey-on-cryptoassets.pdf (last accessed 10 November 2021).

O'Reilly, T. 2007. What is Web 2.0: Design Patterns and Business Models for the Next Generation of Software. *Communications & Strategies*, 1(17). Retrieved from: https://ssrn.com/abstract=1008839.

Pardo-Guerra, J. P. 2019. *Automating Finance: Infrastructures, Engineers, and the Making of Electronic Markets*. Cambridge University Press. https://doi .org/10.1017/9781108677585.

Peng, T. 2020. World's largest sovereign wealth fund indirectly holds almost 600 Bitcoin. *Coin Telegraph*, 20 September. Retrieved from: https://cointel egraph.com/news/worlds-largest-sovereign-wealth-fund-indirectly-holds -almost-600-bitcoin (last accessed: 10 December 2020).

Santiment. n.d..Crypto intelligence is collaborative (home page). Santimant.net (last accessed 12 April 2022).

Shrikanth, S. 2020. 'Gamified' investing leaves millennials playing with fire. *Financial Times,* 7 May. Retrieved from: https://www.ft.com/content /9336fd0f-2bf4-4842-995d-0bcbab27d97a (last accessed: 10 December 2020).

Stiegler, B. 2018. *The Neganthropocene*. Open Humanities Press.

Swartz, L. 2018. What was Bitcoin, What Will It Be? The Technoeconomic Imaginaries of a New Money Technology. *Cultural Studies*, 32(4), 623–650. https://doi.org/10.1080/09502386.2017.1416420.

United States Census Bureau. 2021. Income and Poverty in the United States: 2020. Report no. P60–273, 14 September. Available at: https://www.census .gov/library/publications/2021/demo/p60-273.html#:~:text=Median%20 household%20income%20was%20%2467%2C521,median%20house hold%20income%20since%202011 (last accessed 12 April 2022).

van Dijck J., Poell, T., and de Waal, M. 2018. *The Platform Society: Public Values in a Connective World*. Oxford University Press.

Wittel, A. 2013. Counter-Commodification: The Economy of Contribution in the Digital Commons. *Culture and Organization*, 19(4), 314–331. https:// doi.org/10.1080/14759551.2013.827422.

Zuboff, S. 2019. *The Age of Surveillance Capitalism: The Fight for a Human Future at the New Frontier of Power*. Public Affairs.

CHAPTER 10

Labour Control and Commodification Strategies Within a Food Delivery Platform in Belgium

Milena Franke and Valeria Pulignano

Introduction

Processes of 'datafication' and 'algorithmic control' are central in much recent research on labour platforms, which are defined as online tools that bring together and mediate between workers and customers for the exchange of paid labour (van Dijck, Poell and de Wall 2018; Wood et al. 2018). Arguments from the literature claim that the ways in which platforms technologically steer data collected from users and workers is at the core of 'platform capitalism' (Srnicek 2016). However, in-depth knowledge on the mechanisms enabling platforms to accumulate surplus value based on labour subordination remains somewhat limited. This requires focusing on the labour relationships underpinning 'algorithmic control' within platforms (Gandini 2019), which is the main analytical contribution of this chapter.

We focus on labour commodification, the process by which labour power is bought and sold as a commodity (Marx 1990). Together with Wood et al. (2019), we argue that commodification is key to explaining how platforms

---

How to cite this book chapter:
Franke, M. and Pulignano, V. 2022. Labour Control and Commodification Strategies Within a Food Delivery Platform in Belgium. In: Armano, E., Briziarelli, M., and Risi, E. (eds.), *Digital Platforms and Algorithmic Subjectivities*. Pp. 135–147. London: University of Westminster Press. DOI: https://doi.org/10.16997/book54.k. License: CC-BY-NC-ND 4.0

achieve labour subordination by exposing workers to market exchange. Hence, we ask: what are the strategies labour platforms use to allocate labour efficiently by exposing workers to market exchange? How do the mechanisms and practices underpinning these strategies work and how do they account for the way in which platforms achieve labour subordination?

Understanding 'new' modes of capital valorisation under 'digital capitalism' requires looking at digital data (Srnicek 2016). Research illustrates that platforms optimise efficiency through workers' participation in the production of digital data (Attoh, Wells and Cullen 2019). However, data is not only generated by workers, but also by the platform's users (Van Doorn and Badger 2020). Accordingly, we argue that subordination through labour commodification occurs at the intersection of the relationships between platforms, workers and users (which we define as both individual clients and businesses such as restaurants).

Based on a qualitative study including interviews with workers (in this case couriers), clients, restaurants and the platform management within a food delivery platform (FD-Plat – an anonymised acronym) in Belgium, we illustrate how platforms foster commodification through what we call an 'empowerment cycle' and a 'disempowerment cycle', consisting of a series of recurrent practices and mechanisms that simultaneously support and constrain workers, restaurants and clients. Digital data collection and processing involved in these cycles continually boost the platform's capacity to control users and workers while purportedly providing them with autonomy. We argue that labour control and subordination emerge from these commodification strategies, enabling capital accumulation by the platform. We refer to Wright's (2000) definition of exploitation whereby the subordinated worker is excluded from access to certain means of production. In the following sections, we first theoretically frame our argument, then we present the methodology before setting out the findings. Finally, we discuss and conclude.

Bringing 'Work' Back into Labour Platforms

Current definitions point to labour platforms as technological tools that allow for the organisation of interactions and transactions between users and workers online. This is often referred to as a 'triangular' work relationship (Duggan et al. 2020; Schörpf et al. 2017) where digital technology is key in bringing together supply and demand for labour (Graham and Woodcock 2018). However, conceiving labour platforms merely as 'market intermediaries' (Harris and Krueger 2015) is insufficient to fully grasp platform work. A critical understanding requires positioning platform work within the labour relationships characterising 'platform capitalism', considering them as capitalist relations of production (Joyce 2020; Srnicek 2016). We argue that commodification is an important Marxian theoretical category to clarify how subordination within platform work evolves. By circumventing intervention from trade unions and other labour market intermediaries (Pulignano 2019), labour platforms have acquired unprecedented control over the compensation for and the organisation of work. Labour platforms can hire workers by the task and undercut statutory minimum wages (Huws 2014) while providing no social protection (De Stefano 2016). This all takes place under the 'façade' of self-employment (Shapiro 2020), with *de facto* subordinated workers often misclassified as independent contractors (Cherry and Aloisi 2017). To control workers, platforms often use algorithms and other technological infrastructure to collect and monetise data (Vallas 2019). We argue that digital data management accounts for the way in which novelty is brought to work and performed within labour platforms through commodification. Hence, studying the mechanisms and practices through which commodification occurs is essential to understand how platforms dominate labour processes.

Uncovering Commodification in Platform Work

Platforms collect and process large amounts of data that users generate themselves when accessing platform services (van Dijck, Poell and de Waal 2018). Platforms then offer third parties access to these data (Helmond 2015), or transform data into 'desired' outputs through algorithms. 'Algorithmic management' is often defined as a control system where self-learning algorithms execute decisions, thereby limiting human involvement in the labour process (Möhlmann and Zalmanson 2017). However, together with Moore (2019) we claim that such a view risks reifying algorithms at the expense of underplaying the importance of the capital-labour relations underpinning platform capitalism. It is not the use of algorithms that accounts for platforms tracking workers (Duggan et al. 2020), but rather it is the power of capital over labour that explains how 'algorithmic management' effectively works (Rosenblat and Stark 2016). We identify two implications for the study of platform work.

First, labour platforms repurpose capitalist relations in a new environment where workers are constantly monitored and evaluated (Schor and Attwood-Charles 2017), eliciting a qualitative intensification of work (Wood et al. 2019). Second, platforms govern access to data as a commodity (Jabagi et al. 2019). We argue that generated digital data is then used to increase efficiency in labour allocation and in the decision-making of users. We consider that studying the mechanisms and practices through which this occurs is essential in order to understand the platform as a 'place' where control is enacted upon workers (Gandini 2019). As we will illustrate in the following sections, this points to a need to analytically and empirically reconsider the 'triangular' platform-user-worker relation as one allowing the accumulation of capital from labour exploitation. It also requires acknowledging the importance of digital data, by exploring platforms' commodification strategies. Specifically, we explain how these strategies account for control by simultaneously empowering and dis-empowering users and workers at the intersection of their relationships with the platform.

Research Design and Methodology

Context

Digitalisation has fostered deregulation in Belgium (Basselier, Langenus and Walravens 2018), in turn potentially undermining collective bargaining and the social protection system (Van Gyes, Segers and Henderickx 2009). Notably, the 'De Croo law' allows certain platforms to use the so-called 'peer-to-peer' category, exempting platform work for up to €6,340 per year from taxes and social contributions between 2018–2020. Food delivery platforms benefited from this regulation, and were able to grow rapidly while circumventing work-ers' employment protections. A large share of Belgian workers engaging in food delivery work are young students, economically dependent on their parents. However, others combine platform work with a main job as an employee, or are self-employed in other work, and yet others rely on platform work as their sole source of income (Drahokoupil and Piasna 2019). Looking specifically at FD-Plat, the platform hires couriers under various self-employed statuses or within a peer-to-peer category. Originally, payment for all couriers consisted of a minimum amount for picking up and delivering food plus a variable fee depending on the distance to the client. However, after the Belgian tax authori-ties challenged the classification of couriers under the peer-to-peer heading, FD-Plat switched to a fixed fee for these workers in October 2019 and removed workers' ability to view a client's location before accepting an order.

Data Collection and Analysis

The research was conducted in Leuven, Brussels, Antwerp and Gent, cities with varying degrees of urban concentration. We conducted semi-structured inter-views with couriers, restaurants managers, clients and the platform manage-ment. We interviewed 37 couriers between December 2018 and March 2020, diversifying respondents by employment status and the combination of plat-form work with other employment. Most couriers are men in their twenties (Drahokoupil and Piasna 2019), but we also included five women and some older couriers. Interviews with restaurant managers, clients and the platform management were conducted in early 2020. Five restaurants selling different kinds of food were selected. Clients were one student and two employees who used FD-Plat to order food. Our research also benefited from secondary data, especially the platform's website and a social media community used by couriers.

Additionally, we used participatory observation, with one of the researchers becoming a platform client and using the payment and rating system. This information proved useful to verify and complement data gathered in the interviews. Both primary and secondary data were analysed and encoded following an abductive approach, moving back and forth between data, concepts and categories (Blaikie 2007). In particular, our interest in the concepts of commodification and control informed the analysis, but a much deeper understanding of these phenomena was obtained by analysing the themes emerging from the collected data.

Findings

Cycles of Labour Commodification

FD-Plat's business model relies on collecting and processing vast amounts of data. Data is collected through three digital applications – one for clients, one for couriers and one for restaurants – which monitor all their activities, choices, locations and contact details. Data is analysed by the platform's back-office staff and then used to strategically expand choices and support decision-making by restaurants and clients. Moreover, it is fed into a self-learning algorithm which makes increasingly accurate predictions of users' and couriers' behaviour as more and more data is collected, contributing to increased delivery efficiency. Data collection and processing are at the heart of the platform's market expansion, enabling FD-Plat to enhance efficiency, while at the same time empowering and disempowering both users and couriers through commodification.

The Empowerment Cycle

As shown in the upper right-hand side of Figure 10.1, FD-Plat offers an extensive choice of meals to clients, which can quickly be delivered at any time of the day.

The collection of client data allows for the personalisation of the food delivery service, tailoring the choice of meals and special offers to client preferences. During 2019–2020, FD-Plat used this data to expand to one thousand new restaurants, hence enlarging client choice while increasing competition among restaurants:

> The reason why I started ordering through [name of platform] is because they have such an extensive offer. I don't mind leaving the house to get food, but sometimes the restaurant is far away or it's difficult to pick up the food. Then I use [name of platform] to order, which is much faster. (Client 2)

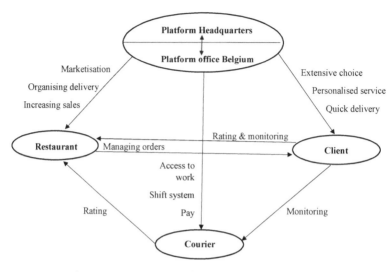

Figure 10.1: The Empowerment Cycle. Diagram by the authors.

As shown by the client ➔ restaurant/courier arrows in Figure 10.1, the client application monitors in real-time when food is being prepared and where the courier is. Clients can rate restaurants using a five-star rating system and, also, possibly adding a comment. The platform processes the collected data and transfers it as 'use value' to restaurants, which can access their ratings and other statistics, such as the 'preparation time statistic' or how well sales are doing. The upper left-hand side of Figure 10.1 illustrates that FD-Plat empowers restaurants through marketisation. For example, the platform's back-office staff in Belgium exchanges data with the company's corporate headquarters (see the circle at the top of Figure 10.1) and uses it to offer targeted marketing advice:

> For example, we tell the restaurant 'Have you heard of this new dish, the poke bowl? It's popular in France, it will come to Belgium as well. Don't you want to include it in your menu?' (FD-Plat management)

The restaurant application enables restaurants to choose the dishes and prices shown to clients, and to manage incoming orders. Moreover, FD-Plat supports restaurants by organising the delivery service on their behalf. As a result, restaurants gain access to a large pool of new online clients, boosting their sales:

> One advantage of working with [name of platform] is that many more people get to know you. (Restaurant 2)

> One third of the dishes we prepare now are for delivery via [name of platform]. (Restaurant 3)

Simultaneously, as shown by the platform ➜ courier arrow in Figure 10.1, FD-Plat provides couriers with access to work through an almost unrestricted recruitment system. Couriers register online and usually access work through a shift system, reserving time slots for the upcoming week. Incoming orders are assigned to couriers by FD-Plat's algorithm, based on real-time data on client demand, restaurants and couriers' availability and location. Couriers can accept or cancel an incoming order and even have the option to cancel orders during the delivery process, hence benefiting from some flexibility:

> What makes working for [name of platform] so attractive is that it is flexible. […] I can work whenever I want […] I can also reject an order if it's too far, I choose that myself. (Courier 8)

Pay for non-peer-to-peer workers is calculated by the algorithm, taking into account real-time data on the street and traffic situation and hence allowing couriers to maximise their earnings, for example by mostly accepting long-distance orders. Finally, couriers can evaluate the delivery process through a rating mechanism. Most importantly, as illustrated by the courier ➜ restaurant arrow, couriers evaluate their waiting time when picking up food at restaurants:

> I have to say that it makes it easier that at the end of your shift you can always say 'this was not a nice delivery because the restaurant took too much time'. I think that [name of platform] is very responsive in this respect. When things go wrong, they will talk to the restaurant and see that things improve. (Courier 25)

The Disempowerment Cycle

At the same time, FD-Plat's rating and monitoring system fosters competition between restaurants as it generates comparisons among clients and couriers regarding time efficiency:

> Preparation time really depends on what I order. For example [name of restaurant] is really quick, it's like 5 minutes. But when I order for example pizza from an Italian restaurant, they take much more time, like 20 minutes. (Client 1)

> If I go to [name of restaurant] I have to wait there for 15 minutes. That is why I prefer accepting orders from restaurants where I only have to wait for 5 minutes, or from those where the food is ready when I arrive. (Courier 12)

As illustrated in the upper left-hand side of Figure 10.2, data on clients' and couriers' ratings are collected by FD-Plat and used to rank restaurants within

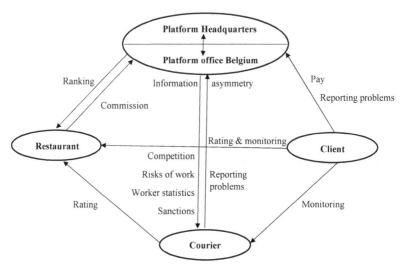

Figure 10.2: The Disempowerment Cycle. Diagram by the authors.

the client application, hence disempowering low-ranking restaurants. Each restaurant pays a commission on orders processed through the platform (usually around 30%). If ratings deteriorate, FD-Plat can increase the commission or even end the contract with the restaurant.

Moreover, as the share of external sales rises, restaurants become increasingly dependent on FD-Plat. Restaurant managers report suffering from the increased workload involved in dealing with incoming orders, which sometimes prompts them to prioritise delivery over serving clients seated, or to hire additional staff. This dependency is magnified by the lack of information on which courier delivers the food, making it harder to deal with delays:

> What often happens is that the order is ready, but the rider hasn't yet arrived. […] Then I think of the client, I think that there is a hot dish waiting and it's not our fault. […] In such cases, we sometimes call the client – we have the number on our tablet – to say that the order is ready, but the rider hasn't turned up yet. (Restaurant 1)

As shown in Figure 10.2, all payments are processed through FD-Plat. Clients pay the full cost (including delivery) to FD-Plat, which in turn pays the courier and the restaurant. Interviews with clients illustrate that they perceive this system as opaque and consider delivery quite expensive, hence they rarely tip the courier:

> I don't tip because each time I order I feel guilty, I'm a student, I can order, I can pay for the food, but if I pay tips also, it will be even more expensive. (Client 1)

Similarly, couriers lack information on who the client is and what their next order or waiting time will be. Peer-to-peer workers are further disempowered by having to accept orders without knowing the client's address, which is only provided to them once they have picked up the order at the restaurant. As illustrated by the courier/client ➜ platform arrows in Figure 10.2, both can report delivery problems to the platform via a chat-system, through both perceive this as largely ineffective as in most cases the answers given by the platform are standardised. Data collected through the chat are processed by FD-Plat to improve the delivery process. As delineated by the platform ➜ courier arrow, FD-Plat strategically fosters competition among couriers. This became particularly visible in 2018–2020, when FD-Plat recruited thousands of new couriers. FD-Plat hires couriers – as stated above under various self-employed statuses – with no social security coverage, hence 'obscuring' control and shifting economic risks to the couriers:

> There is always the major risk of being qualified as an employer. If the riders were then employees, they would lose their flexibility. (FD-Plat management)

Finally, relations with couriers are commodified through the use of individual performance statistics, introducing competition based on data about attendance, cancellation of shifts and working during 'peak hours', when clients place most orders. Bad statistics are sanctioned by deprioritising access to the shift system:

> You book your shifts on Monday and if you have bad statistics, then you can only start booking some hours later than the others. So then the shifts could actually be fully booked. (Courier 13)

> My statistics went down during the summer as I couldn't work then, so I no longer had an advantage over the other couriers. I had to wait a long time to be able to work again. (Courier 26)

Control and Subordination within Labour Platforms

The commodification strategies of empowerment and disempowerment discussed above contribute to labour control and subordination. As the platform fuels competition through the use of data, it restricts couriers' access to work, income and social security. With an easily scalable 'on-demand' workforce at its disposal, FD-Plat is able to efficiently adapt operations to client demand. Couriers' discretion over working time is limited through the use of statistics that induce them to ride on weekends or in bad weather conditions and to keep high attendance rates. FD-Plat restricts access to work and disciplines couriers through increased competition:

Most shifts are booked now, that is a problem. So now it's actually less flexible, I can't simply say 'now I have nothing to do, now I will ride' [...] I don't feel autonomous because I am clearly dependent on whether there is a slot or not. (Courier 17)

In the same vein, platform profits depend on couriers not being in charge of their access to their income. By paying only for completed orders, FD-Plat leaves couriers waiting for orders and/or during the delivery process without an income:

What makes me really angry is when I go to a restaurant where you know you'll have to wait a long time, but because you don't get a lot of orders you accept it. Twenty-five minutes later, you're still standing there, having earned nothing for those 25 minutes. (Courier 31)

FD-Plats' distance-based payment system allows it to allocate couriers across a large catchment area of clients and restaurants. Economic incentives, such as extra pay for 'double orders' or 'bonuses', enable further efficiency gains for the platform. Changing the payment system for 'peer-to-peer' workers to a fixed fee significantly decreased their income. This is maintained through increased information asymmetries as couriers do not know beforehand the distance they have to ride:

Now it's a rate of €4.36 for every order. And I took a few screenshots, I can show you how far we sometimes have to go for that! [...] I lost 60% of my income in this new system. (Courier 37)

Finally, the platform's access to an 'on-demand' workforce is based on excluding couriers from social security:

Once I got sick, I had a fever and I couldn't work. So I didn't respect the assigned hours and [...] I ended up having no more work. [...] I tried to explain to [name of platform] what happened, that I needed to work because I had no more income. They told me that there is nothing they can do because everything works through the algorithm. (Courier 21)

Discussion and Conclusions

The chapter adds to existing research by claiming that digital technology is strategically used by capital to commodify the complex relationships between users and workers and to enact control. Central to this argument is the fact that platforms use digital data to increase efficiency in labour allocation and in the decision-making of clients and restaurants. We examine how platforms commodify the relationships between users and workers by illustrating the competition mechanisms accounting for commodification. We identify an 'empowerment cycle' through which the platform expands users' choices through marketisation and allows couriers to self-manage their working hours, and a 'disempowerment cycle' where the platform simultaneously constrains users and couriers through ratings and information asymmetries.

The platform thus offers freedom while exerting control, which has important implications for the production of subjectivity in platform capitalism (Armano, Teli and Mazali 2020). Our data illustrates that empowerment provides workers with some potential to act as agents, who often report experiencing autonomy in their work and sometimes identify as 'entrepreneurs'. However, we also show how this happens within the context of labour subordination to the platform. The platform controls and exploits workers, hence platform workers also experience exclusion from social protection and limited access to work and income. As labour is commodified, the algorithmic rating, monitoring and data processing mechanisms we identify translate into risks for couriers who continuously compete among themselves and are treated by the platform as 'on-demand' units. However, the same mechanisms also connect 'independently' existing workers and users with each other, giving rise to new relationships between them. The resulting experience of 'connectivity' might prompt workers and users to find new ways to organise and negotiate the conditions of their work (Leondardi et al. 2019).

The contribution of this chapter is twofold. First, we add to the critical strand of sociological literature which analyses the production relations within labour platforms, by illustrating the mechanisms of competition underpinning the commodification strategies through which labour is subsumed. Second, and directly linked to the former, we show how studying commodification is crucial to understanding the nature of 'work' in the platform economy. The current study focuses on one single platform within one single country. We therefore suggest the application of the empowerment-disempowerment cycles to different kinds of labour platforms as a potential direction for future research.

Acknowledgement

This publication is part of two interlinked research projects: RespPecTMe financed by the European Research Council (ERC) under the European Union's Horizon 2020 research and innovation programme (Grant Agreement number 833577), PI: Valeria Pulignano; and 'Precarious work in the on-line economy. A study on digital workers in Belgium and the Netherlands' financed by the Flemish Research Council, FWO (Flemish Research Council Project Number G073919N), PI: Valeria Pulignano.

References

Armano, E., Teli, M., and Mazali, T. 2020. The Production of Neoliberal Sub-jectivity in Platform Capitalism: Comparative Interpretative Hypotheses. *Sociologia della Comunicazione*, 59(1), 106–126.

Attoh, K., Wells, K., and Cullen, D. 2019. 'We're Building their Data': Labor, Alienation, and Idiocy in the Smart City. *Environment and Planning D: Society and Space*, 37(6), 1007–1024.

Basselier, R., Langenus, G., and Walravens, L. 2018. De Opkomst van de Deeleconomie. *NBB Economisch Tijsschrift*, September. Retrieved from: https://www.nbb.be/nl/artikels/de-opkomst-van-de-deeleconomie.

Blaikie, N. W. H. 2007. *Approaches to Social Enquiry* (2nd edn.). Polity Press.

Cherry, M. A. and Aloisi, A. 2017. Dependent Contractors in the Gig Economy: Comparative Approach. *American University Law Review*, 66(3), 635–690.

De Stefano, V. 2016. The Rise of the 'Just-in-Time Workforce': On Demand Work, Crowdwork, and Labor Protection In The 'Gig Economy'. *Comparative Labor Law and Policy Journal*, 37(3), 461–471.

Drahokoupil, J. and Piasna, A. 2019. Work in the Platform Economy: Deliv-eroo Riders in Belgium and the SMart arrangement. *ETUI Research Paper-Working Paper No. 01*. https://www.etui.org/publications/working-papers /work-in-the-platform-economy-deliveroo-riders-in-belgium-and-the -smart-arrangement.

Duggan, J., Sherman, U., Carbery, R., and McDonnell, A. 2020. Algorithmic Management and App-Work in the Gig Economy: A Research Agenda for Employment Relations and HRM. *Human Resource Management Journal*, 30(1), 114–132.

Gandini, A. 2019. Labour Process Theory and the Gig Economy. *Human Rela-tions*, 72(6), 1039–1056.

Graham, M. and Woodcock, J. 2018. Towards a Fairer Platform Economy: Introducing the Fairwork Foundation. *Alternate Routes*, 29(1), 242–253.

Harris, S. D. and Krueger, A. B. 2015. *A Proposal for Modernizing Labor Laws for Twenty-First-Century Work: The 'Independent Worker'* (Discussion paper). Brookings Institute.

Helmond, A. 2015. The Platformization of the Web: Making Web Data Platform Ready. *Social Media + Society*, 1(2), 1–11.

Huws, U. 2014. *Labor in the Global Digital Economy: The Cybertariat Comes of Age*. New York University Press.

Jabagi, N., Croteau, A-M., Audebrand, L. K., and Marsan, J. 2019. Gig-Workers' Motivation: Thinking Beyond Carrots and Sticks. *Journal of Managerial Psychology*, 34(4), 192–213.

Joyce, S. 2020. Rediscovering the Cash Nexus, Again: Subsumption and the Labour–Capital Relation in Platform Work. *Capital & Class*, 44(4), 1–12.

Leonardi, D., Murgia, A., Briziarelli, M., and Armano, E. 2019. The Ambiva-lence of Logistical Connectivity: A Co-Research with Foodora Riders. *Work Organisation, Labour & Globalisation*, 13(1), 155–171.

Marx, K. 1990 [1867]. *Capital*. Trans. Ben Fowkes. Penguin.

Moore, P. V. 2019. E(a)ffective Precarity, Control and Resistance in the Digitalised Workplace. In D. Chandler and C. Fuchs (Eds.), *Digital Objects, Digital Subjects: Interdisciplinary Perspectives on Capitalism, Labour and Politics in the Age of Big Data* (pp. 125–144). University of Westminster Press.

Möhlmann, M. and Zalmanson, L. 2017. *Hands on the Wheel: Navigating Algorithmic Management and Uber Drivers' Autonomy*. ICIS proceedings of the International Conference on Information Systems, 2017, 10–13 December, Seoul. Retrieved from: https://www.researchgate.net/publication/319965259_Hands_on_the_wheel_Navigating_algorithmic_management_and_Uber_drivers'_autonomy.

Pulignano, V. 2019. Work and Employment under the Gig Economy. *Partecipazione e Conflitto*, 12(13), 629–639.

Rosenblat, A. and Stark, L. 2016. Algorithmic Labor and Information Asymmetries: A Case Study of Uber's Drivers. *International Journal of Communication*, 10(27), 3758–3784.

Schor, J. B. and Attwood-Charles, W. 2017. The 'Sharing' Economy: Labor, Inequality, and Social Connection on For-Profit Platforms. *Sociology Compass*, 11(8), 1–16.

Schörpf, P., Flecker, J., Schönauer, A., and Eichmann, H. 2017. Triangular Love–Hate: Management and Control in Creative Crowd-Working. *New Technology, Work and Employment*, 32(1), 43–58.

Shapiro, A. 2020. Dynamic Exploits: Calculative Asymmetries in the On-Demand Economy. *New Technology, Work and Employment*, 35(2), 162–177.

Srnicek, N. 2016. *Platform Capitalism*. Polity Press.

Vallas, S. P. 2019. Platform Capitalism: What's at Stake for Workers? *New Labor Forum*, 28(1), 48–59.

van Dijck, J., Poell, T., and de Waal, M. 2018. *The Platform Society. Public Values in a Connective World*. Oxford University Press.

Van Doorn, Niels and Badger, Adam. 2020. Platform Capitalism's Hidden Abode: Producing Data Assets in the Gig Economy. *Antipode*, 52(5), 1475–1495.

Van Gyes, G., Segers, J., and Henderickx, E. 2009. In het Gelijke onze Verschillen… Het Belgische Collectieve Systeem van Arbeidsverhoudingen Gespiegeld aan Nederland, *Tijdschrift voor HRM/Nederlandse Vereniging voor Personeelsbeleid*, 1, 67–96.

Wood, A. J., Graham, M., Lehdonvirta, V., and Hjorth, I. 2018. Good Gig, Bad Gig: Autonomy and Algorithmic Control in the Global Gig Economy. *Work, Employment and Society*, 33(1), 56–75.

Wood, A. J., Graham, M., Lehdonvirta, V., and Hjorth, I. 2019. Networked but Commodified: The (Dis)Embeddedness of Digital Labour in the Gig Economy. *Sociology*, 53(5), 931–950.

Wright, E. O. 2000. Class, Exploitation, and Economic Rents: Reflections on Sørensen's 'Sounder Basis'. *American Journal of Sociology*, 105(6), 1559–1571.

CHAPTER 11

Algorithmic Prosumers

Elisabetta Risi and Riccardo Pronzato

Introduction: Platforms Everywhere

Today social life is increasingly lived in a digitally saturated world in which everyday activities and consumption practices increasingly occur in and through digital platforms (van Dijck, Poell and de Waal 2018). Within this scenario, social life is not only mediated, but also co-produced and shaped by algorithmic platforms, which work as performative intermediaries and surveillance devices of our online experiences (Bucher 2018). Indeed, platforms 'do not reflect the social: they produce the social structures we live in' (van Dijck, Poell and de Waal 2018, 2), i.e. they intervene in the way social ties are defined through forms of connection that mix social and sociotechnical norms (van Dijck and Poell 2013).

Etymologically, the word 'platform' derives from the Middle French *plate-forme*, i.e. 'a flat form'. That is, a horizontal area that encourages individuals to remain and lean on its surface. According to Gillespie (2010; 2017), this metaphor came into use around ten years ago and has been extremely useful for companies, such as social media services, as it allowed these corporations to promise users a 'open playing field' for participation, to provide advertisers with a limitless and permanent space through which to target users, and to promise regulators a fair and neutral framework for operations: in other words, a flat environment that did not require further external interventions.

How to cite this book chapter:
Risi, E. and Pronzato, R. 2022. Algorithmic Prosumers. In: Armano, E., Briziarelli, M., and Risi, E. (eds.), *Digital Platforms and Algorithmic Subjectivities*. Pp. 149–165. London: University of Westminster Press. DOI: https://doi.org/10.16997/book54.l. License: CC-BY-NC-ND 4.0

Today the 'platformization of the web' (Helmond 2015) is evident, and inside and outside of academia it has become clear that this flatness is only superficial: social, cultural, economic and power relationships are continuously modelled and reproduced by these infrastructures (van Dijck and Poell 2013; Beer 2017), which have become a pervasive presence in everyday life, and indispensable tools for individuals, companies and public institutions (van Dijck, Poell and de Waal 2018; Couldry and Hepp 2017).

As already highlighted by several scholars, critics and activists, these computational architectures constantly monitor and collect data from users in order to produce behavioural predictions (see Couldry and Mejias 2019a; Zuboff 2019). The main inputs that feed these algorithmic procedures underpinning digital platforms are (prod)users' digital traces (Cluley and Brown 2015), which are used with other data points to produce desired outputs that aim to stimulate user engagement, extend datafication processes, produce behavioural models and offer advertisers the opportunity to micro-target consumers ubiquitously and in fine-grained detail.

Everything we do online is datafied and fed into algorithmic procedures. On digital platforms we are ceaselessly exposed to practices of algorithmic identification and individuation (e.g. Prey 2018) whereby we become 'data subjects' (Ruppert 2011), i.e. 'measurable types' (Cheney-Lippold 2017) to recommend content to and from which to extract data. Algorithms *learn* from our digital footprint which content it is that we are most responsive to, and then predicts our future behaviours, thereby determining what we should watch and listen to (Pariser 2011; Seaver 2018a; Airoldi and Rokka 2019).

This process is recursive (Kitchin and Dodge 2011; Beer 2013; 2016). Users decode texts, photos, video, etc., i.e. the outputs of the machine; users react to these stimuli and also share cultural objects, such as pictures, posts and other items. All these activities produce data points that are reabsorbed by the platform to propose new content, which is in turn consumed by users. In other words, users' responses to the outputs of the machine become themselves a new input for the algorithmic infrastructure and are in turn embedded in every new human-machine interaction. Thus, the 'algorithmic culture' (Striphas 2015) that is produced by the platform feeds back to shape new habits of thought and expression.

Given the recursive relationship between individuals and algorithmic recommendation systems, uses (and users) of platforms are encoded into the design and functioning of platforms, especially in the field of cultural consumption and production (Hallinan and Stiphas 2016; Rieder et al. 2018). These data-based models have a dramatic impact on how people derive their sense of self (Cheney-Lippold 2011), as individuals are also subjectified by their relationships with algorithmic media and brought into being by computational processes (Ruppert 2011; Seaver 2017; Bucher 2018). Furthermore, commercial and media industries promote the activity of prod-users' content (Bruns 2008), a process that blurs the distinction between producers and users of content. Indeed, individuals share and create media content, which is then consumed by other users and datafied.

You Have the License, But How Does the Engine Work?

In several countries it is possible to obtain a driver's licence at around the age of 18. Drivers do not have in-depth knowledge of the functioning of the engine, but they are allowed to drive nonetheless. Indeed, most people acquire their driving skills by heuristically and practically learning on a daily basis until they are able to use their vehicles almost unconsciously and without knowing all the internal technical features. Generally, individuals become aware of their car engine in two different circumstances: when the car performs excellently, or when the vehicle malfunctions. In the latter case, the driver understands that there is a problem with the engine, although the issue is often unknown.

The use of algorithmic media in our everyday life often follows the same path. Individuals constantly use these artefacts without reflection or awareness regarding their functioning. Their presence becomes evident only when the opaque mechanisms underpinning these tools surface as errors, unexpected outcomes or disappointing results. When it comes to digital platforms, only developers are aware of the design and working principles of the software, while the general public use these infrastructures and feed them with electricity and personal data.

Several scholars in the field of critical algorithm studies have considered algorithmic media as 'black boxes' (Pasquale 2015b): tools that gather data from users, recommend content to them, predict their behaviours and impact their decision-making processes, but that are almost impossible to put under public scrutiny. Without entering the debate about the possibility of unpacking algorithmic media (e.g. Bucher 2016; Seaver 2017; Bonini and Gandini 2019), it should be noted that users have expectations regarding the functioning of digital platforms, i.e. 'what algorithms are, what they should be and how they function' (Bucher 2017, 30). Nagy and Neff (2015) define these presuppositions as 'imagined affordances', corresponding to expectations about how a platform works, what types of actions users believe are suggested and how these beliefs influence how users approach these technologies. This 'illusion of control' over the platform (Markham, Stavrover and Schlüter 2019) is then disrupted when those expectations are not met, for example when recommended content or an advertisement is considered as mistargeted, or a post does not get as much attention as a user expected (see Bucher 2017; 2018).

These encounters with algorithms highlight that digital platforms 'are not autonomous technical objects, but complex sociotechnical systems' (Seaver 2018b, 378), designed by humans and functioning with and through the data collected from users. These are in turn recursively influenced in their behaviours and feelings by these computational assemblages.

Algorithmic operations appear opaque because the crucial role of the people involved is often obscured and concealed under claims of neutrality (Airoldi and Gambetta 2018) and an unspoken idea of a sort of 'technological unconscious' (Thrift 2005). However, algorithmic media are pervaded by human sensemaking at every point (Seaver 2017): there are people debating computational models, programming algorithmic processes, adjusting the parameters, deciding on which formula to rely on in which context, and so forth (Gillespie 2016). Algorithms are complex socio-technical assemblages, obscure – but not inaccessible – systems which are human 'all the way down' (Heath 2015).

Studying the Engine: An Empirical Contribution

Platforms are not neutral intermediaries, as there are specific norms and values encoded in their design (Airoldi and Gambetta 2018). The main goal of these digital architectures is to favour, organise and monitor interactions between users, in order 'to amass a large and detailed [...] data pool that can then be mined for commercial use' (Barreneche and Wilken 2015, 507). Those favoured interactions become symbolical and cultural practices, behavioural norms and rules, in other words, 'shared cultural imaginaries' (Caliandro and Gandini 2017, 4) that are directly oriented by computational processes. Platforms 'regulate people, processes and places' (Kitchin 2017, 18) and include certain actors in their results, while excluding others, thereby favouring the emergence of a public culture that can be considered the outcome of the intertwinement between human practices and algorithmic procedures (Gillespie 2015; Noble 2018)

If algorithms are a ubiquitous, authoritative, and ideologically biased social presence, however, these infrastructures continue being mainly invisible to individuals, as well as being difficult for researchers to investigate (Beer 2017), given that they often appear to be almost (or actually) inaccessible (Pasquale 2015b; Geiger 2017; Bonini and Gandini 2019). Given this, this chapter focuses on the results of empirical research that aims to analyse media consumption, content production and sharing practices on digital platforms, carried out by Italian students. Thus, this research seeks to address the following research questions:

1. Which media usage practices emerge on digital platforms?
2. What are the practices through which young users share content online?
3. How do individuals relate to algorithmic procedures?

We adopted a qualitative method, specifically the critical pedagogical methods developed by Annette Markham (2019). This approach has a twofold goal: first, it allows the researcher to gather a vast amount of qualitative and first-hand data; and second, by making informants 'autoethnographers of their own digital lives', it favours a proactive process that should empower individuals (Risi, Bonini and Pronzato 2020). Indeed, this critical pedagogical approach aims to increase individuals' awareness regarding their activities that are carried out 'in cultural environments of growing datafication and automated decision-making' (Markham 2020, 227), thereby supporting a self-reflexive process and enhancing data literacy of the participants. In accordance with this research framework, 80 auto-ethnographic diaries of young Italian students were gathered.

The sample included 50 Bachelor of Arts (BA) communication studies students from the IULM University (in Milan, Italy) and 30 BA students from the University of Siena. All the participants were between 20–25 years old. The diaries were compiled in Milan between 27 March and 31 March 2019 and in Siena between the 13 February and 17 February 2020. The sample was gender balanced.

After lectures were held regarding digital platforms and datafication practices, the researchers prepared a narrative analysis sheet, which was then sent to the 80 participants, who were asked to report and reflect on their media consumption practices on a daily basis for five days (see Risi, Bonini and Pronzato 2020). The document included questions aimed at eliciting both reflexive thinking and a highly detailed and accurate description of their relationship with algorithmic media.

After collecting the diaries, they were analysed using open coding techniques generally associated with a grounded theory approach (Corbin and Strauss 2008) in order to shed light on individual practices connected with digital platforms, as well as on the subjectivities of users who spent a significant part of their time on them. The analysis of this contribution also focused on social media platforms and those linked to cultural consumption, such as music and video streaming platforms. This choice was not *a priori* designed but surfaced in a grounded manner from the diaries.

This study aimed to make a contribution to the field of critical algorithm studies. Within this growing area of research, several researchers are focusing on the societal role of metric measurements (e.g. Lupton 2016), and the role of algorithmic platforms in shaping sense-making processes and in the production of subjectivity (e.g. Beer 2016; Bucher 2018). More recent attention has also considered the issue of 'algorithms awareness' (Hargittai et al. 2020; Gran, Booth and Bucher 2020) and the extent to which people are conscious of a life shaped by algorithmic selection mechanisms (Eslami et al. 2015).

At this point, it is necessary to clarify exactly what is meant by 'algorithmic'. The term does not refer only to the algorithm per se, but to the role of algorithmic procedures in the construction and organisation of human knowledge and human experiences. In this case, therefore, 'algorithm' is a synecdoche. That is, we consider a social phenomenon that includes 'not just algorithms themselves, but also the computational networks in which they function, the people who design and operate them, the data (and users) on which they act, and the institutions that provide these services' (Gillespie 2016, 25).

Recently, Bucher (2018) suggested that algorithms should be framed as socio-material entities with dynamic and performative capabilities. This definition further emphasises the recursive relation between individuals and algorithms. Indeed, on the one hand, it recognises the role of computational logics and the people involved in their design; on the other hand, it also acknowledges the agency and sense-making processes of individuals that experience algorithmic operations in their daily life. Thus, this chapter argues that algorithms should be understood not only as the work of those who contribute to their design and implementation, but also as shaped 'through the way they become meaningful, helpful, problematic, opaque in and through what they do on a daily basis as part of the digital infrastructures of everyday life' (Lomborg and Kapsch 2020, 748). The following discussion will explore some of the results of this study, in alignment with this theoretical framework.

We Are the Fuel of the Engine: Looking Underneath Platforms

Cheney-Lippold (2017) claims that 'we are data'. On digital platforms, our complex social activities are transformed into a functional mathematical interaction of variables, steps, and indicators (Gillespie 2016; Zuboff 2019). Within this process, the social is transformed into 'a form that can be continuously tracked, captured, sorted, and counted for value as data' (Couldry and Mejias 2019a, 6). Our online activities are therefore the energy through which the algorithmic engine works. Without user activity, platforms would not function, as the engine (algorithmic procedures) would remain without fuel (data).

This chapter supports the view that platforms work to enact and support forms of datafied subjectivity, which allow a constant appropriation (e.g. Greene and Joseph 2015) and extraction (e.g. Mezzadra and Neilson 2017) of resources from human life in its entirety. However, within this process of datafication, users have expectations regarding platforms and may also actively interact with these algorithmic media (Nagy and Neff 2015; Bucher 2017; 2018).

In this empirical study, informants carried out thick descriptions (Geertz 1973) of their usage practices of algorithmic media. This rich material allowed us to examine not only the use of digital platforms in everyday life, but also the linkages of individuals with algorithmic logics and, more specifically, the role of the subject as an algorithmic prosumer.

Algorithmic Consumers: Platforms and User Agency

In the broadcast age, a typical usage practice connected with television viewing was channel surfing or zapping. This behaviour refers to the practice of viewers switching channels continuously in order to find interesting content or to con-sume snippets of different programmes; content that had been commissioned and scheduled by cultural 'gatekeepers' within the television industry. Today the practice of *scrolling* not zapping has emerged as the most appropriate way to describe the use of digital devices. However, while the content through which viewers zap on TV was selected by traditional top-down gatekeepers, content on digital platforms is filtered by algorithmic procedures that configure users' data feeds and determine what they see. Furthermore, when people use algo-rithmic media, their preferences are transformed into data inputs that power the algorithmic system, which, in turn, will adapt future outputs based on prior user behaviour. This 'socio-technical recursion' (Davies 2018) will enact the user's algorithmic subjectivity, which is ceaselessly reified within the platform (Prey 2018).

> *I was travelling on the train, I scrolled down, paying scarce attention to the contents on my Facebook newsfeed. I stopped only to like two pictures: both posted by a friend of mine.* (Milan, female)

> *Around 3.45 pm I took a break from studying and I went out in the garden to smoke a cigarette, I opened Instagram and I scrolled down my feed.* (Milan, female)

During this episodic consumption, which fills interstitial moments during the day (a trip, a break, a pause), algorithms alleviate 'the burden of choice' (Cohn 2019). No need to think, you just need to scroll until you find something on which you can (briefly) linger. Here the subject is an *algorithmic consumer* who fills time with algorithmic media content. From this acritical acceptance of the proposed content emerges a sort of 'pastoral' power (Foucault 2007). Indeed, algorithms operate as a pastoral technique in the Foucaultian sense, a type of power that optimises its functioning by training the individual to think and behave in a certain way, until such training is accepted by the subject as an internalised and fluid form of self-government.

> *I have lunch at 13.00 and I use YouTube once again. This time the algo-rithm recommends a stand-up comedy clip of Kevin Hart to me that I gladly accept.* (Milan, male)

> *I don't follow this channel, but the video was suggested to me in the home and, given that I'm interested in the topics, I decided to watch it.* (Milan, male)

> *She is another YouTuber that I don't follow but that the algorithm sug-gested to me, probably because in the past I watched the TV series* River-dale. (Milan, male)

Another view that surfaced from the diaries is that algorithmic logics are not only recognised, but also accepted. Indeed, participants appear pleased with the capacity of algorithmic recommendation procedures to identify relevant content for them because this automation relieved them of further decision making. A further key point emerges from the diaries. Algorithmic media undergo a process of *domestication* carried out by individuals. Originally, the term 'domestication' was used by Silverstone (1994) to highlight how television viewing practices were integrated within everyday life. Siles et al. (2019) readapted the concept to Netflix viewing practices and contend that, on the one hand, individuals try to domesticate the use of digital platforms in their daily routine (for example during interstitial moments, or lunch breaks); on the other hand – through datafication – *algorithms domesticate users*, within a process of 'mutual domestication'.

The constant and pervasive datafication of everyday life highlights how platforms do not reveal the subject, nor its data-materialisation, but rather enact a form of algorithmic individuation that is profitable according to platform capitalist logics (Prey 2018; Lüders 2020). User subjectivity is brought into being by algorithmic systems that monitor users and fosters their engagement in order to favour practices of data extraction and exploitation (Couldry and Mejia 2019b).

This process is enabled through a constant categorisation of user behaviour. According to Cheney-Lippold (2011), algorithms do not construct user identities based on fixed demographic data, but rather apply shifting categories which are continuously redefined by statistical (and opaque) correlations, which foster predictive behavioural models. Within this scenario, users have multiple layers of algorithmic identities based on 'statistically-related, largely market research driven' categories (Cheney-Lippold 2011, 170), which are constantly remodulated by competing interpretive machines. The work of 'profiling machines' (Elmer 2004), in fact, is to produce detailed and endlessly shifting consumer profiles in order to anticipate future needs of individuals, whose lives are constantly surveilled (Fuchs et al. 2012) and appropriated (Zuboff 2019).

Algorithmic Producers. Building Algorithmic Selves

While I was making small talk with a colleague, I scrolled down my Instagram feed and I liked a post in which I had been tagged by a friend, and I commented on it with a heart emoji […] I checked how many likes the picture in which I was tagged had obtained. (Milan, female)

At 9.10am I opened YouTube to see a 'like' that a user put on a comment I wrote under a Red Dead Redemption 2 *video.* (Milan, male)

Returning to agency, it should be noted that when individuals play the role of producers of content on social media, they show 'specific senses of agency through the interaction with algorithms' (Siles et. al. 2019, 4). For instance, participants performed 'micro-celebrity' practices (Marwick and boyd 2010), that demonstrate their concern regarding the role of metrics. This result corroborates findings from different authors (Gillespie 2014; Bucher 2017), which highlight that individuals understand and follow, seize and re-modulate social media operational logics to be recognised by the algorithm, in order to be metrically efficient and, therefore, more visible on the platform.

> *I opened Instagram once to see two or three stories and check how many people had seen the story that I had uploaded the same morning.* (Milan, female)

> *Then, I checked the new notifications: I had 6 new followers and 4 likes for the last picture I uploaded a few weeks ago.* (Milan, female)

If individuals are translated into sets of data points and treated as such to feed the algorithm they, in turn, also treat other individuals and content as data subjects. Indeed, 'many of the modern categories with which we think about people and their activities were put in place through the use of numbers' (Lury and Day 2019, 19). This appears evident in our everyday life, for instance, when a restaurant is chosen because of the number of stars an online reservation platform has awarded it, or a product is purchased because of its 'visibility'. In this context, individuals are increasingly called upon to negotiate their reputation and 'to adopt an algorithmic self' (Pasquale 2015a), which is necessarily computational. Indeed, the construction of micro-celebrities is linked to an endless quantification of self. This trend can be framed as the product of the 'society of performance' (Chicchi and Simone 2017; Chicchi 2020), in which measurable performances have become a social imperative. Furthermore, these results highlight how the algorithmic management of personal shared content enhances a neoliberal subjectivity: users publish stories to gain visibility, and then monitor the metrics – the performance of their content within a competitive framework, in which certain actors gain visibility at the expense of others.

> *We went out for a coffee […] my flat-mate asked me for a 'photo session' while she was drinking a coffee.'* (Milan, female)

> *While I'm studying, I upload a story on Instagram with the books placed on the table in the living room, in order to 'inform' my followers that I had started studying.* (Milan, female)

Individuals expect to gain social visibility from their content (Bucher 2012), which is adapted and optimised to reach as many followers as possible. A performative predisposition for being continuously on display emerges from the diaries (Codeluppi 2014). Sharing information about themselves implies giving credit to the judgement of others, the very judgement required by those sharing practices (Bucher 2012; Marwick 2013). Thus, social media users expect visibility as a reward and when they do not obtain it, the outcome is disappointing (Bucher 2012).

> *I published a new picture on my profile, and I spent the following hours checking how many likes and comments it got. I have to admit that every time I decide to update my Instagram profile, I'm almost obsessed with how many likes that picture will get. I cannot avoid it [...] my mood can vary according to the notifications I receive.* (Siena, female)

Metric power manages us (Beer 2016) and convinces us that there are no alternatives. Receiving attention and visibility is a constant reward for scrolling, sharing and producing content. Content is optimised for digital platforms, performances measured with metrics, satisfaction expressed with 'likes' (Gillespie 2014). The subject is satisfied for an instant, for a post produced or consumed, then, it is immediately time to search for a new gratification, within a recursive feedback loop.

Algorithmic Prosumers

Given this scenario, we argue that users on digital platforms can be framed as *algorithmic prosumers*. Both consumption (e.g. scrolling) and production (sharing and producing content) practices are algorithmic as they both feed data extraction and content recommendation procedures. Thus, the relationship between individuals and algorithms is interdependent: on the one hand, users are fed personalised content by algorithms; on the other hand, users feed platforms by sharing and producing their own content.

> *I can confirm that all is algorithmic, nothing is casual. Liking a picture with 'a nice view' will result in at least three pictures with 'a nice view' appearing in your Instagram feed the next day. It's a never-ending loop, in which we users are the engine and the gears – we have a prosumer role.* (Siena, female)

Although only social media platforms feature user-generated-content, individuals may also be framed as algorithmic prosumers even on platforms that do not allow sharing practices. When users consume content (consciously or not), they produce data that platforms collect, analyse and exploit to elaborate their predictively inspired content and assist in their placement and selling of advertisements (Zuboff 2019).

Since the 1970s, companies have involved consumers in productive processes (Codeluppi 2012), while the term 'prosumer' emerged in the 1980s (Toffler 1980) to indicate the idea of consumers working for free for companies and collaboratively participating in the design of goods and marketing strategies (Ritzer and Jurgenson 2010). Recent contributions, such as from Zuboff (2019) and Couldry and Mejias (2019a), completely disprove the idea that there was any 'inability of capitalists to control contemporary prosumers' (Ritzer and Jurgenson 2010, 21) and they highlight what 'the costs of connection' are (Couldry and Mejias 2019b).

On the internet, data about user behaviour is modelled through predictive statistical analyses, which combine different data points to retain individuals within their data loops as much as they can. Search preferences, selected content, every click and second spent lingering on a post is tracked and combined to favour further interactions between users and content, as well as with other users. Not only social media, but every other subscription platform (video and music streaming services, booking apps, etc.) applies the same datafication and surveillance logics to offer personalised content. Thus, we argue that individuals can be framed as algorithmic prosumers as they ceaselessly participate in the improving and shaping of algorithmic processes. The selection of content by personalised media is based on prior user behaviour, which is combined with other data to produce algorithmic outputs, hence, individuals produce data while consuming, and these data inputs will be crucial for their future content consumption and production practices.

I realise that it's not possible to do without these devices that can ruin your life, but, at the same time, they make it better given their speed at connecting you with a public... (Milan, female)

In certain cases, individuals even seem aware of some of the surveillance logics underpinning algorithmic platforms. However, little is done to resist to them. In this scenario, algorithmic media are considered inevitable features of everyday life (Markham 2021) and they emerge as fundamental for the definition of individuals' algorithmic subjectivity. Indeed, users circulate content, join networks in order to participate in collective conversations and to express their opinions and ideas, establish connections with other users, and so on. Users emerge as algorithmic prosumers who both consume and produce content to feed an algorithmic engine, that, in turn, continues working in order to keep them glued to the screen and exploit every possible minute of their everyday life.

Conclusions

Digital platforms have become a ubiquitous and infrastructural feature of everyday life. Today, the boundaries of platforms are merged technical and symbolic fields that delimit specific practices, ways of relating and preside over new processes of signification of 'being together'. The construction and management of sociality that passes through platforms is not defined by a simple transfer of pre-existing dynamics into technological spaces, but it is shaped by the affordances of the platforms themselves, which circumscribe the possibilities and forms of relationships between individuals. Within this framework, platforms emerge as intermediaries that are *not* neutral because their infrastructures embed specific values and ways of relating to the world.

By drawing on 80 auto-ethnographic diaries of Italian students regarding their use of algorithmic media, this study analysed media consumption, content production and sharing practices on digital platforms. Specifically, we argued that the users of digital platforms can be framed as algorithmic prosumers. First, algorithmic consumption was analysed. From the diaries, it emerged that individuals continuously scroll through recommendations on their smartphones which are algorithmically personalised. Here the algorithm alleviates the burden of choice and helps individuals fill daily moments with a never-ending feed of content. In this scenario, individuals entrust their time to recursive algorithmic logics, which exert a pastoral power (Foucault 2007) on users, by which people are individuated and subjectified. Algorithms seem to proffer benevolent guidance and to be capable of guiding individuals in their decision making, always able to offer the ideal choice.

Next, we focused on algorithmic production. It emerged that on social media users perform micro-celebrity practices (Marwick and boyd 2010), and use a form of computational thinking to make sense of their behaviour. On social media it is necessary to be on display (Codeluppi 2012); measured performances are the rule, and metrics appear as an unavoidable feature of social reality (Beer 2016). Thus, it emerged that individuals think about themselves and their relationships via tracked metrics within a neoliberal logic that is encoded into the platform.

Finally, we argued for the merits of understanding users as algorithmic prosumers. On digital platforms, consumption, as well as production, are algorithmic practices that foster datafication and capitalist surveillance logics: users feed algorithmic media and are continuously fed by them within a recursive loop. Moreover, we make the case that individuals are also prosumers on platforms that do not overtly highlight sharing activities. Indeed, data is produced and then used for the exploitation of behavioural predictions (e.g. Zuboff 2019) on every subscription platform, not only social media. If in the 1980s prosumers used to participate in corporate initiatives to collaborate with companies, today individuals constantly participate (often unconsciously) in the remodelling, adjustment and calibration of algorithmic procedures, thereby becoming algorithmic prosumers.

What emerges in this context is an individual whose subjectivity is strictly connected to and enacted by computational processes. Platforms offer content that encourages certain processes of subjectification (see Bucher 2018). In turn, a user's subjectivity becomes highly affected by the content offered by platforms and, at the same time, it remains at the service of these platforms. Given these findings, we suggest that future and cross-cultural research continues focusing on the practices of users to get a better understanding of the relationships between subjects and algorithmic media. Platforms have become a pervasive and often unavoidable feature of our everyday life. To comprehend how they affect social life not only tells us something important about platforms, but also about ourselves.

References

Airoldi, M. and Gambetta, D. 2018. Sul mito della neutralità algoritmica. *The Lab's Quarterly*, 20(4), 25–46.

Airoldi, M. and Rokka, J. 2019. *Algorithmic Consumer Cultures*. Paper presented at Interpretive Consumer Research Workshop, 9–10 May 2019, Lyon.

Barreneche, C. and Wilken, R. 2015. Platform Specificity and the Politics of Location Data Extraction. *European Journal of Cultural Studies*, 18(4–5), 497–513.

Beer, D. 2013. *Popular Culture and New Media: The Politics of Circulation*. Palgrave Macmillan.

Beer, D. 2016. *Metric Power*. Palgrave Macmillan.

Beer, D. 2017. The Social Power of Algorithms. *Information, Communication & Society*, 20(1), 1–13.

Bonini, T. and Gandini, A. 2019. 'First Week is Editorial, Second Week is Algorithmic': Platform Gatekeepers and the Platformization of Music Curation. *Social Media + Society*, 5(4). https://doi.org/10.1177/205630511 9880006.

Bruns, A. 2008. *Blogs, Wikipedia, Second Life and Beyond: From Production to Produsage*. Peter Lang.

Bucher, T. 2012. Want to Be on the Top? Algorithmic Power and the Threat of Invisibility on Facebook. *New Media & Society*, 14(7), 1164–1180.

Bucher, T. 2016. Neither Black Nor Box: Ways of Knowing Algorithms. In S. Kubitschko and A. Kaun (Eds.), *Innovative Methods in Media and Communication Research* (pp. 81–98). Palgrave Macmillan.

Bucher, T. 2017. The Algorithmic Imaginary: Exploring the Ordinary Affects of Facebook Algorithms. *Information, Communication & Society*, 20(1), 30–44.

Bucher, T. 2018. *If… Then. Algorithmic Power and Politics*. Oxford University Press.

Caliandro, A. and Gandini, A. 2017. *Qualitative Research in Digital Environments: A Research Toolkit*. Routledge.

Cheney-Lippold, J. 2011. A New Algorithmic Identity: Soft Biopolitics and the Modulation of Control. *Theory, Culture & Society*, 28(6), 164–181.

Cheney-Lippold, J. 2017. *We Are Data: Algorithms and the Making of Our Digital Selves*. New York University Press.

Chicchi, F. 2020. Beyond the 'Salary Institution': On the 'Society of Performance' and the Platformisation of the Employment Relationship. *Work Organisation, Labour & Globalisation*, 14(1), 15–31.

Chicchi, F. and Simone, A. 2017. *La società della prestazione*. Ediesse.

Cluley, R. and Brown, S. D. 2015. The Dividualised Consumer: Sketching the New Mask of the Consumer. *Journal of Marketing Management*, 31(1–2), 107–122.

Codeluppi, V. 2012. *Ipermondo. Dieci chiavi per capire il presente*. Laterza.

Codeluppi, V. 2014. *Tutti divi: vivere in vetrina*. Laterza.

Cohn, J. 2019. *The Burden of Choice: Recommendations, Subversion, and Algorithmic Culture*. Rutgers University Press.

Corbin, J. and Strauss, A. 2008. *Basics of Qualitative Research*. Sage.

Couldry, N. and Hepp, A. 2017. *The Mediated Construction of Reality*. Polity Press.

Couldry, N. and Mejias, U. A. 2019a. Data Colonialism: Rethinking Big Data's Relation to the Contemporary Subject. *Television & New Media*, 20(4), 336–349.

Couldry, N. and Mejias, U. A. 2019b. *The Costs of Connection: How Data is Colonizing Human Life and Appropriating it for Capitalism*. Stanford University Press.

Davies, H. C. 2018. Redefining Filter Bubbles as (Escapable) Socio-Technical Recursion. *Sociological Research Online*, 23(3), 637–654.

Elmer, G. 2004. *Profiling Machines: Mapping the Personal Information Economy*. MIT Press.

Eslami, M. et al. 2015. 'I Always Assumed That I Wasn't Really That Close to [Her]': Reasoning about Invisible Algorithms in News Feeds. *Proceedings of the 33rd Annual ACM Conference on Human Factors in Computing Systems*, April 2015 (pp. 153–162). Association for Computer Machinery.

Foucault, M. 2007. *Security, Territory, Population: Lectures at the Collège de France, 1977–1978*. Palgrave Macmillan.

Fuchs, C., Boersma, K., Albrechtslund, A., and Sandoval, M. 2012. Introduction: Internet and Surveillance. In C. Fuchs, K. Boersma, A. Albrechtslund, and M. Sandoval (Eds.), *Internet and Surveillance: The Challenges of Web 2.0 and Social Media* (pp. 1–28). Routledge.

Geiger, R. S. 2017. Beyond Opening up the Black Box: Investigating the Role of Algorithmic Systems in Wikipedian Organizational Culture. *Big Data & Society*, 4(2), 1–14.

Geertz, C. 1973. *The Interpretation of Culture: Selected Essays*. Basic Books.

Gillespie, T. 2010. The Politics of 'Platforms'. *New Media & Society*, 12(3), 347–364.

Gillespie, T. 2014. The Relevance of Algorithms. In T. Gillespie, P. Boczkowski, and K. Foot (Eds.), *Media Technologies: Essays on Communication, Materiality, and Society* (pp. 167–194). MIT Press.

Gillespie, T. 2015. Platforms Intervene. In *Social Media + Society*, 1(1), 1–2.

Gillespie, T. 2016. Algorithm. In B. Peters (Eds.), *Digital Keywords: A Vocabulary of Information Society and Culture* (pp. 18–30). Princeton University Press.

Gillespie, T. 2017. The Platform Metaphor, Revisited. *Culture Digitally*, 24 August. Retrieved from: http://culturedigitally.org/2017/08/platform-metaphor.

Gran, A-B., Booth, P., and Bucher, T. 2020. To Be or Not To Be Algorithm Aware: A Question of a New Digital Divide? *Information, Communication & Society*, 24(12), 1779–1796. https://doi.org/10.1080/1369118X.2020.1736124.

Greene, D. and Joseph, D. 2015. The Digital Spatial Fix. *tripleC: Communication, Capitalism and Critique*, 13(2), 223–247. https://doi.org/10.31269/triplec.v13i2.659.

Hallinan, B. and Striphas, T. 2016. Recommended for You: The Netflix Prize and the Production of Algorithmic Culture. *New Media & Society*, 18(1), 117–137.

Hargittai, E. et al. 2020. Black Box Measures? How to Study People's Algorithm Skills. *Information, Communication & Society*, 23(5), 764–775.

Heath, A. 2015. Spotify is Getting Unbelievably Good at Picking Music—Here's an Inside Look at How, *Business Insider*, 3 September. Retrieved from: http://www.businessinsider.com/insidespotify-and-the-future-of-music-streaming.

Helmond, A. 2015. The Platformization of the Web: Making Web Data Platform Ready. *Social Media + Society*, 1(2). https://doi.org/10.1177/2056305115603080

Kitchin, R. and Dodge, M. 2011. *Code/Space: Software and Everyday Life*. MIT Press.

Kitchin, R. 2017. Thinking Critically About and Researching Algorithms. *Information, Communication & Society*, 20(1), 14–29.

Lomborg, S. and Kapsch, P. H. 2020. Decoding Algorithms. *Media, Culture & Society*, 42(5), 745–761.

Lüders, M. 2020. Ubiquitous Tunes, Virtuous Archiving and Catering for Algorithms: The Tethered Affairs of People and Music Streaming Services. *Information, Communication & Society*, 24(15), 2342–2358.

Lupton, D. 2016. The Diverse Domains of Quantified Selves: Self-Tracking Modes and Dataveillance. *Economy and Society*, 45(1), 101–122.

Lury, C. and Day, S. 2019. Algorithmic Personalization as a Mode of Individuation. *Theory, Culture & Society*, 36(2), 17–37.

Markham, A. N. 2019. Critical Pedagogy as a Response to Datafication. *Qualitative Inquiry*, 25(8), 754–760.

Markham, A. N. 2020. Taking Data Literacy to the Streets: Critical Pedagogy in the Public Sphere. *Qualitative Inquiry*, 26(2), 227–237.

Markham, A. N. 2021. The Limits of the Imaginary: Challenges to Intervening in Future Speculations of Memory, Data, and Algorithms. *New Media & Society*, 23(2), 382–405.

Markham, A. N., Stavrova, S., and Schlüter, M. 2019. Netflix, Imagined Affordances, and the Illusion of Control. In T. Plothe and A. M. Buck (Eds.), *Netflix at the Nexus. Content, Practice, and Production in the Age of Streaming Television* (pp. 29–46). Peter Lang.

Marwick, A. E. 2013. *Status Update: Celebrity, Publicity, and Branding in the Social Media Age*. Yale University Press.

Marwick, A. E. and boyd, d. 2010. I Tweet Honestly, I Tweet Passionately: Twitter Users, Context Collapse, and the Imagined Audience. *New Media & Society*, 13(1), 114–133.

Mezzadra, S. and Neilson, B. 2017. On the Multiple Frontiers of Extraction: Excavating Contemporary Capitalism. *Cultural Studies*, 31(2–3), 85–204.

Nagy, P. and Neff, G. 2015. Imagined Affordance: Reconstructing a Keyword for Communication Theory. *Social Media + Society*, 1(2). https://doi.org/10.1177/2056305115603385.

Noble, S. U. 2018. *Algorithms of Oppression: How Search Engines Reinforce Racism*. New York University Press.

Pariser, E. 2011. *The Filter Bubble: What the Internet is Hiding From You*. Penguin Books.

Pasquale, F. 2015a. The Algorithmic Self. *The Hedgehog Review*, 17(1), 30–45.

Pasquale, F. 2015b. *The Black Box Society: The Secret Algorithms That Control Money and Information*. Harvard University Press.

Prey, R. 2018. Nothing Personal: Algorithmic Individuation on Music Streaming Platforms. *Media, Culture & Society*, 40(7), 1086–1100.

Rieder, B., Matamoros-Fernández, A., and Coromina, Ò. 2018. From Ranking Algorithms to 'Ranking Cultures': Investigating the Modulation of Visibility in YouTube Search Results. *Convergence*, 24(1), 50–68.

Risi, E., Bonini, T., and Pronzato, R. 2020. Algorithmic Media in Everyday Life: An Experience with Auto-Ethnographic Student Diaries. *Etnografia e ricerca qualitativa*, 3, 407–422.

Ritzer, G. and Jurgenson, N. 2010. Production, Consumption, Prosumption: The Nature of Capitalism in the Age of the Digital 'Prosumer'. *Journal of Consumer Culture*, 10(1), 13–36.

Ruppert, E. 2013. Population Objects: Interpassive Subjects. *Sociology*, 45(2), 218–233.

Seaver, N. 2017. Algorithms as Culture: Some Tactics for the Ethnography of Algorithmic Systems. *Big Data & Society*, 4(2), 1–12.

Seaver, N. 2018a. Captivating Algorithms: Recommender Systems as Traps. *Journal of Material Culture*, 24(4), 421–436. https://doi.org/10.1177/1359183518820366.

Seaver, N. 2018b. What Should an Anthropology of Algorithms Do? *Cultural Anthropology*, 33(3), 375–385.

Siles, I., Espinoza-Rojas, J., Naranjo, A., and Tristán, M. F. 2019. The Mutual Domestication of Users and Algorithmic Recommendations on Netflix. *Communication, Culture & Critique*, 12(4), 499–518.

Silverstone, R. 1994. *Television and Everyday Life*. Routledge.

Srnicek, N. 2016. *Platform Capitalism*. Polity Press.

Striphas, T. 2015. Algorithmic Culture. *European Journal of Cultural Studies*, 18(4–5), 395–412.

Thrift, N. 2005. *Knowing Capitalism*. Sage.

Toffler, A. 1980. *The Third Wave*. William Morrow.

van Dijck, J. and Poell, T. 2013. Understanding Social Media Logic. *Media and Communication*, 1(1), 2–14.

van Dijck, J., Poell, T., and de Waal, M. 2018. *The Platform Society: Public Values in a Connective World*. Oxford University Press.

Zuboff, S. 2019. *The Age of Surveillance Capitalism: The Fight for a Human Future at the New Frontier of Power*. Public Affairs.

CHAPTER 12

Emerging Forms of Sociotechnical Organisation: The Case of the Fediverse

Jacopo Anderlini and Carlo Milani

Introduction

Shattering events and scandals involving the widespread illegal exchange and exploitation of personal sensitive data by private companies and governments, such as Cambridge Analytica, have had the side effect of putting commercial social media under the scrutiny of a broader audience.

One of the goals of this chapter is to contribute to the rearticulation of the debate around technology and in particular to critically account for the trend of ascribing ethical attributes to it, creating a polarisation between 'good' and 'evil' technologies. Information and communication technologies (ICTs) that open digital spaces for social interactions are probably the most debated: is 'social media' 'good' or 'bad'? In these terms, a technology is mistaken for its specific implementations, in particular what is called commercial social media. Indeed, digital apparatuses are not all the same. Global-scale social media managed by big corporations is often taken as the norm, forming the fabric of the most diffused digital environments, shaping their social relations. These tools, like any other technological tool, are not neutral but embody specific values and inner beliefs, through their underlying architecture. Design and infrastructure

How to cite this book chapter:
Anderlini, J. and Milani, C. 2022. Emerging Forms of Sociotechnical Organisation: The Case of the Fediverse. In: Armano, E., Briziarelli, M., and Risi, E. (eds.), *Digital Platforms and Algorithmic Subjectivities*. Pp. 167–181. London: University of Westminster Press. DOI: https://doi.org/10.16997/book54.m. License: CC-BY-NC-ND 4.0

elements contribute to a precise vision of the world, that (digital) tools help to achieve by enabling certain behaviours. On the one hand, commercial social media promotes competition, mutual conditioning between humans and digital tools, automatisms (Milani and García forthcoming). On the other, Free/Libre and Open-Source Software (FLOSS) for social media seems to open spaces to develop a mutualistic experience of digital relations. In this chapter we want to scrutinise this experience through three different dichotomic tensions, highlighting the relationship between the values and beliefs embedded in digital tools, and the psychosocial beings and relationships they foster: infrastructure (de-centralisation/distribution); design (mutual conditioning/mutual aid); and governance (heteronomy/autonomy).

Recently, academic literature has highlighted an emerging set of practices and projects that try to redefine the very 'nature' of ICTs, rethinking their infrastructure and scale, and the relations they embed between human-to-human and human-to-machine. These practices seem to have foreseen a relationship between humans and apparatuses not based on domination of the first over the latter, but on conviviality (Illich 1973). In this perspective, moving from the idea of appropriate technologies (Pearce 2012), ICTs are considered in their social, environmental, economic and political implications, and in their sustainability. Therefore, digital spaces become profoundly linked with local communities, delineating what has been called the 'organic internet' (Antoniadis 2018), an internet able to embody organic relationships and reciprocal organisms' needs, or 'commons infrastructure' (Baig et al. 2015).

In the wake of these accounts, the key focus of this chapter is the reappropriation of technology intended as a way to conceive 'appropriate' social and technical organisation, in opposition to the forms of exploitation and capture put in place by digital platforms. How do practices of technology reappropriation concur to prefigure new sociotechnical imaginaries (Jasanoff and Kim 2015), shaping not only digital spaces and infrastructures but also social interactions and relations? And in what ways can the reappropriation of social media engender forms of mutualism, not only among human beings (Kropotkin 1902), but even among human and technical beings?

To answer these questions, we will take into account the constitution and development of the 'Fediverse'. The Fediverse can be defined as a network of servers that share a common vocabulary and syntax (the open standard Activity Streams[1]) and a common way to interact between each other (a shared protocol, in this case the open standard Activity Pub,[2] meant for decentralised social networking). In short, the roots of the Fediverse lie in a common language, based on open standards, to exchange messages and to communicate: it is exactly because of this openness[3] – of the protocols to compose and dispatch messages – that servers are able to communicate between each other potentially without limits, besides the ones imposed by themselves. We could think of this as a more complex implementation, in terms of the types of messages and interactions possible between peers, of email messaging. Following these considerations, we can conceive of the Fediverse as more than a social network: a network of networks.

Our case study focuses on a digital community within the Fediverse composed of four instances of Mastodon, a Free and Open-Source Software for microblogging, which allows accounts – user's profiles – to publish short texts and multimedia content, with a limited number of characters. Each installation of the software is a node, called 'instance', which is able to communicate with other nodes in a network. This structure supports the interactions between accounts of different instances. This digital community has been at the centre of our digital ethnographical work since 2018.

Methodology

The research merges the perspective of the genealogy of technology (Milani and García 2017), revising the Foucauldian method of genealogical investigation based on the archive, with digital ethnography (Murthy 2008), intended as a way of studying digital technologies, and the interactions and spaces they produce, taking into account the interconnections between the practices they entail and the underlying technology on which they are based. This methodological perspective, especially when adopted in a multifarious, ever-changing environment, such as the digital social medium called the Fediverse, exposes the researcher to problems, concerns and anxieties we encountered during our research.

As has been widely discussed in the scholarship, digital ethnographies in-the-making involve a high degree of uncertainty and different levels of tension and concerns that, while being a characteristic of ethnographic fieldwork in general (Hammersley 1992; Fabian 1994), have in this context their own peculiarities (Markham and Baym 2009; Hine 2012). In this regard, following Beaulieu (2004), we can summarise epistemological and methodological anxieties in relation to three aspects. First, the accountability of the field: what is 'real' and how to assess it. Second, the presence of the researcher: her role and position, as well as issues concerning her distance, anonymity and identity. Third, the relation of the researcher to the field: how and in what ways the researcher participates with and influences social interactions in a digital space. Another important prompt from Beaulieu's account is related to the apparent opposition between two processes. On the one hand there is the traditional ethnographic practice of transcription, in which the researcher can evaluate and elaborate her experience of the field. On the other hand, available to the researcher is the mechanical capture of digital interactions across different types of media content, in a field – the Mastodon instances analysed – considered totally open to them. While the capture process presents hindrances *per se*, in our fieldwork on the Fediverse we had to predominately rely on transcription, for two reasons: first, to organise the stream of information coming from 'direct messages', 'mentions' and messages that can be restricted to certain digital social groups (i.e., one's 'followers', or the accounts of the same 'instances'); and second, to cope with the ephemeral nature of this type of content, which can always be altered or deleted by its creator. Furthermore, Wilson and Peterson noted that ethnographic accounts of new media have to face the rapid obsolescence of their very object of study (2002, 451). Similarly, we could say that the same happens with methodological and epistemological concerns: the emerging of diverse technologies and, as a consequence, of new forms of social interaction, often overcome and render obsolete existing problems of methodology, while opening up new ones. To face the constantly emerging challenges of the field, we assumed the practice of practiced self-reflexivity (Markham and Baym 2009) throughout the research to periodically assess our ethical and methodological choices in terms of positioning, involvement and influence in our digital relations.

In order to address not only the acknowledged 'messiness' of digitally-mediated interactions (Postill and Pink 2012) but also the specific openness and porosity that are constitutive of the Fediverse, we found ourselves giving form in our practice to a multi-sited – or rather 'decentralised' – ethnography of digital spaces. Building on the ethnographic modes described by Marcus (1995), we aspired to 'follow the flows' using a perspective that extends the idea of 'following the thing' to take into account the digital dimension. Therefore, we focused on the marks and traces that characterise the social interactions in digital spaces, being these streams of information data, signs or messages that circulate along the networks.

Embracing this approach, our digital ethnography moved from the examination of a singular Mastodon instance in the Fediverse to other nodes of this network, following the traces of digital interactions. During the study, we considered a total of four instances, mostly in the Italian or English language, populated by more than ten thousand accounts, of which approximately one thousand were 'active'. We defined as 'active' an account that logs into the platform at least once per week, information that is publicly available from the instance's statistics. The social context in which Mastodon instances initially developed is the Italian anarchist and radical left social movements and the hacking/hacktivism scene, loosely identified here as the heterogeneous consortium of people gravitating around the annual Italian Hackmeeting event (Anderlini 2018; Maxigas 2012). Since May 2018, the authors have been deeply involved in the life of the instances as members and participants, not only in digital interactions and conversations but also in 'offline' events, such as public meetings and gatherings. During this time, we collected field notes and various exchanges with other accounts. In order to respect the anonymity of the people involved, the names of accounts and instances have been removed and messages have been partially rephrased: references to these will be made stating the year and the type of message (DM, peers-only, public).

Infrastructure: (De)Centralisation/Distribution

Roughly speaking, three typologies of network infrastructure exist – *centralised*, *decentralised* and *distributed* – carrying different topologies and enhancing different types of relations. In real world examples, these ideal models are actually mixed, but it is useful to mention their respective characteristics.

Technical terminology almost always gives important clues regarding the social questions that are at stake. Centralised systems use client/server architecture where one or more client nodes are directly connected to a central server. The *client* is also called *slave*, while the *server* is also called *master*. This server-master/client-slave architecture is the most commonly used type of system in many organisations where clients-slaves send requests to company's servers-masters and receive a response. The psychosocial relationship implied by the centralised networks is of a commercial type (clients asking [to] servers) and implies a relationship of submission (slaves to masters). Clients-slaves cannot directly communicate: they need the mediation-permission of the servers-masters.

Centralised systems present a number of advantages both from the client-slave side (e.g. it has a terminal, a hardware directly connected and seamlessly integrated with the company) and the server-master side (e.g. the ease of managing and detaching individual nodes). But there are a number of disadvantages too, with significant implications for the kind of social relations they allow. In particular, vertical scaling on a global scale rapidly reveal its limits.

Decentralised systems address the weaknesses inherent in centralised systems through a replication mechanism, as shown in Figure 12.1. Vertical scaling is also possible in decentralised systems. Each server-master node can add resources (hardware, software) to increase its performance, leading to an overall improvement of the entire system. Performance bottlenecks are better addressed, because the entire load can be balanced. But at the same time complexity increases, bringing with it possible coordination problems. In

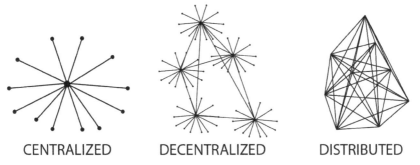

CENTRALIZED   DECENTRALIZED   DISTRIBUTED

Figure 12.1: Different forms of infrastructure. Graphical representation by Jacopo Anderlini.

decentralised systems too, clients-slaves cannot directly get in touch without the server-master agreement and without supervision. From a social point of view, both centralised and decentralised systems are clearly inspired by a domination logic that is also evident from the terminology used. Decentralisation is a technique used to improve system reliability and does not necessarily imply distribution. In fact, commercial social media can rely on a decentralised system of machines (servers-masters), without having to decentralise decision-making or give more autonomy to their users.

A third model is the distributed system. Nodes are connected among them, which means that they create a graph where every single node is directly connected to every other node. In this model, in addition to vertical scaling, horizontal scaling is possible: each node can add resources, resulting in an improvement for the whole network. Typical applications of distributed systems are P2P (peer-to-peer) networks, where each node can function as a server. The fault tolerance is maximised – nodes are autonomous, the network will still be functional even if several nodes disappear. Coordination and consensus are however more expensive and time-consuming because every node has the same importance. The infrastructure of the Fediverse is based on this architectural model: each node of the network could potentially work by itself while still being able to provide basic functionalities. At the same time, the connection with other nodes to form a network allows for a better redistribution of resources and new possibilities of interaction for its users. A certain degree of automation is possible within such a network, for instance if a node asks for more connectivity, the target node(s) can be programmed to automatically provide it.

However, in practice the behaviour of each node is not predictable, each node acts in its own way, with a certain degree of freedom, juggling between the need to help other nodes and the actual availability of resources. Unlike centralised and decentralised systems, there is no single point of contact, no hierarchical leaders who decide for everyone or for significant portions of the network. Each node has its own autonomy, and the greater the node's autonomy in terms of decision-making, the greater the robustness of the network.

Drawing on Gilbert Simondon's perspective on 'technical alienation' (2014), we are convinced that from a technical point of view, and contrary to some widespread representations, automation corresponds to a rather low degree of technical perfection. In contrast, 'open machines' are characterised by their openness: they integrate their 'associated milieu' into their functioning, and can, therefore, tolerate greater interactions with human beings.

The analysis of the architectural dimension of network infrastructures demonstrates how this impacts the material fabric of psychosocial organisation. Power can be centralised, decentralised or distributed. But technology does not determine *per se* the output – distributed networks are not 'better' or 'freer' than centralised networks. They just present a number of design characteristics that open a field of possibilities for the agency of both humans and machines.

Design: Mutual Conditioning/Mutual Aid

The design of digital interfaces is another element through which to understand the characteristics of communication in digital spaces. Interface design has become a 'battleground' that shapes human-to-human and human-to-machine digital interactions in a continuum that goes from dispossession to reappropriation. This continuum plots power relations. From one end, the interface can be put to work to increase behavioural automatism in order to 'free' the user from the freedom of choice: a relation of subjugation and gamified mutual conditioning between the human and the machine. At the other end, the interface can be designed to be convivial, self-organised, be able to open space for a relation between peers that takes into account the reciprocal specificities (humans and machines), and to develop interactions that are founded on appropriate technologies.

An example to better understand the role of the interface in shaping relations in digital spaces is the right to withdraw, to exit a digital space. The question to be asked is: can I close my account(s) on a specific platform? Can I erase all the information gathered by the platform? How much of this 'exit work' is difficult (technically, and in terms of time spent)? From a legal perspective, in 2016 the EU General Data Protection Regulation (GDPR) introduced, in Article 17, a 'right to erasure' – however in practice its application and enforcement seems to be limited to the jurisdiction of EU Member states. For example, an international company can erase personal data only from the EU version of its platform, keeping it available for other versions. However, legal loopholes are only the tip of the iceberg when assessing the problems faced by users who want to withdraw from digital platforms.

In the case of commercial social media, a common experience is the lack of clear information on how to delete personal data, to unsubscribe from the service or simply to log out. The path to achieve these goals usually requires many steps and it is 'hidden' in the interface *by design*. The overall goal pursued by this design is to discourage actions that would harm the interests of the companies running the platforms – especially any such interests that would impact on profits generated by selling data in the context of the data industry. In addition to this, many platforms require, through their interface, input from humans to validate or confirm their actions. This input often evokes emotional scenarios of loss (i.e. 'Do you want to lose all your messages and pictures?'), with a moral twist ('Are you sure you want to unsubscribe? Your friends will miss you!'). This kind of communication is a sort of 'emotional blackmail' based on what scholars have called FOMO – 'fear of missing out' (Przybylski et al. 2013). Indeed, the use of fearful discourses has been a constant in the promotion of closed, centralised advertising commercial ICTs (Sanvitale 2019). On the contrary, the entire digital experience with these platforms is designed to increase the time spent on the platform itself through mechanisms of gamified interactions and positive reinforcements: notifications that quantify social acceptance and boost satisfaction (du Boulay 2019); an interface shaped to minimise the effort and therefore the mediation to perform the action; messages to validate and encourage the digital experience.

The microblogging software Mastodon sits on a different point in this continuum, between a complete mutual conditioning which nullifies the spaces of freedom and the provision of mutual aid aimed at strengthening expressions of freedom. The design of the interface is not fixed but is a negotiable element that every user can transform for herself in the digital space, mitigating (or not)

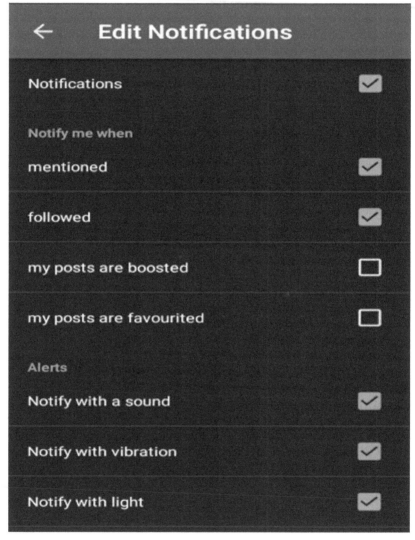

Figure 12.2: Mastodon's Notification Settings. Screenshot by the authors.

the elements that reproduce forms of gamification. Users can change elements of the interface for their accounts but also entire instances can set alternative interface defaults to shape their experience and interactions in the digital space. For example, an instance can decide to hide by default the number of 'followers/followed' or to fix a number for everyone.

The 'stars debate' in the Mastodon community highlights this. 'Stars' are used to *favour* a message written by another user. This action is one of the three that can be performed by accounts on a message, alongside the *retoot*, which disseminates the message amongst one's peers, and the *reply*, which allows users to engage directly in conversation with the author of the message. However, the use of the 'favour' action is ambiguous and has been publicly debated many times in the Mastodon community – at least five times, with long discussion threads on the topic lasting several days. While some users argue that there is no need for it – stating, 'I don't really use it. I don't need the star' (instance-only 2018), others refuse to use it, as a conscious reflection on the potential effects on fellow users, 'I don't want to use it. I don't want to trigger other people. I prefer to engage in a conversation, not to interrupt it with "medals"' (instance-only 2018). Many users, while mostly agreeing with the considerations on gamification, think that the star can be used to praise a message, to express acceptance with a limited risk of reproducing gamified dynamics: 'It is just a way to appreciate the contribution of someone. I am using it in this way, without abusing it' (instance-only 2019). Another common use of the star is less linked to a social dimension and consists in using the star as a bookmark for further reading or as a way to trace interesting conversations for oneself: 'I just star posts that I want to read later or that I want to find again in a while' (instance-only 2019). A widespread practice is the double use, as a bookmark and as a way to appreciate a message, mixing personal use and social acknowledgment.

Every time discussion moved to 'should the number of retoots and stars be displayed below a message by default?', the position varied. One proposal has been to refuse to show them to everyone in order to avoid what is perceived as a simplified interaction and to provide a different experience in comparison to commercial social media: 'I don't think we have to display this information at all. We don't need to quantify appreciation and show it to others' (instance-only 2018). Another has been the partial acceptance of it, limiting the display of information to the author only: 'I want the author of a post I appreciated to see that I liked it' (public 2018). One position that arose was to leave the decision to the individual, using the options, available to everyone, to change the software interface: 'Everyone should decide for herself if she wants to see stars and retoots or not' (public 2018). In general, despite the different positions on the topic, many members of the community showed an interest in actively experimenting with what they perceive as different or new practices in comparison with commercial social media: 'We test. We fail. We go back. We experiment. #gomastodon' (public 2019).

This approach to experimentation has been reflected not only through the individual use of interface elements in the digital space but also in the interactions and mediation of conflicts between different users, with common attempts to 'have a caring role in the conversation' and towards those involved. This diffused attitude towards self-reflection and experimentation in the use of social media, fostered by the possibility of altering the software interface, resulted in an increased self-awareness of users' digital experience. Many reported their experience with a different interface as a way to gain consciousness of digital space and their use of it, and also in comparison with their previous experience with other social media platforms: 'I have disabled notifications for stars for some time now and I can see I felt less urgency to look at notifications for "how many stars I got today" and I am more focused on the discussions. I also engage more in conversations with other people' (DM 2020). This aspect of empowerment of users is visible and also clearly arises in relation to the organisation and governance of the community.

Governance: Heteronomy/Autonomy

Due to its tendency towards a decentralised or even distributed infrastructure, the Fediverse facilitates a more horizontal and distributed governance by redistributing power and thus creating the possibility for more open machines able to shape humans' personal and collective identities – and be transformed by human interactions (Milani 2010). The possibility to have multiple instances using different software, whilst being able to manage with whom to communicate and interact, has allowed the spread of clusters of nodes that are associated by common interests and views. The very nature of the federation is built on the autonomy of each node. In fact, in the Fediverse, the federative process can be instigated directly by users through their interactions with those of other instances. At the time of its creation, an instance A displays only a timeline with the messages of its users. Then, a user of instance A starts to follow the updates of a user of instance B. At this point, instances A and B start to share the public messages of their users between each other. Hence, it is through the activity of users, who interact with those of other instances, that the original instance increases its connections. Each instance shows a federated timeline gathering public messages coming from interconnected instances. This means that the technical possibility to federate with other nodes is also dependent upon users. A technical possibility that opens – but does not open automatically –implies *by design* that there is a space for a more horizontal governance of the instance, from an organisational, political and psychological point of view, and this impacts on the processes of subjectivation of 'users' in the context of digital platforms. They can negotiate their personal data exposure and sharing; users have the power to desert a given role if it does not suit their needs. Their choices, situated in a distributed network context, influence and are influenced by the choices of others, thus helping to shape an appropriate socio-technical environment.

The ownership of the instance is in the hands of those who created and manage it, which can directly create clusters of federated instances – called 'relays' – or they can decide to *silence* or to *defederate* an instance. To silence implies that the messages coming from the excluded instance are not visible in the federated timeline for users of the first instance, while single users can still interact with those of the silenced instance. To defederate means that no interaction is possible, not even between individual users. These possibilities led to widespread initiatives and coalitions between instances to isolate other instances. Specifically, this happened with the 'alt-right', fascist, racist, antisemitic, sexist and transphobic network, 'Gab' (Katz 2018). On this occasion, a huge mobilisation of Fediverse users led to the almost total isolation of Gab and related instances, followed by an official statement by the Mastodon developer team (Mastodon 2019).

This episode highlights how the governance of the Fediverse is the result of actions and interactions between instances and their users and relies on the autonomy of each instance. It is reflected also in the internal management of each node, which can have a dedicated policy and specific rules for its users. In this case, the instances share a policy that excludes 'racist, sexist, fascist and discriminatory contents; nationalist propaganda or from institutional political parties; messages promoting commercial activities; offensive or denigratory messages, intended only to insult or threaten other users on a personal level; links to Facebook content; anything formulated without first thinking that the other users' sensitivities may differ from your own' (public policy 2018).

The founding collectives opened the governance of instances through meetings and a mailing list, to promote the self-organisation of the nodes. Through these tools, and constant conversations within instances, users and collectives experimented with a form of grassroot organisation of a digital space and the building of a variegated community. As previously mentioned, an important topic of discussion and decision-making has been regarding the interface itself: the boundaries of the digital space – an element that in commercial social media is taken for granted as a 'natural' aspect of the platform. Furthermore, the self-organising process has fostered a widespread crucial reflection on digital relations and the development of an ethics of care in order to create a more inclusive digital social space. This has been illustrated particularly in discussions around content moderation, and especially via the actions of administrators of instances to enforce the policy.

Content moderation is a practice broadly used in the regulation of digital spaces. It often reveals disparities between 'technical' and 'non-technical' users, producing relational dynamics that span between the admin 'patronising' and the user 'tipping off'. When instances were first set up, these dynamics had been partially reproduced: instead of engaging in interactions with users violating the policy, most users reported them to the admins. In fact, the admins are the only ones with the technical power to silence an account or remove a message. The ability to silence single users from their personal timeline, however, is available to every account, and this has been a strategy adopted when admins were 'too slow' to take action. During the 2019 instances live meeting, following several digital conversations, the idea of a more direct and collective engagement was discussed: 'Everyone should feel responsible for making this instance a safer space' (instances live meeting 2019). On this occasion, dozens of participants agreed to speak out more in the digital space in order to preserve it. To reduce the damaging effects of conflictual interactions, the idea of a 'white flag' has been adopted: when a discussion escalates and becomes aggressive or hostile, a third user intervenes, not taking sides, but in order to temporarily suspend the exchange: 'Hey guys, this conversation is starting to become a fight :whiteflag:' (public 2020).

The governance of the Fediverse appears as a complex balance between 'admin-users' relationships and instance-to-instance interconnections. Machines, far from being mere neutral supporters of human action, are endowed with specific characteristics and a certain degree of freedom in their associated milieu – in a sense, they belong to evolving companion species (Haraway 2003), involved in processes of identity co-construction. While the technical solutions provided by the software's and protocols' architectures can foster a more autonomous governance of the network, its effective realisation is deeply dependent on users' agency and initiative. Indeed, the Fediverse allows for the direct participation of its users in its management at the level of the infrastructure, a condition that on commercial social media platforms is simply not possible.

Conclusions

In this chapter, through the analysis of infrastructure, design and governance of social media we showed how practices of the reappropriation of technology can be mobilised to foster more autonomous forms of digital organisation encompassing both social and technical aspects.

The Fediverse appears as a *ligne de fuite* (line of flight), an always-changing way of building digital identities, individual and collective, that offers greater degrees of freedom compared to corporate social media. These possibilities of freedom, more open and horizontal, do not imply per se, in a deterministic way, that such communication exchanges and connections are open and horizontal by design, but provide – as technology does – spaces of possibility that can be inhabited or destructured through social relations in a stream of continuous feedback; spaces that still need to be addressed by media studies and STS scholarship. Further research, therefore, should focus on how elements of digital interfaces crucially affect the human perception and experience of digital space and at the same time are reflected in the development of technical tools and environments. In this regard, digital ethnography, as a research practice building on the empathic connections that characterise ethnographic encounters, is a fundamental methodological approach we deem vital to investigate the multifarious socio-technical interactions of this still unexplored field.

In conclusion, in the context of broader reflections on the platformization of societies, our approach emphasises the necessity to rethink human-machine relationships in terms of psychosocial technical alienation. The development of 'open machines', with degrees of freedom and as part of distributed networks, is therefore a crucial phase of a process to favour less alienated activities of subjectivation and the co-construction of identity – a liberated algorithmic self – and, more generally, to imagine networks of appropriate technologies able to enact mutual aid relations to work against platform capitalism or desert it (Mezzadra 2016).

Notes

1   See: https://www.w3.org/TR/activitystreams-core.
2   See: https://www.w3.org/TR/activitypub.
3   For a critical historical account on the concept of open standards see Russell (2014).

References

Anderlini, J. 2018. Hackit 98. *Zapruder. Storie in movimento*, no. 45 (April), 74–83. https://doi.org/10.5281/zenodo.4884627.

Antoniadis, P. 2018. The Organic Internet: Building Communications Networks from the Grassroots. In V. M. B. Giorgino and Z. Walsh (Eds.), *Co-Designing Economies in Transition: Radical Approaches in Dialogue with Contemplative Social Sciences* (pp. 235–72). Springer International. https://doi.org/10.1007/978-3-319-66592-4_13.

Baig, R., Roca, R., Freitag, F., and Navarro, L. 2015. Guifi.Net, a Crowdsourced Network Infrastructure Held in Common. *Computer Networks*, 90 (October), 150–65. https://doi.org/10.1016/j.comnet.2015.07.009.

Beaulieu, A. 2004. Mediating Ethnography: Objectivity and the Making of Ethnographies of the Internet. *Social Epistemology*, 18(2–3), 139–63. https://doi.org/10.1080/0269172042000249264.

du Boulay, B. 2019. Escape from the Skinner Box: The Case for Contemporary Intelligent Learning Environments. *British Journal of Educational Technology*, 50(6), 2902–2919. https://doi.org/10.1111/bjet.12860.

Fabian, J. 1994. Ethnographic Objectivity Revisited: From Rigor to Vigor. In A. Megill (Ed.), *Rethinking Objectivity* (pp. 81–108). Duke University Press.

Hammersley, M. 1992. *What's Wrong with Ethnography? Methodological Explorations*. Routledge.

Haraway, D. J. 2003. *The Companion Species Manifesto: Dogs, People, and Significant Otherness. Vol. 1*. Prickly Paradigm Press.

Hine, C. 2012. *The Internet: Understanding Qualitative Research*. Oxford University Press.

Illich, I. 1973. *Tools for Conviviality*. Harper & Row.

Jasanoff, S. and Kim, S-H. (Eds.), 2015. *Dreamscapes of Modernity: Sociotechnical Imaginaries and the Fabrication of Power*. University of Chicago Press.

Katz, R. 2018. Inside the Online Cesspool of Anti-Semitism That Housed Robert Bowers. *POLITICO Magazine*. Retrieved from: https://politi.co/2qpdV6B (last accessed 22 June 2021).

Kropotkin, P. 1902. *Mutual Aid: A Factor of Evolution*. Heinemann.

Marcus, G. E. 1995. Ethnography in/of the World System: The Emergence of Multi-Sited Ethnography. *Annual Review of Anthropology*, 24(1), 95–117.

Markham, A. N. and Baym, N. (Eds.), 2009. *Internet Inquiry: Conversations About Method*. Sage Publications.

Mastodon. 2019. Statement on Gab's Fork of Mastodon. Joinmastodon.Org. 4 July. Retrieved from: https://blog.joinmastodon.org/2019/07/statement-on -gabs-fork-of-mastodon/ (last accessed 22 June 2021).

Maxigas, P. 2012. Hacklabs and Hackerspaces: Tracing Two Genealogies. *Journal of Peer Production*, 2 (July).

Mezzadra, S. 2016. MLC 2015 Keynote: What's at Stake in the Mobility of Labour? Borders, Migration, Contemporary Capitalism. *Migration, Mobility, & Displacement* 2(1), 30–43.

Milani, C. 2010. Organized Autonomous Networks (Trans. C. Turner). *Cultural Politics*, 6(3), 269–86.

Milani, C. and García, V. 2017. Cryptogenealogia – Primo Frammento per Una Genealogia Della Crittografia (Dai Cypherpunks a Wikileaks). *Mondo Digitale*, 69 (April).

Milani, C. and Garcia, V. Forthcoming. AI Evolution: From Work Automation to Mutual Conditioning. *Journal of Extreme Anthropology*.

Murthy, D. 2008. Digital Ethnography: An Examination of the Use of New Technologies for Social Research. *Sociology*, 42(5), 837–55.

Pearce, J. M. 2012. The Case for Open Source Appropriate Technology. *Environment, Development and Sustainability*, 14(3), 425–31. https://doi.org /10.1007/s10668-012-9337-9.

Postill, J. and Pink, S. 2012. Social Media Ethnography: The Digital Researcher in a Messy Web. *Media International Australia*, 145(1), 123–34.

Przybylski, A. K., Murayama, K., DeHaan, C. R. and Gladwell, V. 2013. Motivational, Emotional, and Behavioral Correlates of Fear of Missing Out. *Computers in Human Behavior*, 29(4), 1841–48. https://doi.org/10.1016/j.chb .2013.02.014.

Russell, A. L. 2014. *Open Standards and the Digital Age: History, Ideology, and Networks*. Cambridge University Press.

Sanvitale, G. 2019. Fear of Falling Behind and the Medicalization of Computer Attitudes in Cold War USA (1960s–1980s)/Angst Vor Dem Zurückbleiben. „Computerphobia" in Den USA Während Des Kalten Krieges (1960er Bis 1980er Jahre). *Technikgeschichte*, 86(3), 227–44. https://doi .org/10.5771/0040-117X-2019-3-227.

Simondon, G. 2014. Psychosociologie de La Technicité. *Sur La Technique (1953–1983)* (pp. 27–129). Presses Universitaires de France.

Wilson, S. M. and Peterson, L. C. 2002. The Anthropology of Online Communities. *Annual Review of Anthropology*, 31(1), 449–67.

CHAPTER 13

A Workers' Inquiry into Canvas and Zoom: Disrupting the Algorithmic University

Robert Ovetz

Introduction

The pandemic has created the ideal circumstances for corporate consultants and 'edtech' venture capitalists, textbook publishers and online education advocacy groups to further automate, outsource and rationalise academic labour. This is being accomplished by widespread deskilling and automation of teaching in colleges and universities that harkens back to the massive privatisation of K-12 education in New Orleans following the 2005 Hurricanes Katrina and Rita and the pandemic.[1] (BCG 2020; Bay View Analytics 2020; Williamson 2020; Hogan and Williamson 2020) In 2020, as self-isolation and quarantines during the 2020 Covid-19 pandemic have suppressed the transmission of the virus, the turn toward remote work using new telecommunications technology such as the Canvas learning management system (LMS) and the Zoom teleconferencing app threatens to also sweep away many of the barriers to the spread of another epidemic – the digital automation and deskilling of teaching in higher education (Bailey 2020; Online Learning Consortium and Cengage

How to cite this book chapter:
Ovetz, R. 2022. A Workers' Inquiry into Canvas and Zoom: Disrupting the Algorithmic University. In: Armano, E., Briziarelli, M., and Risi, E. (eds.), *Digital Platforms and Algorithmic Subjectivities*. Pp. 183–200. London: University of Westminster Press. DOI: https://doi.org/10.16997/book54.n. License: CC-BY-NC-ND 4.0

2020). What we currently face is a confluence of forces that is accelerating the attack on the very academic labour of faculty in higher education, an attack that must be understood in order to devise the necessary tactics and strategies to counter and resist it.

Online education (OLE) in the US has been making slow and steady gains for the past decade. The number of students who have taken at least one OLE class grew from 8 percent in 1999–2000 to 18 percent in 2017 with twice as many in public institutions as in private (National Center for Education Statistics 2011; 2019). Nevertheless, OLE has taken a hit due to devastating reports of the 'online performance gap,' in which online courses in every academic discipline result in higher failure and drop out rates than in person courses, and the much hyped Massive Open Online Courses (MOOC) defeated by faculty at my campus, San Jose State University, after its first and only semester in 2013 (Johnson and Mejia 2014). The widespread reliance on conferencing platforms such as Zoom to move nearly all higher education into OLE has accelerated the process of imposing a new technical composition of academic capital on higher education. This necessitates that faculty and other academic workers shift our organising tactics, strategies and objectives to address the changing organisation of academic labour.

Conferencing platforms like Zoom and LMS's such as Canvas, which are driving OLE, are not neutral technologies. The emergence of OLE coincides with decades of neoliberal assaults on higher education through the commodification of academic knowledge production, adjunctification, austerity, privatisation, entrepreneurialisation and the shifting of costs to students and their families through skyrocketing tuition and fees paid for by massive personal debt. The relentless drive for quantitative assessment of research and teaching is applying intense pressure to further commodify and rationalise cognitive labour (Harvie 1999; 2006) resulting in 'redundancies' of tenured faculty such as those seen at the University of Leicester in the UK where faculty went on strike in 2021 and launched a global boycott of the university (BBC 2021). These represent the external factors placing relentless pressure on higher education to make it more effectively serve capital (Ovetz 1996; Harvie 1999, 106; De Angelis and Harvie 2009; Harvie, Ivancheva and Ovetz 2022). Alongside these external factors is the equally critical internal factor of the fragmentation and rationalisation of academic labour by OLE that threatens to undermine the very craft once thought insulated from attack – the human skill of teaching (Noble 2003).

This chapter offers a workers' inquiry of Canvas and Zoom in the emerging new technical composition of academic capital as the latest phase in response to the recomposition of the power of academic labour that accelerated in the 1960–70s. OLE is predicated on fundamentally shifting teaching and learning from assessment of *comprehension* of content knowledge to measurement of *proficiency* in task completion (Ovetz 2020a). There are two critical aspects to this shift. First, it is made possible by the emergence and ubiquity of artificial intelligence (AI) and communications technologies that are being used to reduce the reliance on full-time tenure track faculty while rationalising academic labour. Second, it is intended to produce more productive self-disciplined students as student labour power to meet the growing demand for precarious 'platform' or 'gig' work. The rise in organising among adjunct faculty in recent years will not be sufficient in itself to halt the emergence of this new technical composition of academic capital by continuing to rely on contract unionism that merely trades wages and benefits for control over academic labour. To know how to organise it is essential to understand the terrain on which academic workers now find ourselves.

A workers' inquiry (Ovetz 2020b) into the new technical composition of academic labour in the university understood through the lens of class composition theory is critically needed. A workers' inquiry is a method for studying the new technical composition of capital which reorganises work as a strategy to decompose the power of workers from previous successful struggles in order to recompose the relations of production so as to restore control over production. This new technical composition is immensely valuable in serving capital's need for workers sufficiently disciplined to carry out platform labour managed by remote algorithmic management tools. Understanding each phase of the class composition is critical for workers to devise new tactics and strategies to recompose their strength and shift power back in their favour (Ovetz 2017).

The Faculty Appendage to LMS

To understand the role of Canvas and Zoom in deskilling and disciping academic labour we can turn to Marx's analysis of the technical composition of capital[2] (1867, 481). His analysis of rationalisation was further applied by Braverman (1974) to the Taylorisation of craft labour at the turn of the twentieth century. Bringing both Marx and Braverman into the classroom, Foucault (1977) applied rationalisation to education as a strategy for the control and disciplining of academic labour.

The technical composition of industrial work, Marx explained, shows that 'not only is the specialised work distributed among the different individuals, but the individual himself is divided up, and transformed into the automatic motor of a detail operation', thereby transforming the worker into an 'appendage' of the machine and the factory (1867, 481–2). Marx's detailed analysis of the deskilling of craft workers in the rational organisation of industrial production in the factory is entirely relevant to understanding the rationalisation of skilled into deskilled academic labour today.

Braverman showed how the worker is transformed into the machine tender by the rationalisation of industrial labour designed by engineer Frederick Taylor. As faculty labour is assessed and rationalised, course design, delivery and assessment (McCowan 2017, 738) becomes fragmented and the pieces redistributed to non-faculty academic staff such as content experts, counsellors, course designers, technical support, programmers, and outsourced to textbook and software companies.

OLE is replete with examples of such rationalisation. In February 2017 I received a spam email from Norton with the subject line 'No time for grading?' promising 'our content, your course.' A May 2020 spam email from Packback further promises the use of AI 'to improve student engagement for community college students...while also automating some of the administrative faculty burden that unfortunately comes with managing discussion.' These two companies are not merely pitching their product to engorge their bottom lines but the rationalisation of academic labour by what Harry Braverman described as the 'separation of conception from execution' (Braverman 1974, 113–114). He noted how this takes place when 'the first step breaks up only the process, while the second dismembers the worker as well, means nothing to the capitalist, and all the less since, in destroying the craft as a process under the control of the worker, he reconstitutes it as a process under his control' (Braverman 1974, 78).

The 'datafication' and 'dataveillance' built into OLE provides a critical element in the rationalisation of academic labour (van Dijck 2014, 198; Williamson, Bayne and Shay 2020, 351). By transforming the complex multivariate aspects of teaching into tasks that measure the 'competency' of students represented in the form of data, OLE serves to operationalise teaching by rationalising it into disassembled components that can be redistributed to specialised staff responsible for highly differentiated technical aspects of the course (Mcfarlane 2011). What Marx and Braverman have taught us is that the rationalisation of labour is not simply about reducing labour costs, although that is of critical concern. The cost of labour is a factor of the *level* of control of labour power. Control is critical if capital is able to transform labour power from potential into actual work. Rationalisation is a strategy for decomposing the power of academic workers in order to discipline and make them work.

Foucault meticulously related how 'the human body was entering a machinery of power that explores it, breaks it down and rearranges it' (1977, 138). According to Foucault, the 'learning machine' exists for 'supervising, hierarchizing, [and] reward' (1977, 147). It breaks down the action of teaching and learning into its key components so that 'to each movement is assigned a direction, an aptitude, a duration; their order of succession is prescribed' (1977, 152). Finally, Foucault noted that the labour of the student and faculty are similarly rationalised as the complex supervisory role of 'the master' who assesses by the exam is replaced by the serialisation and hierarchisation of each task into a series along 'disciplinary time' (1977, 159). Although he died about a decade before OLE was introduced, Foucault might as well have been describing its impact on teaching and learning today.

Canvas and Zoom are two critical tools for implementing deskilling. This new technical composition can be seen in the rapid expansion of OLE run on the Canvas LMS and the delivery of courses through Zoom.[3] In order to understand the current technical composition of higher education a workers' inquiry into academic labour will be explored below by examining the structure and organisation of Canvas and Zoom for the algorithmic management of academic labour.

Canvas and Zoom: A New Technical Composition of Academic Work

A close analysis of the design of the LMS demonstrates how the process of rationalising academic labour is built into the digital architecture of the Canvas LMS. Although faculty appear to have complete autonomy to set up their LMS shell for their course, with a variety of possibilities to match their chosen pedagogy, the very architecture of the LMS is designed to fragment teaching into the delivery of tasks and learning into competency in their completion.

Constructed as a diffused virtual space of an online 'classroom', the Canvas LMS is not intended to simply mimic the in person classroom but replace it with an entirely different logic. Students no longer learn or study but respond to orders called 'prompts' in a virtual space in which their every action is designed to be treated as a measurable task. After 'logging in,' the student moves through the discretely organised spaces of the LMS differentiated by 'modules' that function as timed work spaces in which students write text, post a file, upload a video, download a reading, stream a video, or follow a link to material or work elsewhere, to name a few of the possible tasks. Because these spaces 'open' and 'close' at predetermined times, student work is highly regulated and regimented. A commonly used activity of faculty is to require students to respond to another student's text, work or video post. This not only serves to use students to 'prompt' other students to complete their work, it turns students against one another as little bosses that inform on one another for missing work, such as providing a response to another student's post. In effect, the isolated student virtually moves through the architecture of the LMS, disassociated from personal contact with fellow students, faculty and the physical space of the classroom and campus.

The LMS is designed for the virtually isolated student to self-discipline themselves by completing a sequence of tasks in the predetermined order established by the faculty member, course designer or content specialist. Because each student moves in complete isolation and solitude through the LMS, their 'learning' becomes a series of discrete, disconnected tasks to be completed during the window of time allowed. The apparent similarity of the use of time, such as due dates, to impose work in an in person class is deceptive because the LMS functions to achieve an entirely different immediate objective. Time takes on a different role in OLE by guiding the completion of discrete tasks that substitute for the complex inter-personal relationships that are central features of learning. Because OLE can use AI programmed by technicians to entirely bypass faculty, time becomes the predominant standard of assessing how students complete the now rationalised components of the curriculum. Just as OLE rationalised teaching into its component parts, the LMS becomes the technology for sequencing these parts and using time to measure the intensity and productivity of the tasks which a student completes. The ability to time is the ability to impose and to measure work. Like Taylor's much despised stopwatch, the LMS is the mechanism for solving the transformation problem of turning student labour power into work.

Timing student work effectively assumes the ability to surveil it. In this way, the LMS serves as a mechanism of surveillance foreseen by Foucault's 'eye that sees without being seen,' today called 'dataveillance' or 'a form of continuous surveillance through the use of (meta)data' (van Dijck 2014, 198). In the LMS, students never know with certainty when they are being remotely observed, tracked, monitored, measured and assessed (Ovetz 2017). LMS software that runs the online class provides virtual 'eyes that must see without being seen' – the twenty-first century digital panopticon (Foucault 1977, 171).

An alternative method of measurement to faculty's perceived subjective assessment of the usefulness of student work is provided by the ubiquitous collection of data in the LMS. Just as teaching is shifted to competency, learning shifts to task completion under the guise of dataveillance. Just as the classic classroom 'made educational space function like a learning machine, but also as a machine for supervising, hierarchizing, rewarding' (Foucault 2010, 147), the LMS was designed as a data driven machine for the imposition of academic work.

Canvas's LMS 'learning machine' provides an unprecedented and rich source of granular metadata on both a student and the faculty's current work that can be used to measure, manipulate, predict, quantify and monetise current and future behaviour (van Dijck 2014, 200). From log in to log out, immense amounts of data are available to faculty, or anyone with administrative access, in Canvas and its integrated apps, as well as employers willing to pay for the data harvested by the emerging field of 'educational data mining' (Desai 2020, 1).

Canvas data is being analysed to connect discussion posts to grades in order to profile the personality traits, or what is called the 'social behavior of students' (Desai 2020, 10). Desai used a 'text mining process' to analyse student data mined from Canvas courses, distributed through the unsecured WhatsApp, and processed and stored on an external database (Desai 2020, 9, 25 and 42). Using the real-time Canvas Online Discussion Analyzer (CODA) interface available as a built in Canvas app, researchers conduct a 'sentiment analysis' on the quality of a student's opinion, connectivity among students and faculty, leadership qualities, friendliness, sentiments of opinion on course issues, and other student characteristics in a single course and across multiple courses (Desai 2020, 10, 34). According to Desai, 'CODA recognises the leading students in the discussions based on centrality measures and keyword usage. Centrality metrics correspond to the influence, leadership abilities, connectedness, and friendliness in the student network' (Desai 2020, 33). Promising to provide predictive indications of struggling students and the correlation between effort and grades, it also constructs a profile of soft work skills desired by employers and a surveillance tool that could be used by repressive governments.

LMS harvested data is immensely useful for what it tells us about student work. For example, the 'People' window contains a wide range of detailed real-time and historical data on a student's online work. In it, the 'Access Report' provides precise details about every step a student takes across every part of the Canvas site. The 'Analytics' page gives dynamic bar graphs on four types of X-Y axes or tables with precise days and times on each task, number of tasks completed, number of page views, number of actions taken, interactions with instructors and comparisons to the class median on each graded assignment. In effect, the student can be monitored for the efficiency, intensity, productivity and persistence of their work.

The 'Quizzes' tab provides a range of similar aggregate data in spreadsheet format on how each student engaged with every question in a multiple choice exam. Second by second data is available for every action a student takes while completing an exam under the 'Speed Grader' 'Action Log'. An 'Item Analysis' is available which contrasts how each student performed on every exam question, for example, relative to the other two thirds of the class, and includes the variance, standard deviation, difficulty index and a distractor point biserial correlation. This last factor is intended to identify a reliable answer based on each students' answer choice in order to provide an objective measurement that discriminates between a student who mastered the material on the exam and those that did not. This function allows a students' work to be measured in comparison to other students' outcomes rather than assessed by the faculty according to their own personal attributes of learning, which are notoriously difficult to assess and evade comparability and standardisation.

The Canvas LMS is invaluable for generating vast amounts of data on student work habits, which is critical to the deskilling of academic labour and the shift from learning to competency. In the version of Canvas available to me there are literally hundreds of available integrable apps under 'Settings' that I can request to automate virtually any aspect of the course such as inserting standardised content, grade exams, issue badges, access user and exam data, acquire biometrics, assign peer evaluations, take polls, grading papers, post grading comments and tutor.

The apps Dropout Detective and MyCoursEval stand out for their accumulation of data on both faculty and student work. According to the corporate text embedded in the app, Dropout Detective 'integrates with a school's existing learning management systems and analyses student performance and behavior across ALL courses in which they may be enrolled'. The corporate text for MyCoursEval promises to allow real-time student evaluation of faculty by being embedded in the LMS. Both Canvas apps are just two of many intended to provide immediate dataveillance of faculty and students to evaluate the productivity of their labour by producing daily more than 280 million rows of data. Canvas is hosted on Amazon Web Services servers giving commercial access to mountains of data about student work to anyone who wishes to pay for it. In fact, Canvas's privacy policy discloses the use of cookies, web beacons, and third party hosting to gather, store and link data to 'personally identifiable information' (Marachi and Quill 2020, 421, 423, 425). The integration of data from within and outside the classroom is offered by Solutionpath's StREAM (Student Retention, Engagement, Attainment and Monitoring), which provides a real-time 'engagement score' for students based on in class activity, Radio-Frequency Identification (RFID) card swipes, attendance and even library check outs, providing a ubiquitous surveillance of productivity of all aspects of students' lives (Williamson 2020). Student awareness of the potential of being monitored, even when they are not sure precisely when they are actually being surveilled, is the power of Canvas. This serves as a velvet glove to self-discipline and self-imposed work, which is what makes OLE so valuable as a technology for producing measurable, disciplined labour for platform work. Students who have taken some OLE courses and graduated provide rich data to a future employer of their ability to work and presumably internalise the procedures for working under algorithmic management regimes. The Boston Consulting Group (BCG) and Arizona State University (ASU) asks us to 'imagine the implications for higher education' from the application of 'Amazon's predictive models of human behavior' (BCG and ASU 2018, 3). Perhaps BCG and ASU are unaware that Instructure, the company that owns Canvas, has not just stopped at imagining this integration but is actually doing it.

The persistent problem of student refusal to work can be identified in the high rate of drop outs and F's in OLE courses and poor performance relative to in person classes (Johnson and Mejia 2014, 1; Barshay 2015). This gap is partially attributed to 'difficult to measure' student characteristics such as 'self-directed learning skills,' motivation, ability and time management. Each of these factors can be understood in class terms as tactical refusals of school work (Johnson and Mejia 2014, 8). The prevalence of such refusals raises doubt about whether Canvas has effectively solved the transformation problem of turning labour power into work.

As a result of forcing countless thousands of professors and millions of students online during the 2020 pandemic, the numbers taking online courses reportedly grew 500 percent literally overnight. While the LMS infrastructure was already in a place, a new tool was quickly added to it, even making inroads into the nearly impenetrable arena of public K-12 education. Zoom, Google Hangouts, GoToMeeting, Big Blue Button and Jitsi teleconference tools suddenly moved from being obscure business tools into the mainstream as OLE delivery mechanisms. At the top of the teleconferencing market sits Zoom, which received immense scrutiny due to a takeover bid by a hedge fund in early 2020.

Zoom adds yet another layer of dataveillance of faculty and students that streams into the already immense ocean of data accessible through Canvas, according to Marachi and Quill (2020). Zoom uses AI to scan the location of the user through the camera and microphone, can turn on and override the host's security settings, can turn on the camera without the consent of the user, tracks users even when the app is turned off, installs a local server on users' devices and is vulnerable to hacking now known as 'Zoombombing' (Ovetz 2022). Among the possible sources of data harvested by Zoom could be measures of bodily motion, eye-tracking and emotion detection (Haw 2019). What has escaped all attention, however, is that like the LMS into which it is integrated, Zoom accumulates data that is now available to administrators and potential employers and can be used for measuring and discipling academic labour power. This connection is explicitly illustrated by Instructure's recent purchase of the integrated app Portfolium which directly provides data on student achievement and competency to employers (Marachi and Quill 2020, 428; Hill 2019).

To make their service valuable to potential employers, Canvas and Zoom accumulate data that is being integrated with data from plagiarism detection apps, learning analytics and outcomes, attendance, social media, credit records and other sources of metadata. This data can be further combined with the growing plethora of student IDs with RFID tags and licence plate readers that can track a student's activity and work outside the classroom or LMS. In short, the granular data generated by a student's movement through every module and task of the online course makes the LMS a rich kernel of data on the effectiveness, efficiency and productivity of a student's work. Rather than demonstrate student learning, the massive data being accumulated about each student is designed to measure their work habits, efficiency, productivity and most importantly their willingness to work. 'New organizations have even suggested that it may be possible to quantify the value of every university module, course or career choice and, by consolidating a permanent record of students' qualifications and skills from across the whole educational 'supply chain' – as 'learner wallets' hosted on blockchain technologies – offer AI-enhanced employability advice and enable students to securely share their data with employers' (Williamson, Bayne and Shay 2020, 355). Such rich data on each individual student is likely to follow a student through their lifetime as a commercially available 'work record score' that will determinately shape their life outcomes. The architecture of OLE is designed to provide an alternative to assessment exclusively controlled by faculty and institutions of higher education, what Wang long ago famously denounced as 'monopolies' subject to legally mandated unbundling (Wang 1975). OLE, the Canvas LMS and Zoom are transforming faculty academic labour into less about teaching than a machine tender for the remote monitoring, measuring, assessing, processing and delivery of disciplined unwaged student labour power.

From Online Education to Gig Work

OLE is central to the strategy to impose a new technical composition of capital in higher education (Ovetz 2020a). The US labour market is rapidly moving to contingent part-time, temporary contract work in which increasing numbers of workers, as much as 30–40 percent of the US labour force, work remotely and are monitored and managed by information technology (*The Economist* 2015). This rapid growth of contingent and platform labour is intended to make the Northern labour force become more like workers in the South where about 84 percent of India's 470 million workers, for example, are 'casual' or self-employed, or contingent (Ness 2015, 85). The adjunctification and rationalisation of academic labour in higher education is not an exception to this new global division of labour, it is actually the model for it.

The short-lived MOOC functioned at the extreme end of OLE allowing tens of thousands of students to select an online class from a higher education 'platform' through which an adjunct professor delivers pre-packaged standardised lessons. Students have no interaction with the professor or one another, and take exams 'assessed' by a computer program in order to earn a 'badge'. Although it has all but disappeared from discussion since its high-profile defeat at San Jose State University in 2013, the MOOC remains the ultimate objective of achieving the professor- and classroom-less 'university' by enclosing all public higher education within an Uber-style platform system for distributing courses in which the content specialist is paid by the head according to surge pricing (Hall 2018, 22–29). Those seeking to rationalise college and university teaching are taking the 'long march' through these institutions by using crises like the 2008 recession and the Covid-19 pandemic to accelerate the move to OLE.

Changes in the organisation, methods, processes and strategies for organising work are intended to decompose the power of academic workers (Ovetz 2020a). Because the labour-intensive teaching and learning that comes from human interaction, social relationships and emotional and intellectual exchange is lacking in the LMS, *teaching* is rapidly becoming deskilled into *assessment, measurement* and *monitoring* while *learning* is being replaced by *competency* of *task completion* (Ovetz 2020a).

This deskilling shows itself in the ever-increasing focus on measuring task completion which becomes a self-fulfilling prophecy that is transforming how we define teaching and learning. According to Ben Williamson, Sian Bayne and Suellen Shay, 'The fact that some aspects of learning are easier to measure than others might result in simplistic, surface level elements taking on a more prominent role in determining what counts as success … As a result, higher order, extended, and creative thinking may be undermined by processes that favor formulaic adherence to static rubrics' (Young 2020, 5). Learning itself is being redefined and stripped down to the quantifiable completion of tasks.

The reduction of learning and teaching to task completion and task monitoring is intended to produce a larger and more self-disciplined work force.

Trained to work remotely with no apparent oversight, OLE and precarious gig or platform work have evolved into illustrations of the emerging new technical composition of capital. The need for a larger self-disciplined workforce is the outcome of four decades of educational 'reform' going back to the 1983 National Commission on Excellence in Education's *A Nation at Risk* report. While layoffs, class size increases and budget cuts extract more academic labour from faculty, the other objective of reformers has been to produce more 'work ready' college graduates for the labour market. In class terms, it is a strategy to produce more productive academic workers who can work remotely, submit to precarious 'flexible' working conditions and are self-disciplined by the presence of ubiquitous algorithmic surveillance. To achieve this outcome, the primary impediment must be moved out of the way. That impediment is the relatively well-organised faculty who labour in marginally democratic institutions subjected to shared governance and union contracts which provide them with a semblance of autonomy over the content, delivery and assessment of academic work.

Reformers commonly resort to hyperbole about campuses being populated by unruly students, grade inflating faculty and graduates who can't or won't work. Such language underscores the intention of using OLE to automate the disciplining of labour power in the abstract, or what Marxists call 'immaterial labour'. OLE is the strategic response to what Massimo De Angelis and David Harvie call the struggle over measurement. Such tools 'help shape *the form* of academic labour in both educational and research contexts. They do so by counter-posing the measures of capital, which privilege the meeting of abstractly defined targets (whether these indicate financial viability or consistency with government policies), to the immanent measures of immaterial labourers' (De Angelis and Harvie 2009, 20).

The intense struggle still raging over the form and purpose of academic labour is illustrated by the variety of strategies to measure and standardise immaterial academic labour. Among these approaches include faculty and student 'performance indicators' of 'student success': faculty-student ratios; progression rates; matriculation; retention; degree completion; guided pathways; units earned; student, college and departmental learning objectives; and even access and equity reported in periodic programme reviews required by government agencies and accreditation agencies. The imposition of these new measures of learning reflects the shift from the generation and transmission of knowledge to the competent internalisation of information by students. The professor is transformed from expert to foreman, from directing learning and knowledge generation to managing self-disciplined students completing increasingly standardised 'learning objectives' (Prendergast 2017).

The focus of OLE to produce more and better self-disciplined workers mirrors the technical composition of other sectors of the labour market. The logic of the technology that drives OLE is analogous to the logic of contingent labour, the self-disciplining of labour power that is always available for waged work.

As the proportion of the labour force that are contingent – contract, consultants, gig and platform workers – grows, higher education is being reorganised to produce the labour power to do that work. This emerging division of labour in higher education serves the emerging global division of labour across the spectrum from 'ride sharing' to the work of legal document review. Big Data is being used to rationalise every type of job from the unskilled to the professional, fragment it into its component parts, automate some of the parts and distribute the rest either horizontally to other deskilled workers, or situate them under the control of management. More of the work is distributed to informal 'gig' workers who are considered 'self-employed' because they are intentionally hired lacking any formal legal contractual relationship with the employer of fact. In an updating of the 'putting out' system described in detail by Marx (1867), these workers work remotely carrying out discrete tasks, lack immediately overt oversight by human managers, must possess the self-discipline to always be ready to work and are entirely responsible for ensuring their own reproduction and tools whether they have paid work or not. In his study of class struggle in platform food delivery work, Cant (2019) calls this new technical composition algorithmic management by the 'black box'. The new division of academic labour is designed to serve the global division of labour in which workers of all types – including professors – labour under the conditions of gig work.

Disrupting the Academic Black Box

Academic resistance to these 'reforms' now being pushed by the 'edtech' complex of corporations, administrators, thinktanks and government planners, has been primarily levelled at external factors and through emphasising the impact on loss of 'quality', declining 'outcomes' and high cost while almost entirely missing the primary attack on academic labour.[4] The implications of the rationalisation of faculty academic labour has been apparent since Troutt first pitched the professor-less classroom more than four decades ago in which 'an unbundled system assumes learning can transpire without students having to purchase the teaching function' (Troutt 1979, 255). Today, it is common to read about the 'automation of the profession' in which AI is paired with an entirely precarious faculty of 'machine tenders' delivering 'digitally mediated rebundled teaching' (Czerniewicz 2018). OLE is transforming teaching to be 'focused more on coaching and mentoring and less on content delivery' (Sandeen 2014, 5). The professor-less virtual classroom is attractive to universities that wish to be 'swapping expensive lecturers for cheap, versatile machines that don't go on strike, don't need sleep, and respond to students within nanoseconds' (Haw 2019). As a result, higher education faculty and unions have not yet grasped the full extent of these objectives for expanding OLE. What is missing in faculty union organising and resistance is that edtech advocates are not merely proposing to outsource teaching merely to make profits but to reorganise all of higher education to better subordinate it to global capital accumulation.

The first step to achieving this is to break the control of academic workers over teaching and learning. As Mazoué bluntly puts it, 'If we assume learning is dependent on teaching, and that teaching is an inherently labor-intensive activity, then we will never be able to increase productivity, improve quality, and lower cost simultaneously' (Mazoué 2012, 80). As long as faculty control teaching and assessment of learning, faculty labour is a critical choke point for disrupting the reorganisation of higher education.

LMS driven online education is only the latest 'reform' effort which is intended to rationalise and measure academic labour (Noble 2003). The outcome of a university education is not preordained because the struggle over measurement is a continuation of the struggle over the uses of academic labour. As De Angelis and Harvie remind us, 'capital's constant struggle to impose and reimpose the 'law of value' is always a simultaneous struggle to impose (a single, universal) measure' (De Angelis and Harvie 2009, 27). As the anonymous academics writing as the aptly named The Analogue University put it, 'we need to do more than merely reveal the darker side of these transformative neoliberal relations; we need to find ways to mobilise and actively resist them' (The Analogue University 2019, 1186).

Academic worker organising must take into account this new algorithmic composition of academic capital in order to develop new tactics and strategies to counter it. After three years of higher education nearly all going online, academic workers need to roll back any effort to shift the baseline and stop further deskilling of academic labour. Such organisation must begin with tactical rigidity and the application of leverage at critical choke points up and down the labour supply chain (Bonacich 2003; Alimahomed-Wilson and Ness 2018). Academic workers already possess power over both the operations of the university and the production of disciplined labour for capital. It is yet to be seen if it will be used.

Notes

1 One of the most significant pushes for moving and keeping higher education online is being made by the Boston Consulting Group whose Managing Director and Partner Nithya Vaduganathan has touted her efforts to 'develop strategic plans for scaling personalised learning' (code for online education) and 'supported rebuilding the K-12 system in New Orleans following Hurricane Katrina.' (BCG 2020) In fact, the massive shift to Zoom during the pandemic is modeled after the Sloan Semester online courses for Hurricane Katrina and Rita refugees organised by the Sloan-C project to expand OLE (Online Learning Consortium 2020). Due to disruption of the

education of about 1.6 billion students in 200 countries because of the pandemic, the edtech industry is expected to reap windfall profits estimated to double to $341 billion in total value, with online degree providers doubling in size to $74 billion by 2025 (*Business Insider* 2019; Holon IQ 2020; Hogan and Williamson 2020, 4).

2   Marx examined the technical composition of capital in detail in chapter 25 of *Capital* Volume I (1867, 762–870). The technical composition of capital has gained a resurgence in recent years. It can be understood as the current ratio of technology to human labour and the strategy, rules and processes for organising work and managing workers (Woodcock 2016; Cleaver 2019; Ovetz 2020b).

3   I focus on Canvas as the dominant LMS in the education market at this time.

4   The potential profits from the $600 billion higher education sector is so immense that investments by the 2,861 'edtech' companies then in existence grew 32 percent between 2011–15. Edtech investment in higher education was thirty percent of the total, just behind K-12. Ninety-seven percent of all investment was concentrated in just five countries, with 77 percent of that in the US with Canada, the UK, India and China composing the rest (BCG 2016).

References

Alimahomed-Wilson, J. and Ness, I. (Eds.), 2018. *Choke Points: Logistics Workers Disrupting the Global Supply Chain*. Pluto.

Analogue University, The. 2019. Correlation in the Data University: Understanding and Challenging Targets-Based Performance-Management in Higher Education. *ACME: An International Journal of Critical Geographies*, 18(6), 1184–1206.

Bailey, N. 2020. Disaster Capitalism, Online Instruction, and What COVID-19 is Teaching us about Public Schools and Teachers. Nancy Bailey's Education Website, 16 March. Retrieved from: https://nancyebailey.com/2020/03/16/disaster-capitalism-online-instruction-and-what-covid-19-is-teaching-us-about-public-schools-and-teachers/.

Barshay, J. 2015. Five Studies find Online Courses Are Not Working Well at Community Colleges. *The Hechinger Report*, 27 April. Retrieved from: https://hechingerreport.org/five-studies-find-online-courses-are-not-working-at-community-colleges.

Bay View Analytics. 2020. The Great (Forced) Shift to Remote Learning: A Survey of Instructors and Campus Leaders. Retrieved from: http://onlinelearningsurvey.com/reports/2020_IHE_BayViewAnalytics_webcast.pdf.

British Broadcasting Corporation (BBC). 2021. University of Leicester Staff Join Call for Global Boycott. BBC News, 5 May. Available at: https://www.bbc.co.uk/news/uk-england-leicestershire-56985258.

Boston Consulting Group (BCG). 2016. Following the Money in Education Technology-Infographic. Boston Consulting Group, 13 June. Retrieved from: https://www.bcg.com/en-us/publications/2016/private-equity-following -money-education-technology.aspx.

BCG and ASU. 2018. Making Digital Learning Work: Successful Strategies from Six Leading Universities and Community Colleges. Boston Consulting Group and Arizona State University, 20 April. Retrieved from: https:// edplus.asu.edu/sites/default/files/BCG-Making-Digital-Learning-Work -Apr-2018%20.pdf.

BCG. 2020. Education Experts: Nithya Vaduganathan. Boston Consulting Group. Retrieved from: https://www.bcg.com/en-us/about/people/experts /Vaduganathan-Nithya.aspx.

Bonacich, E. 2003. Pulling the Plug: Labor and the Global Supply Chain. *New Labor Forum*, 12(2), 41–48.

Braverman, H. 1974. *Labor and Monopoly Capital*. Monthly Review Press.

Business Insider. 2019. Global Education Technology Market to Reach $341B by 2025. Holon IQ Press Release, 24 January. Retrieved from: https:// markets.businessinsider.com/news/stocks/global-education-technology -market-to-reach-341b-by-2025-1027892295#.

Cant, C. 2019. *Riding for Deliveroo: Resistance in the New Economy*. Polity.

Cleaver, H. 2019. *33 Lessons on Capital: Reading Marx Politically*. Pluto Press.

Czerniewicz, L. 2018. Unbundling and Rebundling Higher Education in an Age of Inequality. *Educause Review*, 29 October. Retrieved from: https:// er.educause.edu/articles/2018/10/unbundling-and-rebundling-higher -education-in-an-age-of-inequality.

De Angelis, M. and Harvie, D. 200. 'Cognitive Capitalism' and the Rat-Race: How Capital Measures Immaterial Labour in British Universities. *Historical Materialism*, 17(3), 3–30.

Desai, U. 2020. *Student Interaction Network Analysis on Canvas LMS*. (Master's thesis, Miami University). Retrieved from: https://etd.ohiolink.edu/apexprod /rws_olink/r/1501/10?clear=10&p10_accession_num=miami1588339724 934746.

Economist, The. 2015. The On-Demand Economy: Workers on Tap. The Rise of the On-Demand Economy Poses Difficult Questions for Workers, Companies and Politicians. Leader, *The Economist*, 3 January. Retrieved from: https://www.economist.com/leaders/2014/12/30/workers-on-tap.

Foucault, M. 1977. *Discipline and Punish: The Birth of a Prison*. Vintage.

Hall, G. 2018. The Uberfication of the University. *Incite Items for Educational Iconoclasm*, Item 02, June. Retrieved from: https://inciteseminars.com/tag /education/page/2.

Harvie, D. 1999. Alienation, Class and Enclosure in UK Universities. *Capital & Class*, 24(2), 103–132.

Harvie, D. 2006. Value Production and Struggle in the Classroom: Teachers Within, Against and Beyond Capital. *Capital & Class*, 88(1), 1–32.

Harvie, D., Ivancheva, M., and Ovetz, R. 2022. The Political Economy of the Public University. In A. Maisuria (Ed.), *Encyclopaedia of Marxism and Education*. Brill.

Haw, M. 2019. Will AI Replace University Lecturers? Not If We Make It Clear Why Humans Matter. *The Guardian*, 6 September. Retrieved from: https://www.theguardian.com/education/2019/sep/06/will-ai-replace-university-lecturers-not-if-we-make-it-clear-why-humans-matter.

Hill, P. 2019. Instructure: Plans to Expand Beyond Canvas LMS into Machine Learning and AI. *eLiterate*, 11 March. Retrieved from: https://eliterate.us/instructure-plans-to-expand-beyond-canvas-lms-into-machine-learning-and-ai.

Hogan, A. and Williamson, B. 2020. Commercialisation and Privatisation in/of Education in the Context of Covid-19. *Education International*, July. Retrieved from: https://issuu.com/educationinternational/docs/2020_eire search_gr_commercialisation_privatisation?fr=sZDJkYjE1ODA2MTQ.

Holon IQ. 2020. The online degree market is one of the fastest-growing segments of global higher education, which we forecast will reach $74B in 2025. Holon IQ, 1 May. Retrieved from: https://www.holoniq.com/notes/74b-online-degree-market-in-2025-up-from-36b-in-2019.

Johnson, H. and Mejia, M. 2014. Online Learning and Student Outcomes in California's Community Colleges. Public Policy Institute of California, May. Retrieved from: https://www.ppic.org/content/pubs/report/R_514HJR.pdf.

Mcfarlane, B. 2011. The Morphing of Academic Practice: Unbundling and the Rise of the Para-Academic. *Higher Education Quarterly*, 65(1), 59–73.

Marx, K. 1867 [1976]. *Capital: A Critique of Political Economy*, Volume I. Vintage.

McCowan, T. 2017. Higher Education, Unbundling, and the End of the University as We Know It. *Oxford Review of Education*, 43(6), 733–748.

Marachi, R. and Quill, L. 2020. The Case of Canvas: Longitudinal Datafication Through Learning Management Systems. *Teaching in Higher Education*, 25(4), 418–434.

Mazoué, J. 2012. The Deconstructed Campus: A Reply to Critics. *Journal of Computing in Higher Education*, 24(2), 74–95.

National Center for Education Statistics. 2011. Learning at a Distance: Undergraduate Enrollment in Distance Education Courses and Degree Programs. NECR, October. Retrieved from: https://nces.ed.gov/pubsearch/pubsinfo.asp?pubid=2012154.

National Center for Education Statistics. 2019. Number and Percentage of Students Enrolled in Degree-Granting Postsecondary Institutions, by Distance Education Participation, and Level of Enrollment and Control of Institution. NECR, Fall 2017. Retrieved from: https://nces.ed.gov/fastfacts/display.asp?id=80.

Ness, I. 2015. *Southern Insurgency: The Coming of the Global Working Class*. Pluto.

Noble, D. F. 2003. *Digital Diploma Mills: The Automation of Higher Education*. Monthly Review Press.

Online Learning Consortium. 2020. OLC's Historical Timeline. Retrieved from: https://onlinelearningconsortium.org/about/pioneering-higher-edu cations-digital-future-timeline.

Online Learning Consortium and Cengage. 2020. Perspectives: COVID-19, and the Future of Higher Education. Retrieved from: https://onlinelearn- ingconsortium.org/about/digital-learning-pulse-survey.

Ovetz, R. 1996. Turning Resistance into Rebellion: Student Movements and the Entrepreneurialization of the Universities. *Capital & Class*, 58, 113–151. https://doi.org/10.1177/030981689605800106.

Ovetz, R. 2017. Click to Save and Return to Course: Online Education, Adjunc- tification, and the Disciplining of Academic Labour in the Social Factory. *Work Organisation, Labour & Globalisation*, 11(1), 48–70.

Ovetz, R. 2020a. The Algorithmic University: On-Line Education, Learning Management Systems, and the Struggle Over Academic Labor. *Critical Soci- ology*, 47(7–8), 1065–1084.

Ovetz, R. (Ed.), 2020b. *Workers' Inquiry and Global Class Struggle: Strategies, Tactics, Objectives*. Pluto.

Ovetz, R. Forthcoming. Zoombombing Higher Education: Resisting the Online-ification of the University. In J. Ramirez, J. Fehrle, and J. Lieber (Eds.), *(De)automating the Future*. Brill.

Prendergast, A. 2017. Did a Community College Plan to Pass More Students Fail its Teachers? *Westword*, 1 August. Retrieved from: http://www.west word.com/news/community-college-of-aurora-may-pass-more-students -but-did-it-fail-teachers-9317325.

Sandeen, C. 2014. Unbundling Versus Designing Faculty Roles. *Presiden- tial Innovation Lab White Paper Series*, American Council on Education/ Center for Education Attainment and Innovation. Retrieved from: https:// www.acenet.edu/Documents/Signals-and-Shifts-in-the-Postsecondary -Landscape.pdf.

Troutt, W. 1979. Unbundling Instruction: Opportunity for Community Col- leges. *Peabody Journal of Education*, 56(4), 253–9.

van Dijck, J. 2014. Datafication, Dataism and Dataveillance: Big Data between Scientific Paradigm and Ideology. *Surveillance & Society*, 12(2), 197–208.

Wang, W. 1975. The Unbundling of Higher Education. *Duke Law Journal*, 24(1), 53–90.

Williamson, B., Bayne, S., and Shay, S. 2020. The Datafication of Teaching in Higher Education: Critical Issues and Perspectives. *Teaching in Higher Edu- cation*, 25(4), 351–365.

Williamson, B. 2020. Datafication and Automation in Higher Education Dur- ing and After the Covid-19 Crisis. *Code Acts in Education*, 6 May. Retrieved from: https://codeactsineducation.wordpress.com/2020/05/06/datafication -automation-he-covid19-crisis.

Woodcock, J. 2016. *Working the Phones: Control and Resistance in Call Centres.* Pluto Press.

Young, J. 2020. Researchers Raise Concerns About Algorithmic Bias in Online Course Tools. *EdSurge*, 26 June. Retrieved from: https://www.edsurge.com /news/2020-06-26-researchers-raise-concerns-about-algorithmic-bias-in -online-course-tools.

CHAPTER 14

Plat-Firming Welfare: Examining Digital Transformation in Local Care Services

Davide Arcidiacono, Ivana Pais and Flaviano Zandonai

The Platform Firm: A Variety of Organisational Models

The birth of online platforms is transforming every sector of the economy and every facet of society from education to the media and from energy to personal services. The promulgation of notions like 'platform logic' (Andersson Schwarz 2017), 'platform society' (van Dijck, Poell and de Waal 2018), 'platform capitalism' (Langley and Leyshon 2017; Srnicek 2016) or, for the current context most aptly, 'platform economy' (Kenney and Zysman 2016; Kenney, Bearson and Zysman 2019) aims at indicating the novelty of an emerging socio-economic form of organisation (Grabher and König 2020).

The most widely shared definition sees the platform as a digital infrastructure that enables interaction between two or more social groups for the exchange of goods and services (Srnicek 2016); a more analytical definition is proposed by Grabher and van Tuijl (2020, 104) who define platforms as 'programmable digital infrastructures controlled by platform operators who, as non-neutral intermediaries, curate the interactions of interdependent complementors and users'. Research on platforms has mostly been developed within

How to cite this book chapter:
Arcidiacono, D., Pais, I., and Zandonai, F. 2022. Plat-Firming Welfare: Examining Digital Transformation in Local Care Services. In: Armano, E., Briziarelli, M., and Risi, E. (eds.), *Digital Platforms and Algorithmic Subjectivities*. Pp. 201–212. London: University of Westminster Press. DOI: https://doi.org/10.16997/book54.o. License: CC-BY-NC-ND 4.0

the field of media studies, through the study of infrastructures characterised by programmability, connection and data exchange through digital applications. Platforms may be distinguished from infrastructure primarily by the latter feature:

> unlike system builders, platform builders do not seek to internalize their environments through vertical integration. Instead, their platforms are designed to be extended and elaborated from outside, by other actors, provided that those actors follow certain rules. (Plantin et al. 2018, 298)

The emergence of platforms was initially linked to the tourism and transport sectors. More recently, this process has begun to spread into other sectors (Casilli and Posada 2019). Just as McDonald's became the symbol of globalisation (Ritzer 1993), Uber fulfilled the same role for 'platformization': the company's operating logic is being adopted in highly disparate sectors in a quest to create 'the Uber of...' a given sector. Concerns relating to the regulation of work in ridesharing/ridehailing platforms have focused attention mainly on issues in these sectors while aspects relating to the organisation of work and the social implications of the platform model have remained marginal, albeit with interesting exceptions, including Schor (2020), Frenken and Pelzer (2020) and van Dijck, Poell and de Waal (2018). The 'uberization' of the digital economy shows how platforms could embody a neoliberal subjectivity based on individual autonomy and proactive attitudes towards work and social life (Armano, Mazali and Teli 2020). Is this race towards 'uberization' also affecting welfare services? Are welfare platforms available for the last territory for neoliberal subjectivity to colonise? (Couldry and Mejias 2019b)

Our hypothesis is that the 'platform' is not neutral as regards the goods/services they act as intermediaries for. In particular, we would argue that: firstly, the welfare state has specific features that require the construction of organisational models at least in part specifically customised for individual service or for the sector (Flanagan 2019; Ticona and Mateescu 2018; Dupret 2017); and secondly, the users of welfare services have specific characteristics and needs, around which it is necessary to build a dedicated infrastructure.

Any digital transformation brings with it not only the risk of transferring into a non-material dimension what has always been tangible, but also the opportunity to target users previously excluded from the services provided. In traditional services, the main purpose of technology is to direct users' behaviour through standard processes, while in welfare services platforms, it should aim at enabling actors to participate in the design of the process, according to their degree of autonomy and capabilities (Fosti 2016). As welfare services become increasingly digitalised, citizens unable to use standardised digital technologies may start to face new forms of exclusion. When analysing the organisational models of welfare platforms, it is therefore important to take into consideration people's situated uses and practices (Oudshoorn and Pinch

2003), in order to understand how the design of novel digital tools at an institutional level could respond more efficiently to citizens' needs.

The adoption of this approach changes the analytical perspective; it is not a question of verifying the capacity of a sector to move according to an isomorphic logic along a 'platformization' process whose characteristics have been defined from the outside, but rather to investigate how able the sector is at building its own platform model. In this way, we want to observe how welfare platforms offer a novel type of welfare service governance and provision that does not replace the ones we know, but instead can support and integrate them, triggering the redesigning of services, organisation and governance.

Methods

The research was carried out through the analysis of the start-up, management and implementation of platforms as part of a series of community welfare projects. These platform projects were funded by the Cariplo Foundation in the Lombardy Region in Italy.

The territorial limitation of the research must certainly be taken into consideration when evaluating the results achieved. At the same time, literature on the platform model is predominantly based on examples from the United States and this study can contribute to the analysis of the role of local ecosystems in the spread of digital platforms and in their global and local variants. Furthermore, we believe that on this issue, the strong tradition of the Italian 'for benefit' sector can also provide an original contribution to the international debate.

The research focused on five projects: 'Mi fido di noi', a time bank for the exchange of goods and skills; 'La cura è di casa', which aims to provide tools for collecting reports relating to frail, elderly people and the preparation of Care Plans; 'Bacheca digitale', which collects services in the areas of housing, food, work and civic participation to make them available to social workers and direct beneficiaries of the project; 'Family Like' for matching supply and demand for services and events aimed at families with young children; and 'WeMi' which provides a single point of offering welfare services to the home.

The research path took its cue from the platform model as it was implemented in the private sector, and then differentiated with respect to the specificities of welfare, paying particular attention to the role of 'for benefit' and public entities. The objective was not evaluative, and the platform model developed in other sectors was not considered as an ideal end point for welfare. On the contrary, the five cases were used as prototypes to highlight the specific features of the welfare platforms with respect to the organisational model, platform design, operating logic, role of the community, ecosystems and skills of the operators. As an analytical framework, we used the Eurofound report (2018), which identifies 27 criteria for analysing platforms (in particular, for labour-based ones), divided into five groups: the structural characteristics of the platform, the business model, accessibility to the platform, the matching process and the criteria relating to tasks commissioned through the platform. In the following discussion, we use this criteria to analyse the case studies and reflect more generally on the singularity of welfare platforms.

The empirical research was carried out through desk analysis of the platform design and interviews with the platform managers of these five cases in order to investigate in detail their project and their strategies for the implementation of the platform model. The research was carried out between May 2018 and February 2019. We believe that the results are particularly interesting today in light of the phase of social transformation related to Covid-19, which has accelerated the spread of digital services further into the welfare sector. Up until now, digital services have generally been aimed at people with high cultural capital. Following the lockdown (March–May 2020), however, larger sections of the population have begun to expand their use of digital tools, widening the target of digital welfare services and leading to changes in the organisation and design of these services.

Findings: The Emergence of Quasi-Platforms

The analysis of these welfare platforms revealed a gap compared to the standard platform model, that is partly constitutional and not dependent on the evolutionary stage of the platforms being analysed. The most widely known examples of the platform economy mainly follow market logic, not hiding their extractive purposes. The platforms in the field of welfare, on the other hand, offer alternative paths, beyond the public/private dichotomy, rooted in the 'foundational' value of services (Barbera et al. 2015) and intended as a daily infrastructure, but also serving as a bridge to a reconnection (and hybridisation) between existing forms of exchange and value creation.

The platform model in welfare takes on traits that we have summarised as *quasi-platform*, a term that does not indicate the failure to achieve an ideal model but that recalls the literature on welfare *quasi-markets* (as well as that on quasi-unions[1]) (Gori 2014). As in *quasi-markets*, even in *quasi-platforms*, competition is not necessarily driven by the motivation to generate profit and is attenuated thanks to the introduction of authorisation and accreditation systems; furthermore, there may be the commitment of public resources but unlike *quasi-markets*, the purchasing power is mostly in the hands of end users.

This is the trait that most distinguishes *quasi-platforms*. Whereas the platform model is based on users' autonomy and in the traditional welfare model the institution acts as client on behalf of the end user, in quasi-platforms the user is able to use the services, but their agency is supported and conveyed by intermediary organisations. In addition, the platform allows organisations certified through the public accreditation system to offer the same (or similar) services on the market, directly addressing end users. The following table provides a summary of the ideal-typical characteristics that emerged from what we have defined as the *quasi-platforms* model, compared both with the platform model and with traditional welfare services.

Table 14.1: Platforms, Quasi-Platforms and Welfare Services: A Comparison.

	Platforms	*Quasi-platforms*	*Welfare services*
Governance	Coincides with the platform	Exceeds the platform and the policy scope	Coincides with a (social) policy scope
Geographical distribution and size	Reproducibility of the business model	Territorial roots of the offer system (partly transferable)	Customisation of the service model
Market positioning	Open but with a tendency to monopoly	Market encapsulation, with pushes to open	Oligopoly through accreditation systems
Business model	Venture capital percentage on the transactions	Philanthropy subscription	Public redistribution. Cost sharing (by users)
Data	Private property (sale)	Commons (for policy making)	Public (monitoring, evaluation)
Users	Open access	Open access for users only	Closed access
Task complexity	Unbundling of tasks	Supply chain with differentiation between operators and volunteers	Specialisation of the service and user segmentation
Social risks	Indirect/market protection	Detection and response to new social risks	Advocacy on needs and policy implementation
Matching supply/demand	User's choice through the mediation of the algorithm	Mix between organisational mediation and service evaluation	Prevalence of organisational mediation
Reputation systems	Opaque algorithms	Supply: integration with accreditation systems. Demand: social scoring linked to activation mechanisms.	Supply: external assessment of the quality of services. Demand: evaluation of direct or indirect users.

A central point concerns governance, which in the platform model coincides with the platform itself since the platform has an autonomous legal form. In all the cases examined, the platform is not a company, it has no autonomous legal nature; it is promoted and managed by a public administration, or by a third sector organisation, or by a network of associations.

In our cases, in three of the projects the platform is owned by the local administration ('WeMi', 'La Cura è di casa' and 'Bacheca Digitale'). In all these cases, the owner is therefore different from the operators and, at least for the moment, only accredited operators have access to the platform. For Family Like, the platform's credits are held by a cooperative: the platform is therefore owned by an operator but open to a network of operators who can publish their own content. Finally, 'Mi fido di noi' is the platform of a District of Solidarity Economy (Brianza in Lombardy) and therefore owned by a network of operators and is open for citizens to use in order to exchange time, skills, information and material goods. In this regard, quasi-platforms also go beyond the vertical governance of local welfare systems centered on relatively limited social policies. While the organisations using the standard platform model are mainly start-ups, quasi-platforms are more frequently part of an organisational transformation process.

As regards geographical distribution, conventional platforms are based on economies of scale (*scaling wide*). This dynamic generates *winner-takes-all* mechanisms, which lead to the creation of monopolies. In all our cases, the geographic distribution is currently only local but it is interesting to also consider the potential of platforms for the construction of long networks and wider markets for services that have traditionally been organised – and not only provided – at local level. In quasi-platforms, 'deep scaling' logics, based on the local adaptability of mechanisms that have proven their effectiveness elsewhere, could also prove to be effective here (Bloom and Chatterji 2009). This can happen by means of different strategies: the repositioning of the platform in a multi-local key, leveraging the transfer of skills acquired in the 'pilot area' in particular with regard to the enhancement of the offer and community building actions; the adaptation of non 'site specific' platforms (for example corporate welfare) to the characteristics of the context, for example through the involvement of local providers; or the construction of clusters by suppliers according to a multi-homing strategy.

The need to quickly reach many users leads platforms to make significant investments in marketing, supported through venture capital. Once fully operational, platforms usually take a percentage of transactions and sell data. In quasi-platforms, initial investments are lower and are mainly supported by philanthropic investments. In all the observed cases, the projects have not yet reached financial sustainability: the number of users is limited, and this does not allow the adoption of business models based on fees on transactions. For this reason, the platforms seem to exclude models based on user payment. The only exception is 'Mi fido di noi', which requires annual membership to the Solidarity Economy District (10 euros).

'Bacheca digitale' and 'Family Like' offer a bulletin-board of services and transactions take place directly between the user and the association/ organisation. The 'WeMi' case is particularly interesting for two reasons. Firstly, that operators accustomed to working only with the public administration have instead turned directly to the end user for the first time, with consequences for price formation mechanisms. Secondly, by showcasing the prices of the services, the platform has created a competition mechanism amongst operators.

'Mi fido di noi' is the only platform where payment is made directly on the platform, using a complementary currency, called 'Fido'. It is interesting to note that while using only time as a criterion for defining the value of the service, the assessment of the value of the 'fido' was parameterised to the cost of labour (one hour = 10 fido = 10 euros). The criterion relating to market positioning must necessarily be redefined in platforms that act mainly in the context of redistribution. As we have seen, if the platform model were to be adopted, some cases examined could move in the direction of hybridisation with market logic and enter a sector already occupied by private platforms – for example 'WeMi' operates in the same field as private platforms for babysitting or caregivers.

The sector is, by definition, one of welfare, with some specific characteristics: projects that see the direct involvement of local administrations are more oriented towards social services, even at a low threshold (home services for 'WeMi'; services for the elderly for 'La Cura è di casa'; services for home, work, food, participation for 'Bacheca digitale'), whereas the other two projects are oriented towards a type of service which is less assistance-oriented (support for parenting for 'Family Like'; exchange of services/skills/knowledge for 'Mi fido di noi'). Platforms that allow for the provision of services insist on incorporating welfare dimensions but do so within a market logic. One of the most interesting aspects of quasi-platforms is that – whilst organising the provision of services to protect against traditional risks – they can detect new social risks. This is a potential competitive advantage even as regards traditional welfare systems, where the response to risk sometimes appears slower, moving from advocacy action that only later turns into a standard offer of services.

The matching of supply and demand on platforms is entrusted to users in a negotiation between the parties mediated through an algorithm, which is generally not transparent. In welfare quasi-platforms there is a form of mediation by the organisations that deliver the service. This is due both to the adoption of supply accreditation mechanisms and, on the demand side, to the use of social scoring mechanisms linked to user activation logics (albeit still functioning in an embryonic stage in the projects examined), which are intentionally absent in the traditional welfare system.

As for data protection and management in the platform model, access is open and profiles are visible to both sides. In quasi-platforms, the operators' accreditation system and the protection of users' privacy lead more often towards more closed and anonymous models, even if there are pressures in the direction of open processes, especially when services do not involve fragile users. Currently, the only platform that allows access to service users is 'Mi fido di noi'; it is a peer-to-peer platform with user profiling, but the information is accessible only to members using a 'club' logic (Buchanan 1965). On the other platforms, operators log in with an organisational profile, not linked to individual identity. An exception is 'La cura è di casa', which provides an individual profile for each operator but information is protected with levels of visibility consistent with the operator's profile.

The platforms divide up complex tasks, also segmenting them into micro-activities; on quasi-platforms this process is less evident. In the logic of a 'pure' platform, there is no selection of service providers based on skills or professionalism; everyone offers what they can and they are evaluated on results in terms of customer satisfaction. In an area such as social services, platforms (or quasi-platforms), on the contrary, incorporate the professional logics of the relevant sector. In 'La Cura è di casa' there is a division of labour between simpler tasks attributable to volunteers (also on the basis of their preferences) and more complex tasks reserved for professional operators.

Matching up is the platforms' core activity and additional services vary according to the service offered; among the most common are insurance and pre-screening but they are generally limited. A more specific element of quasi-platforms is the investment in training, especially of operators and users including in 'educational' terms (culture of use, consumption behaviour, etc.), with even higher levels of intensity than in traditional social welfare systems. This path is considered functional to the success of organisational transformation processes, though it is less necessary in market platforms, where users select themselves according to their needs and skills.

Furthermore, platforms enable digital communities, which generally correspond to a low sense of belonging and where the building up or strengthening of social capital is a by-product of other processes, activated mainly for instrumental reasons. They often take the form of a brand community, especially when users perceive the related services as part of an innovative lifestyle. In the case of traditional welfare systems, the community relationship is significant, incorporating not only those of a professional nature, but also, in a broader sense, the social aggregations that carry out advocacy action regarding the quality of services and the innovation of responses to old and new needs. Quasi-platforms, at least in this initial phase of their life cycle, are based on the central role of the communities of practices of professional operators of social services that work to respond to specific needs. Automation and algorithmic management assume peculiar features in quasi-platforms: welfare platform managers refuse to lose control over key processes (such as selection and matching, performance control and assessment, or knowledge sharing) and this reduces the occurrence of the phenomena of 'machinic dispossession', a concept introduced by Delfanti (2019) to identify the tendency to expropriate the knowledge of workers and incorporate it in machinery such as computer programs. In our case studies we did not find any significant process of knowledge and expertise transfer from humans to machines. In particular, the platform managers claimed they were able to maintain stronger control in the transition to platform organisation and avoid the most disruptive forms of algorithmic management. They viewed the idea of disintermediation as not entirely applicable or even desirable for the welfare sector. They focused more on the importance of continuous mediation and tuning into the needs and practices of the operators and volunteers that operate in direct contact with the beneficiaries of care services.

Finally, as regards the ecosystem of digital platforms, it is often a largely artificial construction aimed at safeguarding the competitive advantage of the platform, for example through the colonisation of other networks in order to guarantee the diversification of the business model and, at the same time, the dominance of one's own network. In the case of quasi-platforms, ecosystems refer to a more 'generative' logic linked to the growth of new initiatives that do not necessarily pertain to this infrastructure, but which nevertheless contribute to creating favourable conditions in socio-cultural and political terms, notably for the development of this sociotechnical innovation. This is a further evolutionary stage indicated even with respect to traditional welfare systems in which the ecosystem 'agglutinates' to a great extent around the governance of a policy which, as mentioned above, concerns a sectoral and territorial policy. In fact, the quasi-platform model not only acts as a 'reforming' element of the classic welfare system, but, moreover, can try to intercept needs and resources that for a variety of reasons escape the purview of the current structure (Fosti 2018).

Conclusions

In conclusion, we have established the variants of the platform organisational model, starting with the welfare sector which, due to the characteristics of the goods/services provided and the specific nature of the users, can be considered an extreme case compared to what is considered 'standard' in the platform model. Our analysis confirmed the distinct nature of welfare platforms, which can be traced back to some common elements that we have summarised as 'quasi-platforms': a form of governance that goes beyond the platform, the territorial roots of the supply system, encapsulation in the market, business models based on philanthropy or subscriptions, and featuring instead data as commons, a differentiation in the tasks of volunteers and operators, a matching based on a hybrid between organisational mediation and evaluation of the service and reputational mechanisms integrated with accreditation systems. This analysis is rooted in a broader debate about the social model that has underpinned European welfare states since the Second World War and the identification of the guiding principles of a 'digital welfare state' for the twenty-first century (Huws 2020).

Platformization is often associated with processes of commodification of care work. In the Lombardy Region, where the case studies examined are located, this would seem to be continuous with a process of privatisation of the public care service which, as demonstrated by Muehlebach (2012), has also determined 'the emergence of a new mode of social and moral subjectivity, new assumptions about citizens' rights and duties, and new conceptualisations of human agency, affect, and will' (17). However, we analyse digital platforms not only as a problem – because they exacerbate the problems of fragmentation of labour and poor social protection – but also as a possible solution. The cases presented here move towards those that Ursula Huws (2020) has defined 'digital platforms for public good', referring to the use of new digital technologies 'not just to enhance and expand existing welfare services but also to bring into being entirely new services that can contribute to the development of a new kind of welfare state' (147). These are local experiments, or pilot schemes, similar to those presented by Cottam in her book (2018), which – albeit in an embryonic form – show new possibilities and offer new discourses on the future of the welfare state.

The projects examined concern very 'tailor-made' experiences and structures dealing with precise objectives and territories. This is a choice that characterises the quasi-platform model but which in itself does not exclude the possibility of transferring it to other contexts by proceeding through locally rooted mechanisms. This model which, as we have seen, is characteristic of local platforms exhibiting strong hybridisation between market logics, redistribution and reciprocity, can therefore be analysed in more general terms and could be adapted to different sectors or socio-economic contexts. As for the limitations of the research, in addition to those relating to sampling, it is useful to remember that this analysis was carried out starting with the functionality of the sites studied and interviews with the designers and managers of the platform, whereas the implications for users were identified indirectly. It is hoped that these first results will stimulate further research, aimed at verifying the stability of the hypotheses formulated here in other sectors and territories and investigating more directly the consequences in terms of subjectification processes.

Note

[1] Quasi-unions are organisations that have emerged to represent the interests of otherwise unrepresented people in their work lives and in their relationships with their employer. They have a distinctive approach and play a key role in domains where traditional trade unions have not been very active.

References

Andersson Schwarz, J. 2017. Platform Logic: An Interdisciplinary Approach to the Platform-Based Economy. *Policy & Internet*, 9(4), 374–394. https://doi .org/10.1002/poi3.159.

Bloom, P. N. and Chatterji, A. K. 2009. Scaling Social Entrepreneurial Impact. *California Management Review*, 51(3), 114–133.

Armano, E., Mazali, T., and Teli, M. 2020. The Production of Neoliberal Sub-jectivity in Platform Capitalism. Comparative Interpretative Hypotheses. *Sociologia della Comunicazione*, 59(1), 106–126. http://digital.casalini.it /10.3280/SC2020-059006.

Casilli, A. and Posada, J. 2019. The Platformization of Labor and Society. In M. Graham and W. H. Dutton (Eds.), *Society and the Internet: How Networks of Information and Communication are Changing Our Lives*, (2nd edn.). Oxford University Press.

Cottam, H. 2018. *Radical Help: How We Can Remake the Relationships Between Us and Revolutionise the Welfare State*. Virago Press.

Couldry, N. and Mejias, U. A. 2019. *The Costs of Connection: How Data is Colo-nizing Human Life and Appropriating It for Capitalism*. Stanford University Press.

Delfanti, A. 2019. Machinic Dispossession and Augmented Despotism: Digital Work in an Amazon Warehouse. *New Media & Society*, 23 (1), 39–55.

Dupret, K. 2017. Working around Technologies—Invisible Professionalism? *New Technology, Work and Employment*, 32(2), 174–187.

Eurofound. 2018. *Employment and Working Conditions of Selected Types of Platform Work*. Publications Office of the European Union. Retrieved from: https://www.eurofound.europa.eu/publications/report/2018/employment -and-working-conditions-of-selected-types-of-platform-work (last accessed 22 June 2021).

Flanagan, F. 2019. Theorising the Gig Economy and Home-Based Service Work. *Journal of Industrial Relations*, 61(1), 57–78.

Fosti, G. 2016. Sharing Welfare? In E. Polizzi and M. Bassoli (Eds.), *Le polit-iche della condivisione: La sharing economy incontra il pubblico* (pp. 71–97). Giuffrè.

Frenken, K. and Pelzer, P. 2020. Reverse Technology Assessment in the Age of the Platform Economy. *Built Environment*, 46(1), 22–27.

Gori, C. (Ed.), 2014. *Il welfare sociale in Italia: La situazione attuale e le prospet-tive future*. Carocci.

Grabher, G. and König, J. 2020. Disruption, Embedded: A Polanyian Framing of the Platform Economy. *Sociologica*, 14(1), 95–118.

Grabher, G. and van Tuijl, E. 2020. Uber-Production: From Global Networks to Digital Platforms. *Environment and Planning A: Economy and Space*, 52(5), 1005–1016.

Huws, U. 2020. *Reinventing the Welfare State: Digital Platforms and Public Policies*. Pluto Press.

Kenney, M. and Zysman, J. 2016. The Rise of the Platform Economy. *Issues in Science and Technology*, 32(3), 61.

Kenney, M., Bearson, D., and Zysman, J. 2019. The Platform Economy Matures: Pervasive Power, Private Regulation, and Dependent Entrepreneurs. SSRN Scholarly Paper ID 3497974. https://papers.ssrn.com/sol3/papers.cfm?abstract_id=3497974.

Langley, P. and Leyshon, A. 2017. Platform Capitalism: The Intermediation and Capitalisation of Digital Economic Circulation. *Finance and Society*, 3(1), 11–31.

Muehlebach, A. 2012. *The Moral Neoliberal: Welfare and Citizenship in Italy*. University of Chicago Press.

Oudshoorn, N. and Pinch, T. (Eds.), 2003. *How Users Matter: The Co-Construction of Users and Technologies*. MIT Press.

Plantin, J-C., Lagoze, C., Edwards, P. N., and Sandvig, C. 2018. Infrastructure Studies Meet Platform Studies in the Age of Google and Facebook. *New Media & Society*, 20(1), 293–310. https://doi.org/10.1177/1461444816661553.

Ritzer, G. 1993. *The McDonaldization of Society*. London: Sage.

Schor, J. 2020. *After the Gig: How the Sharing Economy Got Hijacked and How to Win It Back*. University of California Press.

Srnicek, N. 2016. *Platform Capitalism*. Polity Press.

Ticona, J. and Mateescu, A. 2018. Trusted Strangers: Carework Platforms' Cultural Entrepreneurship in the On-Demand Economy. *New Media & Society*, 20(11), 4384–4404. https://doi.org/10.1177/1461444818773727.

van Dijck, J., Poell, T., and de Waal, M. 2018. *The Platform Society: Public Values in a Connective World*. Oxford University Press.

CHAPTER 15

Performed Subjectivities in Ranking and Recommendation Systems

Tatiana Mazali and Nicoletta Gay

There is a delicate balance between
appropriating new technologies
and being appropriated by them.
(Pasquale 2015, 43)

Digital Labour in Creative and Cultural Industries

Digital creativity has long been viewed as a space which offers unprecedented possibilities for socio-economic development. This is well exemplified by the early dotcom era and subsequently by the support given to industries that fall under the umbrella term of Creative and Cultural Industries (CCI), which was first coined by the United Kingdom's Department for Culture, Media and Sport (DCMS) in the late 1990s. It is often used in relation to urban development policies linked to the rhetoric on creative classes (Florida 2002). Until now, digital creativity and its professions seemed to almost exclusively inhabit sectors clearly defined by Information and Communication Technologies (ICT); however, it also inhabits those which are more difficult to define (but which are of no less importance) to the Creative and Cultural Industries, which can be considered 'factories without walls' of informational capitalism.

How to cite this book chapter:
Mazali, T. and Gay, N. 2022. Performed Subjectivities in Ranking and Recommendation Systems. In: Armano, E., Briziarelli, M., and Risi, E. (eds.), *Digital Platforms and Algorithmic Subjectivities*. Pp. 213–224. London: University of Westminster Press. DOI: https://doi.org/10.16997/book54.p. License: CC-BY-NC-ND 4.0

Now, the digitisation of processes also plays a pivotal role in the production chains of physical goods. As a result, the digital sphere is becoming more and more important; this is clear if we look at the push towards the systemic and structural digitisation of production and consumption processes. Within this framework, the digital sphere offers directions and transversal affordances which, to a certain extent, are shared by the different sectors which produce 'ideas' (the CCIs) and 'things'. A shared language, a regulating system which is as abstract (think of the binary code) as it is concrete (think of the ability of the digital sphere to influence behaviours, content, subjects and objects).

Let us now focus our attention on sectors where digital creative work has historically developed, in the CCIs; in other words, the beating heart of the creative economy. What sets these industries apart is a greater centralisation of creative-cognitive functions in the production cycle, but also greater circularity and interaction between the production and consumption phases. John Hartley (2005) defines digital creative work as the convergence between creative arts (connected to individual talent) and mass cultural industries, in the context of new digital media technologies. As a result, digital creative work is closely linked to the media world (communication environments) and to the discourse between individual creativity – which aims to personalise processes and products – and creativity in mass cultural production, which aims to serialise and scale processes and products, as often occurs in the movie industry, large broadcasting agencies and, today, in digital media factories.

The map of digitally-related creative professions is the result of hybridisations within the new media ecology, which has been heavily redefined by new actors of the internet economy. Fondazione Rosselli's 14th Report on Communications in Italy (Barca and Zambardino 2012) includes a study on the new structures deriving from the co-dependencies of traditional media and internet actors, and highlights that these co-dependencies exist and change as a result of the different stages of internet development:

1. 'The Age of Discovery'. This era was characterised by substantial deregulation of social and economic flows.
2. 'The Age of Experimentation' (up to the dotcom bubble of the 1990s). In this era, users continue to enjoy the use of free content, while traditional content producers remain wary of transferring their content online for fear of not finding profitable business models.
3. 'The Age of Consolidation'. Our current era, which is characterised by a more articulated value chain. The market and its users are more mature and have a greater propensity to experiment with services behind a paywall.

The Age of Consolidation coincides with the switch to Web 2.0 and the popularity amongst users of sharing and co-creating. In this trend towards the hybridisation of genres, services and business models, we are seeing a shift on behalf of network players from distributors to producers of creative content (a prime example of this is Netflix). This transformation also represents the shift to platform capitalism (Vecchi 2017; Srnicek 2016), which transcends the CCI sectors and leads to the creation of new business set-ups and work opportunities, such as the 'platformization' of capital-work relationships.

Within this context of technological innovation, traditional media professions are 'hybridised' with ICT professions. Work profiles that require hybrid skills, which encompass technology, communication and marketing, are emerging; these include titles such as web designers, webmasters, user experience analysts and social media managers. 'Cloud' managers and Big Data and mobile content specialists are among today's most sought-after professional figures. If we were to map these professions, we would see that the required skills are an ICT specialisation combined with textual, visual and audiovisual communications expertise.

In terms of what work looks like in this hybrid industry, we are seeing the combination of 'individualisation' and 'recircularization' of work. Within the media sector, we have observed a growth of content produced by individuals or small-scale productions, but also collaborative and almost always project-based (short-range, intermittent) productions, which often straddle the commercial and non-commercial spheres, and which may be paid or free (Terranova 2000). This tendency is occurring concurrently with the crisis of both cultural institutions and traditional media (Banks, Gill and Taylor 2013). Digital creativity professionals are in strong demand, particularly in strictly ICT professions (Aica et al. 2017) and over time they have quite simply become paradigmatic professions of contemporary work.

Indeed, as highlighted by several studies carried out on digital creative work (for Italy, see Mazali 2016), these professions, and the people behind them, are subjected to certain dynamics we find in the broader employment sector today: employment precarity (Gill and Pratt 2008); work stress and anxiety, which are linked to increased rates of subjective and objective precarity (Gill and Pratt 2008); the tendency to establish forms of self-exploitation (Ross 2009) dictated by the need to build and maintain a high digital reputation; the high affective content of the work (Hardt 1999), which exacts a significant emotional toll in order to carry out one's job, but also the growing demand placed on the worker to fully embrace and commit to the business project; the push towards personal capitalism (Bonomi and Rullani 2005); and finally, the tendency – and need – to adapt to platform capitalism's rules of exchange (to give an example in the creative field, think of the growing importance of freelance marketplaces such as Fiverr or Dribble).

These features, which place attention on individuals, fit into new collective configurations which characterise contemporary digital culture: participatory culture (Jenkins 2006) and the active role of the public in 'media making' (Boccia Artieri 2012) constitute a significant part of today's media productions; the short-circuit between production and consumption leads to the creation of hybrid content makers who are both professional and non-professional, and are also referred to as 'proams' – professional amateurs (Flichy 2010). This leads to an unprecedented tension between different kinds of 'service providers' (for example, the presence of proams leads to the lowering of the cost/value of creative products, which has a detrimental effect on actual professionals); the implementation of crowd modalities to self-finance creative projects or to conduct job searches are new practices for professional growth, which very quickly lead to possible perverse effects, as in the case of the gig economy (Graham and Shaw 2017).

In this complex digital work landscape, creative professions were among the first to be subject to the logic of the algorithms which feature in online reputational mechanisms, rating processes, evaluations and measurements. Within transformations of labour practices, creative workers were also among the first to showcase the critical aspects of the so-called 'algorithmic self' (Pasquale 2015) or 'data self' (Horning 2012) or 'quantified self' (Moore 2018), which emerge from the process of sharing, being shared, having automated recommendations, and being processed by algorithms. This is because it is vital for digital creativity professionals to use the affordance of social networks and platforms to showcase their creative work.

To maintain a competitive advantage or simply to remain visible on the network stage, it is therefore necessary to adopt an algorithmic self, at the service of self-promotional strategies. The algorithmic self of digital creatives is based on two socio-technical systems: building a digital reputation and establishing recommendation mechanisms. The former involves a person's individual sphere and enables the creation of a digital subject that will compete in the network's arenas; it entails the construction of affordances of the techno-subject. Using a gaming metaphor, we could say that reputation mechanisms correspond to the features that a player assumes when playing a character. The latter corresponds to the superstructure of social networking relational logics; in the videogame metaphor, the recommendation mechanisms are the playing field and its rules.

Both systems are socio-technical: they are the 'machinic regulation' (Deleuze and Guattari 1980) *and* the subjects' space of action. From the workers' perspective, one's reputation can be a field of empowerment (it can be somewhat guided), and recommendations can be a field of 'alienation', that is a place of complete depersonalisation, a playing field where only automatic machines play. Between these two extremes there are many nuances, and professionals are afforded the possibility to at least partially guide the outcomes of these socio-technical systems.

To understand how creatives can orient reputation and recommendations in their favour, let's now analyse one of the most important platforms in terms of global penetration and self-promoting strategies: Facebook. In particular, we will look at how Facebook operates reputation and recommendations systems within its algorithm.

Facebook's Algorithm

In 2017, Evan Williams, co-founder of Twitter and platforms such as Blogger and Medium, when interviewed by the *New York Times* (2017) on the topic of social networks, said:

> I think the internet is broken. I thought that, once everybody could speak freely and exchange information and ideas, the world is automatically going to be a better place, but I was wrong about that.

The problem is that the internet rewards extremes. Or rather, Facebook's algorithm interprets our digital behaviours as precious indicators of what it believes may be more interesting, relevant and engaging for us. Its end goal is to dissuade us from leaving the platform's walled garden and its entire ecosystem (Facebook owns Messenger, WhatsApp, and Instagram). This same principle governs the algorithms of platforms such as LinkedIn (owned by Microsoft) or YouTube (owned by Google).

Also in 2017, John Evans, TechCrunch's opinion columnist, stated that: 'At Facebook's scale, behavioural targeting doesn't just reflect our behaviour, it actually influences it. The way Facebook's News Feed works is that the more you 'engage' with posts from a particular user, the more often their posts are shown to you. The more you engage with a particular kind of post, the more you will see its ilk. It's just showing you what you've demonstrated you're interested in. The problem applies to all social networks with 'smart' algorithmic feeds that optimise for engagement. Facebook is just the largest and most influential by far' (TechCrunch 2017).

According to Lovink (2016), the crux of the matter is the invisibility of the internet rather than its omnipresence: digital is the new, comforting, unquestioned general rule, and social media are not monstrous machines, but rather (soft) tools of influence: private companies offering the public communication and information management services which, judging by their reach, have an undeniable impact on opinions and behaviour.

While the debate about the very nature of these tools is still ongoing, with some placing social media in old categories – are they containers of content or creators of content?, are they public or private spaces? – the sheer volume of information and data we produce and consume is continuing to grow exponentially (Internet Live Stats). The algorithms on the different platforms are purposefully designed to decide what we can or want to see of this infinite mass of data, adopting different and sometimes extremely complex criteria to make those decisions. Over the years, Facebook has repeatedly issued statements about how its News Feed algorithm (de facto, its recommendation system) actually works.

In 2016, Adam Mosseri, then VP of Product Management for News Feed, emphasised that the goal of the News Section was to connect every person with what is most 'important' to them and only them (Mosseri 2016). Basically, each News Feed is built completely around the actions of the individual user, which can be more or less public (from the comment on a post to the amount of time spent on it). No two News Feeds are the same, even if two platform users like the same things and have the same friends. Concretely, when a user or a Page publishes a post, the system generates a real auction among the various posts published by the friends and pages followed by a given person when that person connects to Facebook. The algorithm then attributes a relevance score to each individual post and arranges the various possible posts on this basis (sometimes deciding not to show them at all). The factors that regulate the News Feed algorithm (over 100,000) are constantly updated, but among the main ones used in 2016, we find those which constituted the Edge Rank from the very beginning (TechCrunch 2010), which are: affinity, weight and time decay. These are influenced by:

- The Content Poster: how often we interact with the Page/user who posted it;
- The Content Type: how often we interact with that type of content (images, videos, links, text, etc.);
- Post Interactions: comments, likes, shares; and
- Post Publishing Time: how recent the update was.

However, in 2018, Mark Zuckerberg's priority was 'putting people at the centre' (Zuckerberg 2018), thereby modifying the algorithm to prioritise posts that generate conversations and create meaningful interactions among platform users such that:

- The format is less important than the content;
- Friends and family posts are prioritised over public content (Pages); and
- Greater importance is given to the territorial and local aspects of posts and responses (geolocalisation).

As Adam Mosseri, VP News Feed at Facebook, indicated in 2017 (SocialMediaExaminer 2017), Facebook's algorithm uses four steps to help it decide how to rank your content in the news feed:

1. *Inventory*: When you first open your news feed, Facebook's algorithm takes an inventory by looking at all of the stories posted by your friends and the pages you follow.
2. *Signals*: Facebook then considers all available data and tries to make an informed decision about how interested you may be in a certain story. Both 'context signals' (such as time and place of access, type of connection, access device) and 'content signals' (which specifically relate to individual posts) are taken into consideration.

3. *Predictions*: Facebook then uses these signals to help make predictions and calculate the probability of certain outcomes; for example, how likely you are to comment on a story, share a story, spend time reading a story, and so on.
4. *Score*: Facebook consolidates the information to calculate a 'relevance score,' a number that represents how interested Facebook thinks you may be in a certain story. Facebook does not really know how interested you are in a certain story; it's an educated guess at best. There are, however, content signals that are weightier than others: particular attention is given to the so-called 'meaningful interactions', such as, for example, if the link to the post has been shared on Messenger; if the post has generated multiple comments (responses) from the same people (thus activating a conversation); if we interacted with a post of a page shared by a friend, and so on.

The algorithm has undergone further changes over the years (Wallaroo 2020); however, it has actually seen an organic drop in the visibility (reach) of the content published in the Pages, spaces specifically designated for the communication of companies, institutions and freelancers. From January 2016 to mid-July 2016, publishers' Facebook Pages experienced a 52% decline in organic reach (Martech 2016) – and it has continued to decline over time.

Today, the average reach of an organic Page post hovers around 5.2% (Wearesocial 2020). That means roughly one in every nineteen fans sees the Page's non-promoted content. The easiest way to boost distribution and direct sales is to boost the advertising budget: it's no secret that most social platforms operate on a pay-to-play model for brands. The more you pay, the more you are seen, and the more your brand sells. Since 'carriers have become personal brands that need to be managed in a virtual age' (Gioia et al. 2014), building a good personal branding strategy today on Facebook (as with other social platforms) means being able to create a digital identity that draws the attention of a specific audience, provides compelling and distinct content (becoming a credible voice in a specific field relevant to the interests of a specific audience), reaches (gathering a community of followers) and generates meaningful engagement (Khamis, Ang and Welling 2017). In concrete terms, this means:

- Investing time and specific skills in content creation and curation activities.
- Investing time, skills and budget in digital advertising.
- Fostering interactions with the reference community (better comments, like, and shares).
- Using a tone that makes the posts 'conversational'.

Individuals stand out from the crowd by articulating their unique value proposition and adopting a professional approach in a consistent manner. It takes time to build trust, earn credibility and forge a relationship, yet this is increasingly important for those who want to develop their own personal brand. To achieve this, it is essential for digital creative professionals to understand the 'languages' of the different platforms and the functioning of their algorithms. These are the current 'golden rules', which are also subject to sudden changes that platforms make to their algorithms, to ensure that digital reputation mechanisms are also tools of effective empowerment for creative workers.

However, we must not forget that these same mechanisms can lead to 'alienation', i.e. maximum depersonalisation, as shown by the example of the evolution of the Netflix algorithm discussed below; unless individuals communicate in an obviously human manner, with the algorithms being prepared to analyse, rank and propose human behaviours, rather than the content itself.

Humanising Algorithms?

The digital reputation and personal branding dynamics of digital creative professionals are part of the broader dynamics of media platform recommendation systems. The Netflix algorithm is emblematic in this respect. Ed Finn (2018), when analysing the evolution of Netflix's recommendation systems, noted that the first version of their algorithm, called Cinematch, fully represented the logic of algorithmic culture 1.0, that is an algorithm based on 'a straightforward statistical linear models with a lot of data conditioning. In other words, the algorithm relied on users rating movies on a single five-star scale. Cinematch didn't care about lead actors, directors or genres. 'It was a mathematical approach to recommendations, one that ignored the complex position of Hollywood entertainment and movie rentals as culture machines' (Finn 2018, 88). The problem inherent in the 'algorithm 1.0' approach – based on a stochastic logic of abstraction and probability – is that 'while everyone could see that it was doing a better job, nobody could quite explain why' (Finn 2018, 90).

In 2012, Netflix claimed to have changed the Cinematch algorithm by inserting logics that went beyond the five-star model, making it much more complex and more interrelated with other platforms, including Facebook. In addition, Netflix introduced a video content tagging system that was not carried out by a machine, but by real people. The word 'tagger', originally referred to as automatic content markup programs, is now a Netflix 'job title'. Todd Yellin, Vice President of Product Innovation, the man who conceived the system, called the platform's new 2.0 algorithmic logic the 'Netflix Quantum Theory' platform, from the word 'quanta', which indicates the dozens of microtags that taggers are asked to identify within the videos. Netflix's anonymous taggers are a clear example of human work at the service of the machine culture that underpins today's computational efficiency. This example also reminds us that in the field of creativity, whether produced or consumed, algorithms have shown that they need people, because creativity cannot only be 'efficient', it must also be 'fulfilling'. Unfortunately, as Netflix's emblematic example suggests, the human role is currently limited to 'serving' the machine and instead of the machine being humanised, the person is 'machinised'.

In this scenario, it seems increasingly urgent, on the one hand, to empower computer designers and, on the other, to overcome single-disciplinary specialism (which has led the technological development of intelligent machines in a pre-dominant way) and shift towards a fully socio-technical approach. In light of the growing debate on artificial intelligence – also visible in the media cover-age of the ethical considerations of algorithms (Ouchchy, Coin and Dubljević 2020) – actions and reflections on ways of making algorithms less 'unfair' have started to appear. By way of example, some IT development directions for the implementation of 'socially responsible' algorithms are working to design more socially responsible artificial intelligence agents to mitigate biases that are inad-vertently incorporated into algorithms (Vetrò et al. 2019); both 'independent' and 'institutional' organisations are monitoring the impact of algorithms in order to spread awareness and suggest guidelines for their governance (Algo-rithm Watch 2020; Agid 2018). On the one hand, the aim of new branches of study on algorithm development is to pay further attention to the ways in which artificial intelligence technologies can trigger positive effects in terms of reducing the existing social, economic and cultural differences through the adoption of equity criteria and methods that embed interdisciplinary concepts into algorithmic systems. On the other hand, we have to know that one cannot talk about 'better algorithms' without first clarifying the distinction between algorithmic equity and social justice. Otherwise, the emphasis will be placed on whether or not to find a technological 'fix' to a problem that is, in fact, socio-political by nature. Techno-mathematical solutions are certainly important, but the question is not only limited to the algorithmic aspect.

Lastly, it should be said that it is not just a matter of 'opening the black box', or in other words, making the functioning of the algorithms transparent, because the problem inherent in some machine learning techniques is that they generate algorithms that are not predetermined, and that are paradoxically and constitu-tionally incomprehensible; such machine learning training techniques produce algorithms based exclusively on numerical weights in a neural network.

There is a research agenda needed that once again calls into the question the accountability of developers and researchers in creating 'explicable' machine learning techniques, algorithms designed so it is possible to explain why they produce a certain set of results. However, underlying these efforts, an inescap-able question remains: if this technology is itself non-transparent, due to the fact it is the result of a process that is ultimately unknown in its deepest ganglia, is it right to develop it at all? And, moreover, to use it?

Final Remarks

Analysing the characteristics of digital work to understand its specificities within the Creative and Cultural Industries means confronting the affordances of the digital medium. It is not a simple tool, but a common 'language': a regulation system, both abstract (binary code) and material (the ability of the digital medium to mould behaviours, contents, objects and subjects). Among the digital affordances that condition the subjects/workers of the digital creativity value chains, an important one is represented by the algorithms of the reputation and recommendation systems, necessary tools for creatives to maintain their 'market position'.

From the workers' point of view, digital reputation can be an area of empowerment (it can be somewhat guided); however, recommendations can be 'alienating' and create a space of maximum depersonalisation, a playing field where automatic machines play. Between these two extremes there are many possibilities, and the chance for professionals to influence, at least in part, the outcome of these socio-technical systems.

To understand if and how creatives can orient reputation and recommendations in their favour, the rules and grammars of the Facebook platform in terms of influencing self-promoting strategies were analysed in detail, focusing on its algorithm and how it has evolved over time. The lesson we learn is that it costs digital creative professionals a lot to maintain their own digital visibility in terms of time and money, since controlling or 'bending' the Facebook algorithm for one's own ends requires investing time and specific skills in content creation and curation; investing time, skills and budget in digital advertising; fostering interactions with the target community (better comments and shares, instead of likes); and using a tone that makes the posts 'conversational'.

While these are currently the rules to ensure that digital reputation mechanisms are tools of empowerment for creative workers, we must not forget that these same mechanisms can be 'alienating', or depersonalising, as highlighted by the Netflix recommendation algorithms, one of the most powerful and pervasive media platforms for creative audiovisual content.

While the analysis of the Facebook algorithm has allowed us to understand how to 'humanise' its use, looking more closely at the Netflix algorithm tells us that algorithms must evolve considering the complexity of the processes they want to automate. For the time being, this evolution seems to be based on a balance between automation and human intervention to the complete detriment of the human. On platforms such as Netflix, the role of humans is designed to 'serve' the machine. More than humanising the machine, the individual is 'machinised'. To address this criticality, IT designers ought to be made responsible and foster an ethical and conscious approach to the development of algorithms as soon as possible. Some initiatives are moving in this direction, tracing the way to make algorithms intelligible, reducing the bias inherent in algorithmic design, and controlling the social impacts of algorithms.

References

Agid – Agenzia per l'Italia Digitale. 2018. *Libro Bianco sull'Intelligenza Artificiale al servizio del cittadino.* https://ia.italia.it/assets/librobianco.pdf.

Aica, Assinform, Assintel and Assinter. 2017. *Osservatorio delle Competenze Digitali: Scenari, gap, nuovi profili professionali e precorsi formativi.* Available at: https://www.assinteritalia.it/ProxyVFS.axd/null/r15297/Report

-integrale-Osservatorio-Competenze-Digitali-2017-pdf?ext=.pdf&v=8401 (last accessed 15 December 2020).

Algorithm Watch. 2020. *Automating Society Report 2020*. Available at: https://automatingsociety.algorithmwatch.org (last accessed 15 December 2020).

Banks, M., Gill, R., and Taylor, S. (Eds.), 2013. *Theorising Cultural Work. Labour, Continuity and Change in the Cultural and Creative Industries*. Routledge.

Barca, F. and Zambardino, B. 2012. *XIV Rapporto Iem. L'Industria della comunicazione in Italia. I nuovi attori 'sopra la rete' e la sostenibilitá della filiera di Internet*. Fondazione Rosselli. Available at: https://www.unipa.it/persone/docenti/d/paolo.dibetta/.content/documenti/2012_XIV_rapporto_IEM.pdf.

Boccia Artieri, G. 2012. *Stati di connessione. Pubblici, cittadini e consumatori nella (Social) Network Society*. FrancoAngeli.

Bonomi, A. and Rullani, E. 2005. *Il capitalismo personale. Vite al lavoro*. Torino: Einaudi.

Deleuze, G. and Guattari, F. 1980. *Mille piani*. Castelvecchi.

Finn, E. 2018. *What Algorithms Want: Imagination in the Age of Computing*. MIT Press.

Flichy, P. 2010. *Le sacre de l'amateur: Sociologie des passions ordinaires à l'ère numérique*. Editions du Seuil.

Florida, R. 2002. *The Rise of the Creative Class*. Basic Books.

Gioia, D. A., Hamilton, A. L., and Patvardhan, S. D. 2014. Image is Everything. *Research in Organizational Behavior*, 34, 129–154.

Gill, R. and Pratt, A. 2008. Precarity and Cultural Work In the Social Factory? Immaterial Labour, Precariousness and Cultural Work. *Theory, Culture & Society*, 25(7–8), 1–30.

Graham, M. and Shaw, J. (Eds.), 2017. *Towards a Fairer Gig Economy*. Meatspace Press.

Hardt, M. 1999. Affective Labor. *Boundary 2*, 26(2), 89–100.

Hartley, J. (Ed.), 2005. *Creative Industries*. Wiley-Blackwell.

Horning, R. 2012. Notes on the 'Data Self'. *The New Inquiry*, 2. February. Available at: https://thenewinquiry.com/blog/dumb-bullshit (last accessed 11 December 2020).

Internet Live Stats. http://www.internetlivestats.com. 7 December 2020 (last accessed 11 April 2022).

Jenkins, H. 2006. *Convergence Culture: Where Old and New Media Collide*. New York University Press.

Khamis, S., Ang, L., and Welling, R. 2017. Self-Branding, 'Micro-Celebrity' and the Rise of Social Media Influencers. *Celebrity Studies*, 8(2), 191–208.

Lovink, G. 2016. *Social Media Abyss: Critical Internet Culture and the Force of Negation*. Polity Press.

Martech. 2016. Facebook organic reach is down 52% for publishers' Pages this year, 6 July. Available at: https://martech.org/facebook-organic-reach-drop-steepens-52-publishers-pages (last accessed 11 April 2022).

Mazali, T. 2016. *Digital Workers. I professionisti delle industrie creative*. Aracne.

Moore, P. V. 2018. *The Quantified Self in Precarity: Work, Technology and What Counts*. Routledge.

Mosseri, A. 2016. Facebook for Developers, News Feed: Getting Your Content to the Right People, 12 April. Available at: https://developers.facebook.com/videos/f8-2016/news-feed-getting-your-content-to-the-right-people (last accessed 15 December 2020,).

New York Times, The. 2017. The Internet Is Broken': @ev Is Trying to Salvage It, 20 May. Available at: https://www.nytimes.com/2017/05/20/technology/evan-williams-medium-twitter-internet.html (last accessed 15 December 2020).

Ouchchy, L., Coin, A., and Dubljević, V. 2020. AI in the Headlines: The Portrayal of the Ethical Issues of Artificial Intelligence in the Media. *AI & Society*, 35, 927–936.

Pasquale, F. 2015. The Algorithmic Self. *The Hedgehog Review*, 17(1), 30–45.

Ross, A. 2009. *Nice Work if you Can Get it: Life and Labor in Precarious Times*. New York University Press.

SocialMediaExaminer. 2017. The Facebook Algorithm Demystified: How to Optimize for News Feed Exposure, 31 May. Available at: https://www.socialmediaexaminer.com/facebook-algorithm-demystified-how-to-optimize-for-news-feed-exposure (last accessed 15 December 2020).

Srnicek, N. 2016. *Platform Capitalism*. Polity Press.

TechCrunch. 2010. EdgeRank: The Secret Sauce That Makes Facebook's News Feed Tick, 23 April. Available at: https://techcrunch.com/2010/04/22/facebook-edgerank (last accessed 15 December 2020).

TechCrunch. 2017. Facebook is Broken, 4 June. Available at: https://techcrunch.com/2017/06/04/when-you-look-into-the-news-feed-the-news-feed-looks-into-you (last accessed 15 December 2020).

Terranova, T. 2000. Free Labor: Producing Culture for the Digital Economy. *Social Text*, 18(2(63)), 33–58.

Vecchi, B. 2017. *Il capitalismo delle piattaforme*. ManifestoLibri.

Vetrò, A., Santangelo, A., Beretta, E., and De Martin, J-C. 2019. AI: From Rational Agents to Socially Responsible Agents. *Digital Policy, Regulation and Governance*, 21(3), 291–304.

Wallaroo. 2020. Facebook Newsfeed Algorithm History. Last Updated: December 9, 2020. https://wallaroomedia.com/facebook-newsfeed-algorithm-history (last accessed 15 December 2020).

Wearesocial, Hootsuite. 2020. Digital 2020 April Global Statshot Report, 23 April. Available at: https://datareportal.com/reports/digital-2020-april-global-statshot (last accessed 15 December 2020).

Zuckerberg, M. 2018. Facebook post, 19 January. Available at: https://www.facebook.com/zuck/posts/10104445245963251 (last accessed 15 December 2020).

CHAPTER 16

The Social Costs of the Gig Economy and Institutional Responses: Forms of Institutional Bricolage in Italy, France and the Netherlands

Maurizio Franzini and Silvia Lucciarini

Introduction

Innovations certainly produce benefits, but they also come with social costs that impact in several areas. This is particularly evident in relation to work, where innovation modifies features such as volume, wages and quality (Kalleberg 2011). The extent, scope and duration of these costs are highly dependent on economic institutions and their relationship with policies (Davidson and Potts 2016). Indeed, states have, previously, been able to limit these negative social repercussions on labour through institutional evolution; in particular, the collective actions of intermediate bodies (Hall and Soskice 2001) have enhanced social cohesion and reduced inequalities. This is one crucial reason why capitalist systems have been able to reproduce themselves and persist over time, even in the face of changing socio-economic and institutional contexts (Streeck 2011; Crouch 1999; Peck and Theodore 2007; Calhoun et al. 2013). It

How to cite this book chapter:
Franzini, M. and Lucciarini, S. 2022. The Social Costs of the Gig Economy and Institutional Responses: Forms of Institutional Bricolage in Italy, France and the Netherlands. In: Armano, E., Briziarelli, M., and Risi, E. (eds.), *Digital Platforms and Algorithmic Subjectivities*. Pp. 225–237. London: University of Westminster Press. DOI: https://doi.org/10.16997/book54.q. License: CC-BY-NC-ND 4.0

thus makes sense to ask three questions among others: *what are the social costs of today's wave of 'digital' innovation? How is the institutional context evolving? Is that evolution sufficient to curb such costs or are further structural changes needed?*

Given the increasing diversification of the labour force, part of this debate has focused specifically on aspects of the status of workers, in particular how to ensure non-standard workers are able to access existing social protections, and how to develop new standards to recognise digital skills that can enhance workers' position in the labour market (Iversen and Soskice 2019). With the current boom in freelance work in all its various forms, scholars are called on to investigate not only transformations in organisational structures but also systems of both collective representation and action (Grimshaw 2016). Some studies have focused on national regulatory systems and on the channels of representation offered by both formal entities and informal collective actors (Vandaele 2018) to the 'digital' self-employed, or 'new self-employed', as some scholars have termed them (Daskalova 2018).

Our main concern is whether institutions have changed in a way that would enable the reduction of the burden of socio-economic costs of these 'digital innovations' and, if so, what these changes should be. Historically, trade unions have been the main actor working to defend and extend workers' rights and to protect and improve working conditions. Several other quasi-collective (Ostrom 1990) actors have emerged as self-employed workers increased in number, but these are not always coordinated with unions, particularly in the field of social and mutual aid cooperatives and of professional associations (Bellini and Lucciarini 2019). These emerging actors make the overall landscape of workers' identity and representation much more complex. To date, scholars have studied these new organisations for self-employed (SE hereafter) workers predominantly by framing them as external to the traditional system of industrial relations, or as bottom-up initiatives with limited powers of action (Vandalae 2018).

In this chapter, which is based on fieldwork with gig workers conducted in three countries, we argue that the role of the state, which has been crucial in the 'classic' system of industrial relations, should also be considered and analysed in relation to today's new organisations for SE workers. In particular, since we focus on mutualistic cooperatives (MCs, hereafter)[1] in Italy, the Netherlands and France we devote particular attention to the role that the state can and does perform in moulding the activities of MCs, as clearly illustrated by our comparative empirical analysis. Members of these MCs are mainly gig workers (in particular on and off-platform, see OECD 2019), a population that has come to face specific risks due to emerging new technologies, such as precarization and instability (Brynjolfsson and McAfee 2011). Evidence from the fieldwork also shows that responses to this challenge have the character of 'institutional bricolage' (Streeck and Thelen 2005; Mahoney and Thelen 2010; Carstensen 2015; 2017). Old and new institutional actors perform new functions to adapt configurations of rules and practices to respond to new conditions and increasing uncertainty. Actors innovate, reworking the existing institutional arrangements, within their limited cognitive and social resources, and as far as they perceive their actions as legitimate (Cleaver and de Konnig 2015), in a gradual institutional change trajectory, where bricolage strategies could represent the first step (Streeck and Thelen 2005). Also in this perspective, the role of the state can be of paramount importance.

The Gig Economy and the Self-Employed: Towards Experimental Forms of Representation and Protection

The term gig economy essentially refers to a labour market characterised by short term, 'on-demand' jobs and/or by the practice of dividing work into tasks, each of which is carried out autonomously and often without knowing what the final output of the production process will be, all in the context of an ever-increasing fragmentation of working conditions (ILO 2015). The gig economy includes both traditional jobs (messenger, porter, gardener, etc.) and new jobs stemming from today's broader processes of digitisation, carried out mainly by SE workers and almost always through the intermediation of platforms (European Commission 2018).

Both atypical and solo-SE workers were already on the rise; however, due to their wide-ranging effects, platforms have contributed greatly to fuelling this trend (Eurofound 2017a; 2017b). Moreover, the labour market position of SE workers is intensely bifurcated, with yawning gaps not only between skilled and unskilled workers but also among professional categories, which are themselves characterised by high variability (Gallie 2013). It is becoming clear, however, that old institutions and policies (including welfare) are not capable of counteracting and limiting the socio-economic costs that gig workers may end up facing as a result of innovation.

In this respect the first consideration is that the main actors historically engaged in protecting workers' rights – trade unions – have faced difficulties for some time now. The second consideration, in terms of institutional effectiveness or lack thereof, is linked more specifically with regulatory models and forms of social protection. Many European countries have responded to the growth of self-employment by extending measures to regulate this field, proceeding along a path of progressive hybridisation between subordinate and autonomous work. In particular, some protection schemes that once applied only to employees have been extended to SE workers (Eurofound 2017a). This phenomenon has occurred in many European countries, but policies have not converged towards a single model; in fact, differences between countries have remained quite significant, each one shaped by different historical trajectories (Pernicka 2006). In general, the regulatory system for SE workers is deeply flawed (Conen and Schippers 2020), in particular in terms of the safeguards it provides. These safeguards do not protect SE workers from fluctuating market trends and, broadly, operate in ways that makes workers themselves responsible for facing the different risks that they may encounter throughout the life cycle, risks which had previously been socialised in various ways. In particular, SE workers are forced to continuously 'transition' between jobs and clients and must be particularly 'adaptive' because platforms' organisational systems are based on changing structures and rules as well as frequent innovations. If not curbed, this complexity calls for a system of safeguards that is not easy to implement and certainly has not yet been put in place. In addressing this phenomenon, Grimshaw et al. (2016) suggest that SE workers face 'protection gaps', particularly if their jobs are intermittent, or they work in sectors affected by frequent waves of innovation, even if solely at the level of organisation. Yet even in this outdated context we can begin to see signs of institutional change, both technological and organisational.

While it is true that labour fragmentation and the de-standardisation of workers (Hyman and Gumbrell-McCormick 2017) have undermined the associative capacity of collective actors and weakened collective action, it is also true that new forms of intervention and collective action can still develop. In fact, these drives towards de-collectivisation have actually led to a reconsideration of collective actors, formal and informal, and their capacity to represent workers' interests. Further, the study of new collective actors representing SE workers, such as MCs, seems useful to understand aspects of organisational and institutional experimentations facing the disruptive tendencies in the labour market (Levesque et al. 2020).

To define the activities these organisations carry out, it may be useful to draw on the well-known concept of 'capabilities' introduced by Amartya Sen (1999) and as employed in some analyses of new representational forms (see Westerveld 2012) as representing an opportunity made *actually* possible. We thus distinguish between 'collective capabilities' and 'collective solidarities'. *Collective capabilities* refer to a MC's capacity to identify aggregating elements among workers that unite them and whose interests do not necessarily belong to the same professional universe or productive sector, nor share the same workplace. This capacity constitutes the basis for inter-professional associational building, rooted in ideas that respond to different logics – 'instrumental' and 'proactive' – that MCs have developed by leveraging two specific rhetorics:

a) *a negative rhetoric*, with organisations seeking to 'fill' gaps in the protection system, on the one hand, and to counteract the extreme individualisation and atomisation of workers, on the other, making an effort to reconsolidate a collectivity based on professional identities;

b) *a positive rhetoric* through which organisations not only aggregate SE workers but offer them a collective system in which different professional specialties are respected in their specificity and, in ways that will be outlined below, provides them with working conditions and protections that are similar to those of traditional, non-precarious work.

Collective solidarities instead refers to the goods and services these organisations offer, services that substantially broaden workers' access to protections for which they would not otherwise be eligible, and strengthens their ability to participate in the market.

We investigate what interests these organisations represent, a question which will allow us to better understand this composite agglomeration of workers and their desires and needs; what strategies they enact; and above all, how they relate to the state. The main purpose of investigating these questions is to assess the prospects of striking a better balance in the future between the risks SE gig workers face and the protections they can enjoy.

Research Methods and Case Study Selection

Our research was conducted at three new worker-representative organisations within the world of mutual aid and cooperatives, and representing numerous SE workers; of these, an ever-growing share are involved in new, as well as traditional, 'gig' jobs. Data was collected between April 2018 and June 2019 through the period of the research via 45 in-depth interviews divided as follows: nine with street-level bureaucrats (SLB); nine with managers of organisations; and 27 with workers hired, enrolled or working in the organisations, (therefore three SLB, three managers, and nine workers per case study). The interviews aim to shed light on three dimensions: internal organisational structures and functions (management level); the rhetorics the organisation uses to communicate with potential members (SLB level); and whether workers' desires and needs are fulfilled, or not, by the organisation, and the associational narratives (factors influencing membership choice) and the respective strong and weak points influencing these narratives.

The three organisations – selected on the basis of their scope of influence and number of members – are Smart in Italy and the Netherlands, and Coopaname in France. Smart is a Belgian Foundation and a European network of cooperatives created in 1998 that represents a wide range of freelancers (artists, creatives, trainers, riders, consultants). The Italian branch has been active since 2014; the Dutch branch since 2016. The former associate almost six thousand workers, the latter two thousand (but there are organisational changes in progress, as we outline below). Both are financially supported by a Belgian parent company; in Italy, the first two years of start-up were also co-financed by the Cariplo Banking Foundation. Coopaname, on the other hand, has been active since 2004. It is an *activité et d'emploi cooperative* set up as a *societè cooperative ouvriere de production* (Scop) and financed through national and regional public funding. It includes almost one thousand workers, located in the Île-de-France area.

In the Italian case, Smart.it is mainly composed of workers in the performing arts sector, such as stage and screen actors; workers who participate in the peripheral labour market are a second group primarily hired for small gigs in events for public and private clients. This membership does not include workers associated with publicly owned theatres or large private events, as these 'dependent' workers still maintain stable professional relationships or work as employees. The Dutch branch of Smart, in contrast, represents digital workers, in particular web designers and web content managers, who freelance and therefore are not eligible for the forms of protection guaranteed by the basic government insurance scheme for subordinate work. The heterogeneity of the French organisation, Coopaname, derives mainly from the fact that it represents both digital workers (in particular web designers, web content managers and musicians) and traditional ones (especially small-scale artisans). We will clarify the reasons for this heterogeneity below when explaining how the state provides financial support to this organisation.

Cooperatives' Logic and Actions

In presenting our main findings, we begin by outlining the associative composition of the three organisations, showing that the Italian and Dutch memberships are highly internally homogeneous while Coopaname is more heterogeneous. The three organisations share the same kinds of mechanisms that make it advantageous for them to represent SE workers and that operate to represent SE workers and for the workers to choose such representation.

From the workers' point of view, as mentioned above, access to a subordinate employment contract has the advantage of making them eligible for forms of protection they could not otherwise access. The organisations can also provide other benefits, in particular in the form of financial planning advice that allows members to identify all possible fiscal deductions they might claim, for instance, and thus reduce their net tax burden. Other benefits may consist of personalised guidance as well as shared projects and initiatives. This guidance is of great benefit, especially for the more vulnerable workers. On the one hand, younger workers cooperate in developing strategies that combine on and off-platform work, and in gaining information on different platforms and their reliability. On the other hand, guidance helps older workers in developing digital skills and navigating the employment market. Workers have pinpointed the 'compass' role of those organisations, in establishing wages benchmarks for one-off and specific gig work, as well as internal systems of ratings of platforms and employers. The information on wages aids the process of professionalisation, especially in new digital sectors where there are no formal skills. The rating system protects workers from 'bad gigs', and reinforces in MC members both the sense of belonging and in-group behaviour. From the point of view of the organisations, the economic advantage lies in the fact that they take a share of what their member-workers earn from each job, using these revenues to cover their costs. This share amounts to approximately 10–12% of total revenue and it is important to underline that, currently, it is individual workers who themselves must find work, without help of the MCs, who then deduct their fee from the payments workers receive for each job. It should be added that for organisations that are part of a larger company, support from the parent company is put into a small mutual fund to supplement the wages of member-workers. The result of this arrangement is that the actual capacity of these organisations to carry out mediation in the market is currently limited; therefore, they can be considered primarily service organisations.

However, this is not the only funding these organisations receive. In fact, Smart.it is also supported by contributions from the Belgian parent company, and funding from the Unicredit Banking Foundation. Unlike Coopaname, it does not receive financing from the state. In fact, the French state supports Coopaname with national and regional funding but on the condition that it also represents traditional place-based workers, specifically those located in Île-de-France. It is this condition that explains the heterogeneous nature of Coopaname members and makes it clear that such public support is not aimed exclusively at platform workers, but rather at providing protection and inclusion to more traditional workers. Thanks to Coopaname's activities, however, such coverage is essentially indistinguishable from the kind of protections that it provides to digital gig workers through mutual aid operations. In the Netherlands, the situation is more complex and currently undergoing a process of adjustment. A previous incarnation of the organisation had revealed a problem stemming in part from the characteristics of the social protection system for Dutch workers. Specifically, workers remained SE because the level of contributions the Dutch welfare system required for dependent workers was too high for Smart.NL to cover, effectively preventing the organisation from hiring its members. On one hand, this kept the MC from growing and developing a role of mediation and representation, reducing its operations to services alone. On the other hand, it created lines of division within the 'collective' represented by this MC: discouraging the membership of young freelancers engaged in occasional gig work and interested in retaining their status as independent workers, and encouraging the participation of older workers with stable clients, as a group potentially interested in transforming their status from autonomous to dependent workers. This strategy began in 2017 and gave rise to a selection process aimed at retaining only the 'strongest workers' as organisation members, i.e. workers in a position to afford the high costs of insurance. In the meantime, the MC and the government engaged in negotiations to determine how to implement such coverage. The result of these developments has been to exclude and penalise more short term and temporary freelancers, who are usually also the youngest workers. We will discuss this problem in more depth in the next section. Here, it is important to note that Smart.NL has responded to this problem by trying to reinforce the professional standing of its member-workers and, together with the state, is carrying out an awareness-raising campaign aimed specifically at improving their professional image and increasing low wages. This would help ensure they have the resources needed to cover the costs of the country's insurance system. Smart.NL's tendency to use the salary levels and the prices it charges for its own services as a criterion for filtering membership of the organisation can be understood in relation to this problem.

The external dimension of the organisation has to do with its ability to relate to other entities and state bodies, in particular lobbying and seeking to exert influence to modify the system governing self-employment benefits, safeguards and practices. Of course, such activity depends in part on the state's stance towards these organisations. An implication of what has been discussed above is that the main differences between the three organisations lies precisely in their relationships with the state. It thus makes sense to lay out some clarifications about these relationships before presenting our conclusions.

State Action and Forms of Institutional Bricolage

It is key that we examine the logics, action strategies and perspectives of these new organisations, including the way they relate to pre-existing institutions, if we are to assess the prospect of limiting precariousness and instability. The state can affect the extent and effectiveness of these organisations' operations in a variety of ways. One of these is, of course, through transfers or (advantageous) taxation. However, the state can also have an impact on the rules and regulations that may either facilitate or hinder the work carried out by these organisations. The results of our study are quite revealing in this respect. In the case of *Italy*, the state appears to be practically absent: it does not interact with Smart.it nor does it provide any type of economic support; instead, as outlined above, such support comes from other sources. This absence is part of a wider pattern of non-intervention by the Italian state in relation to self-employment, traditional or not, and creative work in particular. Indeed, the relative weakness of this professional sector (and especially its digital side) in the labour market probably contributes to obscuring how important it actually is for development. Given this context, an MC has limited room for manoeuvre. As our results clearly show, their activity is almost exclusively aimed at converting gig workers into subordinate workers through employment contracts and finding ways to cover the various costs that this conversion entails.

The *French* case is different and could be described as a model of inclusive, locally based development supported by public funding in that it also includes traditional workers (the small-scale craftspeople mentioned above). Moreover, the state also fosters dialogue between Coopaname and traditional trade unions, sponsoring joint initiatives whose main objective is to promote inclusion through local employment. The state thus plays a more engaged role in France, and this improves the effectiveness of the MC's work. Turning to the *Dutch* case, Smart.Nl can generally be seen as a model of state-led professional consolidation. As outlined above, the state is committed to fostering a shift on multiple levels, including culturally, that would allow digital workers to earn higher wages in the market. This development would apply in particular to web designers. Such a commitment is, of course, commendable in that it aims to redefine work and its legitimacy, while also trying to put a stop to the short term expediencies used to lower labour costs to boost profits and (although this is not always the case) investment in innovative sectors. However, the overall assessment must also take into account that the most vulnerable of the digital workers are facing a series of difficulties that lead them to be excluded from Smart.NL, as previously discussed. These difficulties stem from the high costs of accessing the country's insurance schemes for employees, which this organisation would only be able to cover if the revenues from its activities were greater. This seems to be a weakness, and for the Dutch state to resolve it would require the raising of wages, especially of the most vulnerable, which is not an easy task. The alternative is, of course, to reconsider the requirements for workers' accessing social insurance, considering that the most vulnerable gig workers are not entitled to protection as self-employed workers and cannot obtain such protection by being 'converted' into employees by the MC.

Therefore the intensity of state involvement and the forms it takes varies greatly. Across these diverse cases, institutional bricolage takes the form of an unprecedented hybridisation between two of the MC's functions, with mutual aid principles merged with the principle of public social security. The strategy of transforming SE workers into employees is possible only if access to benefits is a straightforward process, that is, when the threshold of contributions from workers is low as in the Italian and French cases. The requirements in the Dutch case, however, are high enough that this conversion has proved impossible; as a consequence, the MC is pursuing professionalisation and fair wages in order to make it possible.

Conclusions

The few analyses of MCs available to date have focused mainly on their internal organisation and relationships with traditional trade unions (Vandalae 2018). Their relationship with the state, on the other hand, has been investigated very little or not at all. This is a serious shortcoming in light of the results of our research, as described here.

Through a comparative analysis, we have analysed institutional change processes in national gig labour markets (off and on platform). The new challenges involved in ensuring fair working conditions for SE workers are at the centre of debates in countries throughout Europe (De Stefano 2016). This issue touches on aspects of social inclusion and economic competitiveness, driving us to reflect on just how well economic institutions are able to govern and regulate. It also shines the spotlight on the capacity of democratic actors that are sorely tested by today's more fragmented socio-economic system, as a consequence of risks inside and outside the labour market (Sabel 2001).

The three cases we have investigated show how institutional change mechanisms are triggered in the face of social problems not adequately addressed by previous structures. Change is stimulated when these new actors enter the scene and their functions are redefined in interaction with other actors in the same arena, in particular the state and unions (De Munck and Ferreras 2012). MCs are positioned to perform three main functions: to act as collective actors, to increase employment opportunities, and to stabilise income. They carry out quasi-union activities – that is lobbying and influencing to improve their members' conditions by putting pressure on public actors. They function as agents of 'professionalisation' in that they delimit the boundaries of certain emerging professions, asserting closure regimes to workers in related occupational ecosystems, and promoting fair wages.

However, the main way MCs operate is by working to convert SE workers into subordinate workers, and this approach entails several problems all of which are related to the difficulty of covering costs that such a conversion involves. MCs bring together mutual aid and social security principles in the form of a 'bricolage', and the result is extremely fragile. SE workers can only access limited welfare benefits, as the intermittence of their contracts undermines their ability to pay contributions. Such contributions continue to constitute the main axis along which countries calculate the extent and duration of social protection benefits. In none of the three cases does the state act directly to facilitate this SE-dependent conversion, nor does it seem that the state has actually supported these workers, either by increasing the strength of their position in the market or by improving the protections they are eligible for as self-employed gig (intermittent) workers. Beyond the specificities of the individual case studies, our analysis has shown that mutual aid cooperatives can indeed make a significant contribution to greater labour protection, but such solutions may prove fragile in the absence of other, complementary interventions. In this respect the role of the state could be of paramount importance in many different ways: not only by providing financial aid but also by adapting the design of welfare systems, by bolstering fruitful cooperation among the various actors involved, and by limiting some of the vulnerabilities in the labour market itself.

Recent studies on employment precariousness have underlined the importance of the systemic dimension, showing that the disruptive effects of employment precariousness can be mitigated by generating a 'virtuous circle' with the power to restore solidarity through the participation of workers, employers, unions and 'inclusive' institutions; they also show that the effects of precariousness can be exacerbated by fragmented and particularistic actors and institutions (see Doellgast, Lillie and Pulignano 2018 regarding this virtuous vs. vicious theoretical framework). Although our research did uncover interesting strategies for combating job insecurity, the analysis shows that attempts to prevent such conditions are still fragmented and fragile: a case in point is the regulatory framework itself, with its neglect of a group of workers that is increasingly important in Europe. This neglect could be framed as a democratic issue rather than a capitalistic one (Iversen and Soskice 2019).

Note

[1] MCs are relevant actors in the arena of self-employed workers and freelancers (Murgia and de Heusch 2020).

References

Bellini A. and Lucciarini, S. 2019. Not Only Riders. The Uncertain Boundaries of Digital Creative Work as a Frontier for Emerging Actors in Interest Representation. *Partecipazione a Conflitto*, 12(3), 845–870.

Brynjolfsson, E. and McAfee, A. 2011. *Race Against the Machine: How the Digital Revolution is Accelerating Innovation, Driving Productivity, and Irreversibly Transforming Employment and the Economy*. Digital Frontier Press.

Calhoun, C. 2013. What Threatens Capitalism Now? In I. Wallerstein, R. Collins, M. Mann, G. Derluguian, and C. Calhoun (Eds.), *Does Capitalism Have a Future?* (pp. 131–162). Oxford University Press.

Carstensen, M. 2015. Bricolage as an Analytical Lens in New Institutionalism. In F. Panizza and T. Spanakos (Eds.), *Conceptual Comparative Politics* (pp. 46–67). Routledge.

Carstensen, M. 2017. Institutional Bricolage in Times of Crisis. *European Political Science Review*, 9(1), 139–160.

Cleaver, F. 2012. *Development Through Bricolage: Rethinking Institutions for Natural Resource Management*. Routledge.

Cleaver, F. and de Koning, J. 2015. Furthering Critical Institutionalism. *International Journal of the Commons*, 9(1), 1–18.

Conen, W. and Schippers, J. 2020. *Self-Employment as Precarious Work: A European Perspective*. Edward Elgar.

Crouch, C. 1999. *Social Change in Western Europe*. Oxford University Press

Daskalova, V. I. 2018. Regulating the New Self-Employed in the Uber Economy: What Role for EU Competition Law? *German Law Journal*, 19(3), 461–508.

Davidson, S. and Potts, J. 2016. The Social Costs of Innovation Policy. *Economic Affairs*, 36(3), 282–293.

De Stefano, V. 2016. *The Rise of the 'Just-In-Time' Workforce: On-Demand Work, Crowd Work And Labour Protection In The 'Gig-Economy'*. ILO Conditions of Work and Employment Series no. 7. International Labour Office.

De Munck, J. and Ferreras, I. 2012. The Democratic Exchange as the Combination of Deliberation Bargaining and Experimentation. In J. De Munck, C. Didry, I. Ferreras and A. Jobert (Eds.), *Renewing Democratic Deliberation in Europe: The Challenge of Social and Civil Dialogue* (pp. 149–169). Peter Lang.

Doellgast V., Lillie, N., and Pulignano, V. 2018. *Reconstructing Solidarity: Labour Unions, Precarious Work, and the Politics of Institutional Change in Europe*. Oxford University Press.

Eurofound. 2017a. *Exploring Self-Employment in the European Union*. Office of the European Union.

Eurofound. 2017b. *Classifying Self-Employment and Creating an Empirical Typology*. Office of the European Union.

European Commission. 2018. Platform Workers in Europe: Evidence from the COLLEEM Survey, EUR 29275 EN, Luxembourg.

Gallie, D. 2013. *Economic Crisis, Quality of Work, and Social Integration: The European Experience*. Oxford University Press.

Grimshaw, D., Johnson, M., Keizer, A., and Rubery, J. 2016. *Reducing Precarious Work in Europe Through Social Dialogue: The Case of the UK*. Project Report for the European Commission, European Work and Employment Research Centre, University of Manchester.

Hall, P. A. and Soskice, D. (Eds.), 2001. *Varieties of Capitalism: The Institutional Foundations of Comparative Advantage*. Oxford University Press.

Hyman, R. and Gumbrell-McCormick, R. 2017. Resisting Labour Market Insecurity: Old and New Actors, Rivals or Allies? *Journal of Industrial Relations*, 59(4), 538–561.

ILO. 2015. Non-standard forms of employment – Report for discussion at the Meeting of Experts on Non-Standard Forms of Employment (Geneva, 16–19 February 2015). International Labour Organization.

Iversen, T. and Soskice, D. 2019. *Democracy and Prosperity: Reinventing Capitalism Through a Turbulent Century*. Princeton University Press.

Kalleberg, A. 2011. *Good Jobs, Bad Jobs: The Rise of Polarized and Precarious Employment Systems in the United States, 1970s–2000s*. Russell Sage Foundation.

Levesque, C., Murray, G., and Morgan, G. 2020. Disruption and Re-Regulation in Work and Employment: From Organisational to Institutional Experimentation. *Transfer: European Review of Labour and Research*, 26(2), 135–156.

Mahoney, J. and Thelen, K. (Eds.), 2010. *Explaining Institutional Change: Ambiguity, Agency, and Power*. Cambridge University Press.

Murgia, A. and de Heusch, S. 2020. It Started with the Artists and Now it Concerns Everyone: The Case of Smart, a Cooperative of 'Salaried Autonomous

Workers'. In S. Taylor and S. Luckman (Eds.), *Pathways into Creative Working Lives*. Palgrave Macmillan.

OECD. 2019. Employment Outlook 2019: The Future of Work. Retrieved from: https://www.oecd-ilibrary.org/employment/oecd-employment-outlook-2019_9ee00155-en (last accessed 22 June 2021).

Ostrom, E. 1990. *Governing the Commons. The Evolution of Institutions for Collective Action*. Cambridge University Press.

Peck, J. and Theodore, N. 2007. Variegated Capitalism. *Progress in Human Geography*, 31(6), 731–772.

Pernicka, S. 2006. Organizing the Self-Employed: Theoretical Considerations and Empirical Findings. *European Journal of Industrial Relations*, 12(2), 125–42.

Sabel, C. F. 2001. A Quiet Revolution of Democratic Governance: Towards Democratic Experimentalism. In *OECD Governance in the 21st Century* (pp. 121–148). Organisation for Economic Co-operation and Development (OECD).

Sen, A. 1999. *Development as Freedom*. Oxford University Press.

Streeck, W. 2011. Taking Capitalism Seriously: Towards an Institutional Approach to Contemporary Political Economy. *Socio-Economic Review*, 9(1), 137–167.

Streeck, W. and Thelen, K., (Eds.), 2005. *Beyond Continuity: Institutional Change in Advanced Political Economies*. Oxford University Press.

Vandaele, K. 2018. Will Trade Unions Survive in the Platform Economy? Emerging Patterns of Platform Workers' Collective Voice and Representation in Europe. ETUI Research Paper – Working Paper 2018.05. Retrieved from SSRN: https://ssrn.com/abstract=3198546 or http://dx.doi.org/10.2139/ssrn.3198546 (last accessed June 22, 2021).

Westerveld, M. 2012. The 'New' Self-Employed: An Issue for Social Policy? *European Journal of Social Security*, 14(3), 156–173.

The Editors and Contributors

The Editors

Emiliana Armano, sociologist and independent researcher, received her PhD in Sociology from the University of Milan, Italy. Her research focuses on the intertwining of work processes and the production of subjectivity in the context of the platform economy, with a social inquiry and co-research methodological approach. Recent publications include (with Arianna Bove and Annalisa Murgia) *Mapping Precariousness, Labour Insecurity and Uncertain Livelihoods: Subjectivities and Resistance* (Routledge, 2017).

Marco Briziarelli is Assistant Professor in the Department of Communication and Journalism at the University of New Mexico, USA. He studies critical approaches to media and communication theory, especially as these fields intersect with broader issues in political and social theory, intellectual and cultural history. He is also interested in media and social movements and the critical conceptualisation of digital labour. His work has appeared in *tripleC: Communication, Capitalism & Critique, Communication and Critical/Cultural Studies, Journal of Communication Inquiry, Critical Studies in Media Communication, Continuum: Journal of Media & Cultural Studies, Journalism* and *The Handbook of Global Media and Communication Policy* (2011). He is also the author of *The Red Brigades and the Discourse of Violence: Revolution and Restoration* (2014) and co-author of *Reviving Gramsci: Crisis, Communication, and Change* (2016).

Elisabetta Risi, PhD in Information Society, is Research Fellow of the Department of Communication, Arts and Media of IULM University, Italy. She teaches disciplines related to the critical study of society and media and her research interests include contemporary forms of job insecurity, and the relationship between communication practices, identity and social change. Among her recent publications are: 'Emerging Resentment in Social Media: Job Insecurity and Plots of Emotions in the New Virtual Environments', in E. Fisher and T. Benski (Eds.), *Internet and Emotions* (2012) and, with E. Armano, F. Chicchi and E. Fisher, 'Borders and Measures of Emerging Work: Gratuitousness, Precariousness and Processes of Subjectivity in the Era of Digital Production' (2014, Special Issue), *Sociologia del Lavoro*.

The Contributors

Jacopo Anderlini is a Postdoctoral Researcher at the University of Genoa, Italy. His main research interests are border studies, refugee studies, migration, critical theory on technologies, social and political philosophy. He is currently investigating transformations in the government of mobility – its infrastructures and logistics – at the southern borders of Europe. He is part of CIRCE, a research group focused on the analysis of digital technologies, and of many self-organised collectives that support the right to move.

Davide Arcidiacono is Associate Professor in Economic Sociology at the University of Catania, Italy. His research focuses on digital transformation, the sharing economy, deregulation and work transitions. Among his recent publications are (with M. Duggan, 2020), *Sharing Mobilities: Questioning Our Right To The City In The Collaborative Economy*; with P. Borghi and A. Ciarini, 'Platform Work: From Digital Promises to Labor Challenges', in *Partecipazione e Conflitto* (2019); and (with G. Reale, 2018) 'Open Data as a Commons? The Disclosure of Public Sector Information from a Comparative Perspective', in *Rassegna Italiana di Sociologia*.

Alberto Cossu is a sociologist and media scholar who researches at the intersection between digital media and activism, qualitative and digital methods, collaborative and digital economies. He is a Lecturer in Media and Communication in the Department of Media and Communication, University of Leicester, UK. Before joining the University of Leicester, he was Lecturer in New Media and Digital Culture at the University of Amsterdam, The Netherlands, and previously a Research Fellow at the Department of Social and Political Sciences, University of Milan, Italy, where he also obtained his PhD. He is currently conducting a research project on the practices and cultures of cryptoeconomics.

Patrick Cingolani teaches sociology at the University of Paris, France, and heads the Laboratoire de Changement Social et Politique (LCSP). His theoretical research focuses on social figures of precariousness as well as the micropolitics of emancipation. His book publications include *L'exil du précaire* (1986); *Morale et société* (1995); *La république, les sociologues et la question politique* (2003); and *La précarité* (2005). In his latest book, *Révolutions précaires* (2014), he analyses the strains between the living conditions of workers who are engaged in cultural fields and neoliberal deregulations.

Niccolò Cuppini is a Researcher at the University of Applied Sciences and Arts of Southern Switzerland. He is part of the research path 'Into the Black Box – A Collective Research on Logistics, Spaces, Labor'. He is Editor of the magazine *Scienza & Politica* and collaborates with the Academy of Global Humanities and Critical Theory. He works on numerous international projects between the United States, Latin America, Africa and Europe on research ranging from logistics to the economy of digital platforms, from urban studies to the history of political theory.

Joseph Flores is Lecturer in Communication Studies at Gonzaga University, USA, having received his doctorate from the University of New Mexico in 2020. His interests focus on social media, political outreach movements, propaganda and in particular, political communication. Currently, Joseph's research lies at the intersection of political communication and conspiracy theories, with special attention devoted to the political economy of social media and its overall relationship to American politics. He has also been involved in mentorship work for first-generation and Latinx students and is an advocate for teaching media literacy.

Milena Franke is a doctoral researcher for Fairwork Belgium at KU Leuven conducting research on digitalization and new forms of employment in Belgium. Her research focuses on worker control and orientations and their working conditions. She works on the European Research Council funded project 'Researching Precariousness across the Paid /Unpaid Work Continuum' (ResPecTMe) and the Flemish Research Council funded project 'Precarious Work in the Online Economy: A Study on Digital Workers in Belgium and the Netherlands'.

Maurizio Franzini is Professor of Economic Policy at the Sapienza University of Rome, Italy, where he is also Director of the PhD School in Economics and Director of CIRET, the Interuniversity Research Center 'Ezio Tarantelli'. He is also Director of the online journal *Menabò di Etica e Economia* (www.eticaeconomia.it); and coordinator of the Research Area 'Economy-Environment Interaction' of the European Association for Evolutionary Political

Economy (EAEPE). Formerly he was Director of the Department of Economics and Law (2008–2013); Director of CRISS, the Interuniversity Research Center on the Welfare State (2003–2012); consultant to the Italian Labour Minister; and scientific coordinator of several European and national research projects. His current research interests include inequality and redistribution in advanced countries, economic institutions and well-being, cooperation and reciprocity and environmental policies.

Mattia Frapporti is a Research Fellow in the Department of Arts at the University of Bologna, Italy, whose research topics include European integration, contemporary logistics and history, political thought and urban studies.

Nicoletta Gay is a digital strategy consultant and contract Professor at the Polytechnic University of Turin, Italy, and PhD in History and Valorization of Architectural, Town Planning and Environmental Heritage. She teaches on the MA in Cinema and Media Engineering at the Polytechnic of Turin. Since 2014, as a freelancer, she has been training and consulting in digital strategy and marketing for companies, research centres, institutions and freelancers.

Heiner Heiland is Research Associate in Sociology at the Institute of Sociology, Technical University Darmstadt, Germany. His research analyses labour processes, organisational forms and resistances in platform economies.

Daniela Leonardi is a PhD student in Applied Sociology and Social Research Methodology at the University of Milan Bicocca, Italy. Her research interests include processes of subjectivation, conflicts and struggles in the workplaces using a co-research methodological approach.

Silvia Lucciarini is Associate Professor in the Department of Social and Economic Sciences at the Sapienza University of Rome, Italy, where she teaches Economic Sociology. She holds a PhD in urban policies and local design. Since 2012 she has been Professeur Invité of the Minerve Excellence Program at the Lumière 2 Lyon University, France, where she teaches comparative welfare and work policies in Italy and France. Since 2015 she has been Co-Director of the Laboratoire International Associé (LIA) at the University of Aix-Marseille, France. Currently, she is the Italian Contact Point for the European Research Council funded project, ResPecTMe, and she is co-coordinator of the Sustainable Food Procurement for Schools: Challenges and Opportunities in Italy, France and the UK project, funded by the British Academy.

Tatiana Mazali is Associate Lecturer in the Sociology of Media and Communication at the Polytechnic University of Turin, Italy. She currently teaches Interactive Media and Media Economy in Cinema and Media Engineering. Since 2012 she has led research projects on the impacts of digital media and digital culture on labour and workers, focusing on digital workers and professions, creative and cultural industries and the industry 4.0 paradigm. She is a Board Member of the European Sociological Association's Research Network on Sociology of Communications and Media Research (RN18). She is also a member of the Editorial Boards of *Work Organisation, Labour and Globalisation* and *Digitcult@Scientific Journal on Digital Cultures*.

Andrea Miconi is Associate Professor in the Department of Media, Arts and Communication at IULM University of Milan, Italy, and was previously Visiting Lecturer at University of São Paolo (2007–2011) and Adjunct Professor at the University of Italian Switzerland (2013–2016). Dr Miconi was coordinator of the Master's Program in Management of Creative Processes at IULM University (2007–2010); coordinator of the IULM University Unit in the Tempus Project 'e-MEDia, a bottom-up approach for the design and pilot of a joint Master Course in Cross-Media Journalism' (2013–2017); a didactic coordinator of international exchanges (between IULM and Tunisian, Brazilian and Lebanese universities); an expert peer reviewer for Italian National Scientific Evaluation (CINECA); and a member of the Scientific Board, PhD Program in Visual and Media Studies (IULM).

Carlo B. Milani is Research Associate at ERTIM – Institut National des Langues et Civilisations Orientales, Paris, France – and Researcher at the International NGO, NetHood. His research activities focus on power in human-machine interactions. He develops the hacker pedagogy approach at CIRCE and appropriate technologies at alekos.net.

Annalisa Murgia is Associate Professor in Sociology at the Department of Social and Political Sciences of the University of Milan, Italy, coordinating the ERC project 'SHARE – Seizing the Hybrid Areas of Work by Representing Self-Employment'. She recently co-edited the volumes *Platform Capitalism e confini del lavoro negli spazi digitali* (with E. Armano and M. Teli, 2017) and *Mapping Precariousness, Labour Insecurity and Uncertain Livelihoods: Subjectivities and Resistance* (with E. Armano and A. Bove, 2017).

Robert Ovetz is Senior Lecturer in Political Science at San José State University, USA. He is author of *When Workers Shot Back: Class Conflict from 1877 to 1921* (2018), editor of *Workers' Inquiry and Global Class Struggle: Strategies, Tactics, Objectives* (2020) and author of *We the Elites: Why the US Constitution Serves the Few* (2022). He is the Book Review Editor for the *Journal of Labor and Society*. Robert studies credible strike threats in the USA, which can be reported at https://strikethreats.org. Follow him at @OvetzRobert.

Ivana Pais is Full Professor in Economic Sociology at Università Cattolica del Sacro Cuore, Italy, where she is also Director of TraiLab (Transformative

Actions Interdisciplinary Laboratory). Her research interests focus on platform economy and digital labour, and her recent publications include (with D. Stark, 2020), 'Algorithmic Management in the Platform Economy', in *Sociologica*.

Maurilio Pirone is a Postdoctoral Fellow at University of Bologna, Italy. They are part of the Horizon2020 Project PLUS (Platform Labour in Urban Spaces) and are a member of the 'Into the Black Box' research collective.

Riccardo Pronzato is a Research and Teaching Assistant at the Department of Communication, Arts and Media at IULM University, Italy, where he is currently conducting PhD research within the Communication, Markets and Society doctoral programme. He obtained a summa cum laude Master's Degree (MSc) in Sociology and Social Research from the University of Trento, Italy, with an interdisciplinary thesis in cognitive sociology regarding online advertising targeting children. Currently, his major research interests include digital sociology, online media platforms, critical algorithm studies, online political communication, as well as cognitive and socio-narrative approaches.

Valeria Pulignano is Professor at the Centre for Sociological Research at KU Leuven, Belgium. She is Chief Coordinator of the European Sociological Association's Work, Employment and Industrial Relations Network, Chief Editor of 'Work, Employment and Organizations' in *Frontiers of Sociology*, Co-Researcher at CRIMT (Centre for Globalisation and Work – Canada), and Associate Fellow of the Industrial Relations Research Unit (IRRU) at the University of Warwick, UK. She is currently grantee of the European Research Council's (ERC) Advanced Grant RespecTMe and PI of the FWO 'Precarious Work in the Online Economy: A Study on Digital Workers in Belgium and the Netherlands', with her research focusing on work, comparative European employment/industrial relations and labour markets dualization and inequality.

Lawrence Quill is Professor of Political Theory at San José State University, USA. He was a Technology and Democracy Fellow at the Center for Research in the Arts, Social Sciences, and Humanities (CRASSH) at Cambridge University in 2015 and 2017. He is the author of a number of books and articles, most recently 'Technological Conspiracies: Comte, Technology, and Spiritual Despotism' that appeared in *Critical Review* (2016). His current research focuses on the contribution of political theory to understanding the impact of technology on self, society, and politics.

Ned Rossiter is a media theorist noted for his research on network cultures, the politics of cultural labour, logistical media, and data politics. He is Professor of Communication and Director of Research at the Institute for Culture and Society, Western Sydney University, Australia, where he holds a joint appointment in the School of Humanities and Communication Arts. He is the author of *Organized Networks: Media Theory, Creative Labour, New Institutions* (2006), *Software, Infrastructure, Labor: A Media Theory of Logistical Nightmares* (2016) and (with G. Lovink, 2018*) Organization after Social Media*. He is currently writing a book with Soenke Zehle entitled *The Experience of Digital Objects: Automation, Aesthetics, Algorithms*.

Hasmet M. Uluorta is Associate Professor of International Development and World Politics at Trent University, Canada. His research focuses on the US model of development and digitisation, seeking to clarify why consent may be forthcoming despite the existence of hyper-contradictions. He is author of *The Social Economy: Working Alternatives in a Globalizing Era* (2009).

Flaviano Zandonai has twenty years' experience as a practitioner in the field of social enterprise, carrying out research, training, consulting and publishing. Currently, he is Open Innovation Manager in the CGM cooperative group. Recent publications include (with M. Busacca, 2019), 'Trends and Challenges of The Italian Third Sector in The Field of Community Asset Regeneration' in *Paco – Partecipazione e Conflitto*, and (with F. Battistoni and P. Cottino, 2018), 'Regenerating the Commons: Policy Design Models Beyond CSR', in *Social Regeneration and Local Development: Cooperation, Social Economy and Public Participation*, edited by S. Sacchetti, A. Christoforou and M. Mosca.

Soenke Zehle, media theorist, writes, teaches and curates, with a focus on collaborative arts-and-technology research. He is Lecturer in Media Theory at the Academy of Fine Arts Saar (HBKsaar), Germany, and is also Managing Co-Director of K8 Institut für strategische Ästhetik gGmbH, the Academy's non-profit company for thinktank, transfer, and training activities, as well as an affiliate researcher at the Ubiquitous Media Technologies Lab of the German Research Center for Artificial Intelligence (DFKI). Between 2012–2018 he also worked as Managing Director of the Academy's Experimental Media Lab, xm:lab. Current research interests include collective intelligence design and speculative design futures literacies (the www.anticipate.network is currently coordinated and hosted by the Academy's xm:lab and K8) and open technologies.

Index